The Catholic Church and the World Religions

The Catholic Church and the World Religions

A Theological and Phenomenological Account

Edited by
Gavin D'Costa

t&t clark

Published by T&T Clark International
A Continuum Imprint
The Tower Building, 11 York Road, London SE1 7NX
80 Maiden Lane, Suite 704, New York, NY 10038

www.continuumbooks.com

All rights reserved. No part of this publication may be reproduced or transmitted in any form or by any means, electronic or mechanical, including photocopying, recording or any information storage or retrieval system, without permission in writing from the publishers.

Copyright © Gavin D'Costa, with contributors, 2011

Gavin D'Costa and contributors have asserted their right under the Copyright, Designs and Patents Act, 1988, to be identified as the Authors of this work.

British Library Cataloguing-in-Publication Data
A catalogue record for this book is available from the British Library.

ISBN: 978-0-567-21280-1 (Hardback)
      978-0-567-46697-6 (Paperback)

Typeset by Newgen Imaging Systems Pvt Ltd, Chennai, India
Printed and bound in India

Contents

Preface	vi
List of Abbreviations	viii
Notes on Contributors	ix
Chapter 1	
CATHOLICISM AND THE WORLD RELIGIONS: A THEOLOGICAL AND PHENOMENOLOGICAL ACCOUNT	1
Gavin D'Costa	
Chapter 2	
CATHOLICISM AND JUDAISM	34
Roy H. Schoeman	
Chapter 3	
CATHOLICISM AND ISLAM	71
Christian W. Troll SJ	
Chapter 4	
CATHOLICISM AND HINDUISM	106
Martin Ganeri OP	
Chapter 5	
CATHOLICISM AND BUDDHISM	141
Paul Williams OP	
Chapter 6	
CATHOLICISM AND THE NEW AGE MOVEMENT	178
Stratford Caldecott	
Index	217

Preface

This book is written for all those who want to know what the Catholic Church teaches about the four major world religions (Judaism, Islam, Hinduism and Buddhism) and the more recent phenomenon of New Age Religions. The authors hope that it will help Catholics and Christians from all denominations, and we dearly wish it may be read by those from the religions we speak of. We wish to be accountable to all. While we write as Catholics and write from within our own tradition, this is not an unecumenical gesture. From where else could we start? But Christians of all stripes will find that we draw on a common biblical, patristic and medieval heritage and struggle with the questions that every thinking Christian faces in our modern pluralist society. Those from other religions might wish to see how one of Christianity's largest denominations views them! They may wish to see whether there is a respectful understanding of their tradition, a proper and reverent appreciation, and even if there are any interesting questions being put to them.

The Catholic Church has developed a positive and critical approach to the world religions since the mid-1960s. It is positive in being sincerely open to truth, goodness and beauty in the religions and cultures of the world, knowing that from these profound seeds of truth it may be challenged to learn and grow more faithful to God in its own practices. It is positive in seeking to work together with world religions to establish justice and peace in a troubled world. It is positive in seeking to build bridges between all peoples knowing that our common humanity is marked by God's image. It is positive in being forced to be humble in the knowledge that the Spirit moves where it will. It is critical in also holding that Christ is the source of all truth, goodness and beauty and that in knowing Christ all truth everywhere comes to its completion, fulfilment and organic interrelatedness. It is critical in thus challenging the world religions in a fraternal and respectful spirit, regarding questions of truth, both in doctrine and in ethics. And of course, it is humble (or should be), in the light of its own history when it has failed to live according to the standards of the Gospel in relation to these religions. Since the mid-1960s Catholic theologians along with the magisterium have developed this approach in all sorts of theological directions. This opening chapter will examine the Catholic theological approach to the world religions.

The rest of the book then looks at religions in particular in their complex changing historical and phenomenological development. Each author presents a clear, helpful and objective picture of one particular religion. This will allow readers who are unfamiliar with that religion to learn about that religion. This will allow experts to be comfortable that the assessment that follows is based on an accurate, sympathetic and historically sound footing. It will allow those from other religions to see whether their face is reflected in this account. Each writer then turns to a Catholic assessment of that religion, such as is possible in a brief essay. They affirm that which is held in common and seek to build further bridges. They probe and question that which raises difficulties for the respectful Christian. The value of this part of the book is that it applies the theological orientation initially outlined, to the particular – and flushes out the challenges and the joys that await Christians in dialogue with the religions.

Each writer provides some readings that will help the interested reader to move further in their searching. Some of us have provided notes to our essays, but all the chapters can be read as they stand without the notes so that the reader can get to the heart of the matter. All of the chapters can also be read independently.

Gavin D'Costa

List of Abbreviations

AG	*Ad Gentes*
CCC	*Catechism of the Catholic Church*
Compendium	*Compendium of the Social Doctrine of the Church*
DH	*Dignitatis Humanae*
DI	*Dominus Iesus*
FR	*Fides et Ratio*
GS	*Gaudium et Spes*
LG	*Lumen Gentium*
NA	*Nostra Aetate*
RM	*Redemptoris Missio*

Notes on Contributors

Stratford Caldecott is Editor of Second Spring journal for the Thomas More College of Liberal Arts and Humanum for the John Paul II Institute for Studies on Marriage and Family. Caldecott's research interests are in the relationship between faith and culture, philosophy and history of education, and fundamental theology and interreligious dialogue. His most recent publications include *Beauty for Truth's Sake: On the Re-enchantment of Education* (2009); *Catholicism and Other Religions: Introducing Interfaith Dialogue* (CTS, 2009); ed. *Tolkien's* The Lord of the Rings: *Sources of Inspiration* (2008); and *The Seven Sacraments: Entering the Mysteries of God* (Crossroad, 2006). Caldecott is a member of Editorial Board of the Catholic Truth Society.

Gavin D'Costa (editor) is Professor of Catholic Theology at the University of Bristol. His research has been on the Christian theology of religions, with special reference to Catholic dogmatic questions. He is author of six books, and editor of four on the theology of religions (see, for example, *The Meeting of Religions and the Trinity*, 2000; and *Christianity and World Religions. Disputed Questions in the Theology of Religions*, 2009). D'Costa advises the Catholic Church nationally and internationally on theology and other religions as well as the Anglican Church. He is a lay Catholic.

Martin Ganeri OP is the Director of the Centre for Christianity and Interreligious Dialogue at Heythrop College, University of London. His research interests are in Indian religions, Indian Christianity, comparative theology and Catholic relations with other religions. His most recent publications include 'Catholic Encounter with Hindus in the Twentieth Century: In Search of an Indian Christianity', *New Blackfriars* (2007); 'Knowledge and Love of God in Ramanuja and Aquinas', *Journal of Hindu Christian Studies* (2007); 'The Catholic Magisterium and the World Religions', in *A Catholic Shi'a Dialogue: Ethics in Today's Society*, ed. Anthony O'Mahony, Timothy Wright, Mohammad Ali Shomali (2008). Ganeri is the Prior of Blackfriars, Cambridge, and a member of the English and Welsh Bishops' Conference Committee for Relations with Other Religions.

Roy H. Schoeman's research interests are the role of Judaism in salvation history as understood and taught by the Catholic Church, how the Church's understanding of that role has changed over time, and the conversion of the Jews, particularly with respect to such conversion being a necessary precondition for the Second Coming. His recent publications include *Salvation is from the Jews: The Role of Judaism in Salvation History from Abraham to the Second Coming* (2003) *and Honey from the Rock: Sixteen Jews Find the Sweetness of Christ* (2007). Schoeman received his Jewish training under some of the most prominent Rabbis in contemporary American Jewry, including Rabbi Arthur Hertzberg, Rabbi Arthur Green and Rabbi Shlomo Carlebach, a prominent Hasidic Rabbi. His secular education included a B.Sc. from MIT and an MBA magna cum laude from Harvard Business School, where he also served on the faculty.

Christian W. Troll SJ is Honorary Professor of the Study of Islam and Christian-Muslim Relations at the Philosophisch-Theologische Fakultät SJ, Sankt Georgen, Frankfurt/Main, Germany. His work has focused on an analysis of modern Islamic thought and of central issues in contemporary Christian-Muslim relations. He has published widely in numerous languages and his publications include *Sayyid Ahmad Khan. A Reinterpretation of Muslim Theology*, 1978, *Muslims Ask, Christians Answer*, 2005, and *Unterscheiden um zu klären. Orientierung im Christlich-islamischen Dialog*, 2008. Troll is a Jesuit priest and member of the Sub-commission on Interreligious Dialogue of the German Bishops' Conference.

Paul Williams OP is Professor of Indian and Tibetan Philosophy and founding co-director of the Centre for Buddhist Studies, University of Bristol. His work has focused on Madhyamaka Buddhist philosophy and has also has written on Western philosophical and mystical theology. Williams is sole editor of the eight-volume series for Routledge *Buddhism: Critical Concepts in Religious Studies* (2005), the co-author (with Anthony Tribe) of *Buddhist Thought: A Complete Introduction to the Indian Tradition* (2000), and the author of five other books including *The Unexpected Way: On Converting from Buddhism to Catholicism* (2001). Williams is a lay member of the Dominican Order.

Chapter 1

Catholicism and the World Religions: A Theological and Phenomenological Account

Gavin D'Costa

Introduction

I write as a Roman Catholic theologian which has a variety of entailments – in fact, two for the purposes of this introductory chapter. First, this means that my job as a theologian, shaped by the Church's teachings, is to convey the teachings of the Catholic Church on the matter at hand.[1] I hope this will not deter non-Catholic Christians from reading as it is my conviction that every one doing theology comes from 'somewhere' which entails specific allegiances and commitments, authority sources and special texts, and so on. We need to learn from each other. Even the theologian who says they are not aligned to any church and are simply open to the truth have authoritative starting points. This is one of the great insights from postmodern philosophy, or rather it is an insight that helped call into question one of the 'idols' of modernity: that is, it is possible to do objective research without any presuppositions or biases.[2] To 'think with the Church' allows ample room for critical exploration and development of arguments and engagement with a wide range of issues and is not a simple act of repetition, although the latter is also part of the theologian's job.[3]

Second, while it is my primary job to outline what the Church teaches, this is no easy task, for all texts require interpretation. I will begin with teachings from the 'magisterium' on our topic – by which I mean the universal councils of the Church, the bishops speaking together, authoritative statements from pontifical offices within the Vatican and certain teachings by popes.[4] However, with every text we have disputed interpretations among Catholic theologians, so occasionally I will refer to these debates. But this chapter is also interpretative in my arguing that one can formulate a basic orientation towards the religions of the world from authoritative Catholic sources.

In what follows, I will first outline the biblical and historical background to arrive at a proper understanding of contemporary (Vatican II and after) Catholic teaching on this matter.

The Roman Catholic Teaching on Other Religions

Biblical[5] and early church background

Three interesting attitudes to the religiously pluralist reality are discernible within the first few centuries that continue to shape contemporary Catholicism. First, there was a clear emphasis on the necessity of faith in Christ for salvation, echoing John 14.6: 'I am the way, and the truth, and the life; no one comes to the Father except through me.' This faith had an ecclesial dimension, including the necessity for baptism into Christ's body, so that membership of the church (in the case of adults, always assuming active faith and love in the person's heart) was required for salvation (Acts 2.23, 41, 8.12–13, 16.15, 31–33; Mt. 28.19; 2 Cor. 5.17; Gal. 6.15, 3.27; Rom. 6.3–4). This first emphasis meant that Christianity was a vigorous missionary religion with an explicit desire to convert all peoples. This also found expression in the famous axiom *extra ecclesiam nulla salus* teaching (no salvation outside the Church), which was taught at the Council of Florence in the fifteenth century, but originates from as early as the second century and was consolidated by St Augustine. It is still taught in the Roman Catholic Church (see below). This missionary drive excluded no religion or culture, although Jewish rejection of the Gospel was always an embarrassment in the early days of the Church and eventually led to a strong anti-Jewish polemic.

The necessity of faith and baptism into Christ presupposed that God created the world good and that the fall brought about death and alienation between humans and God (Gen. 3; Rom. 5.12–21; Lk. 11.21–22; Jn 16.11). This breach between God and humanity was initiated by Adam and Eve and meant that all humans were born into sin. There were different models employed to understand the transmission of this 'original' sin and much discussion on the matter of those infants who died without baptism. However, the basic drama relates to the history of restoration of the broken covenant between God and humans which begins in Israel and comes to its full and eschatological completion in Christ. It is important to note that until the last century there has generally been what might be called a salvation-pessimism about the fate of non-Christians. That is, there is an assumption that because of sin, non-Christians will be lost. This salvation-pessimism was never part of a formal magisterial teaching. The nineteenth century onwards can be characterized by a salvation-optimism, which is always in danger of playing down the power of sin and exalting the power of human goodness. Doctrinally, human goodness, while being a wonderful reality, is biblically insufficient for salvation: men and women cannot save themselves by their own righteousness.

Second, various early Christian intellectuals had learnt greatly from Greek philosophy and could not help but wonder at the wisdom they had found there: truths that were consonant with revelation, moral exhortation of a high order, and indeed, philosophical frameworks that allowed for the sophisticated explication of Christian revelation and for its defence against philosophical attacks. Such apologists developed three crucial theories to explain pagan wisdom: the *prisca theologia* (ancient theology), the *praeparatio evangelica* (the preparation for the Gospel) and the *semina verbi* (the seeds of the Word). The first held that all pagan wisdom was actually an explicit or unacknowledged borrowing from the Old Testament – a theory of a form of intellectual plagiarism. The latter two theories, by contrast, argued that God provided knowledge in nature and in cultures that prepared people for the truth of the Gospel, and such truth, goodness and beauty outside of Christianity are always derived causally from God's Word. These truths prepared the person for salvation through cultivating the good life but they were not in themselves saving revelation – which came through Christ. Such truths found their fulfilment and culmination in Christ.

Third, the early Christians were faced with the question of the righteous of Israel: were they lost because they were born before the time of Christ? This was unthinkable to many who knew the devout and holy patterns of some of their own parents and grandparents. The saints of Israel had valid faith in God, for they partook of the very covenant which is the root upon which the Church was grafted (Rom. 11.11–24). Ideas of the justice of God (in tandem with passages like Acts 2.7; Rom. 10.6–7; Eph. 4.8–9; 1 Pet. 3.18–20) led to the notion that these righteous awaited the coming of Christ, who as the creed has it, *descendit ad inferos*, 'descended into hell', where he preached salvation to the righteous so that they might be saved.[6] This scenario led to the idea of the *limbus patrum* (the limbo of the fathers) as a kind of metaphoric 'space' for the righteous who died before Christ. In the third century Clement of Alexandria and others argued that righteous pagans had also been in the *limbus patrum*, which suggested the possibility of salvation for all the righteous, not just the righteous Israelites. Augustine likewise insisted on an invisible church from the time of Abel composed of the righteous. For all these thinkers, the assumption was that after Christ came, no one was in an analogous position to these righteous gentiles and pre-Christian Jews.

Together, these three attitudes run throughout Christian history, leading to three central points in Catholic teaching: (1) the necessity of Christ and his Church for salvation; (2) the justice of God towards the righteous before (and obviously after) the coming of Christ, but historically the application was related to those before Christ; (3) the possibility of goodness, truth, and beauty being present in pagan traditions, but never in a manner equal to Christ and his sacramental presence in his Church. However, the modern period introduces a new hermeneutical context within which these teachings are interpreted, but the changes of interpretative context began much earlier.

The medieval and early modern period

Until the age of discovery in the fifteenth century it was generally assumed by many theologians that after the time of Christ everyone knew the Gospel. If a person was not a Christian they had explicitly rejected the truth of God. This meant that Jews and eventually Muslims (from the seventh century onwards) were seen as wilful sinners, apostates and heretics, rather than genuinely 'other' as we tend to view these and other traditions today. The age of colonialism also brought on a development in doctrinal theology with the discovery of the 'new world' in which millions of women and men had never heard of the Gospel through no fault of their own, and some lived impressive moral lives closely related to their religious practices. It was difficult to rely on Thomas Aquinas' (thirteenth century) speculation that, were there to be a young boy bought up by wolves (and who thus had never heard the Gospel), God's justice would require that an angel would visit him or that he would have interior revelation.[7] The evidence indicated that angels had not visited non-Christian peoples *en masse* and private interior revelations were unrecorded. New thinking was required in a new context. But it is important to note the continuity of dogmatic focus on the necessity of Christ and the Church for salvation, while taking serious consideration of other new factors.

The sixteenth-century Dominicans of Salamanca, Francisco de Vitoria and Domingo de Soto planted the seeds for later Catholic theology on this topic in two significant ways. Vitoria (*c.* 1492–1546) was outraged by the behaviour of some of the Spanish missionary *conquistadores* in South America and argued that unless the Gospel was presented properly, without violence, threat and coercion, both before and after its preaching, the hearers were under no obligation to accept it and could not be enslaved as a result of their non-acceptance. Bartolomé de Las Casas (1484–1566) was also deeply critical of certain Spanish military and political authorities for their clear exploitative ambitions and disregard for the natives and their blindness to some peace-loving elements within the Indian civilization. Las Casas obviously thought mission to be essential, but he also thought it must be conducted justly. Through Spain's violent *encomienda*, entire communities were forcibly reduced to slavery by being entrusted to

Spanish conquistadores to whom they were required to pay for their tuition in the Spanish language and instruction in the Catholic faith. Contemporary Catholic missionaries are deeply sensitive to questions of justice and peace; indeed, some missionary groups are today in danger of playing down the necessity of the Gospel and church for salvation. Second, Soto (1494–1560) argued that implicit faith in Christ would suffice for those 'who had never heard the gospel' but who had followed the natural law evident in creation through the use of their reason prompted by grace. This teaching came about through information seeping back from the mission field which called for a serious encounter with the phenomenon of non-Christian religions. This meant that the necessity of the church for salvation was contextualized, while nevertheless still being viewed as binding. This position, with various qualifications remains the official Catholic position today.

The modern period

There are five important European factors that mark the modern period that provide a context for understanding contemporary Catholic sensibilities. The implications of all five factors are deeply disputed between those who call for radical change including in doctrine, others who argue for change because of contemporary circumstances, thus viewing issues of doctrinal continuity as irrelevant, and those who wish to be pastorally sensitive to new situations while continuing to draw from the major doctrinal traditions of the past. While the actual situation is very complex and cannot be reduced to these three positions, of these three, this book follows the latter sensibility. In what follows I attempt to be more descriptive than evaluative. First, there was the end of 'Christendom'. Europe slowly became secularized, initially through the so-called wars of religions when Catholics and Protestants slaughtered each other (and themselves); and later through the nation-state's overcoming of these differences through a unitary identity found in belonging to the state rather than a particular religion.[8] The second factor that marks the modern is the profound crisis of two world wars fought in the heart of Christian Europe. Christians slaughtered each other savagely. Partly because of this, many Europeans had little confidence in the cultural resources of their ancient religion, turning to other traditions, new, old or newly recreated 'antiquity', including the sometimes highly individualized 'New Age Religions'.[9] Some found solace in modern science that was perceived to have more authority than religions in its claims. Science also had vast instrumental power and seemed to offer possibilities of 'redemption' for millions of people in poverty. Others turned to ethics without religion, drawing on the strong Kantian Enlightenment trajectory that emphasized the centrality of ethics rather than historical revelation. Some intellectuals turned to the 'East' which had been particularly idealized by German Romanticism. This mythical 'East' seemed to offer something different from war and destruction.[10] A third factor was the Holocaust. The slaughter of nearly 6 million Jews at the heart of a Christian culture raised deep questions about Christianity's attitude to the religious 'other' as well as its own complicity in European anti-Semitism.[11] A fourth factor was the critique of missions from the viewpoint of secular modernity. Many liberal Europeans saw Christian mission as culturally arrogant, failing to learn from the deep wisdom of the East, bearing responsibility for the destruction of primitive and ancient cultures, and falsely valuing Christianity over other religions. Fifth and finally, many 'prophetic' voices within Catholicism saw the future as requiring a deeper assimilation to modernity. This latter issue is still unresolved in the Catholic Church although popes John Paul II and Benedict XVI have developed a trenchant critique against many aspects of modernity that should certainly call into question any uncritical assimilation.[12] This background helps in part to understand the importance of our topic for dogmatic, apologetic and pastoral reasons. It is also the background that prompted the Second Vatican Council to address the issue of other religions in two of its documents.

The Second Vatican Council (1962–1965)

In the light of the Second Vatican Council I will outline the major teachings that relate to my topic.[13] [I will argue that we find central dogmatic continuity with the ancient faith but also deepening insights and developments of understanding in the modern magisterial pastoral orientation towards other religions.]

The most important dogmatic statement (in contrast to a pastoral document or declaration) on this question is to be found in *The Dogmatic Constitution on the Church*, 16 (*Lumen Gentium*, 1964 – subsequently *LG*). Before turning to section 16 in detail, it needs contextualizing. *LG* 1–7 reiterates previous teachings. It starts with the basic Christian story: God created the world which was good. After the fall humans seek the living God and yearn for that original communion which has been lost. That restoration begins in Israel and the broken relationship is fully and finally restored in the second Adam, Christ, who is founder of the Church.

As the *Catechism of the Catholic Church* puts it: 'Although to some extent the People of God in the Old Testament had tried to understand the pathos of the human condition in . . . *Genesis*, they could not grasp this story's ultimate meaning, which is revealed only in the light of . . . Christ. We must know Christ as the source of grace in order to know Adam as the source of sin. The Spirit-Paraclete, sent by the risen Christ, came to "convict the world concerning sin" (Jn. 16:8), by revealing him who is the Redeemer.'[14]

The document then expands on the Trinitarian foundation of the Church through the Father, and the Son who founded the Church through the power of the Spirit (2–4). It recognizes the way the kingdom is made present in the Church, in its sacramental character but also in the works of charity that follow conversion of the heart, mind and will to God (5). It shows how the Church is prefigured in the Old Testament (6) and then reflects upon New Testament images of the Church (7), leading to the conclusion that the Church is the sacramental mediator of saving grace: 'Christ, the one Mediator, established and continually sustains here on earth His holy Church, the community of faith, hope and charity, as an entity with visible delineation (*)[15] through which He communicated truth and grace to all' (8). It is then stated that this unique church of Christ 'subsists [*subsistit*] in the [Roman] Catholic Church'. This term 'subsists' replaced the term 'is' [*est*] in the original draft, and there has been much discussion about the significance of 'subsists'. Some see 'subsists' as an intended weakening and thus change from 'is', while others see a nuancing and deepening of 'is' to take proper consideration of other Christian churches and communities.[16] The sentence just quoted continues: 'although many elements of sanctification and of truth are found outside of its visible structure. These elements, as gifts belonging to the Church of Christ, are forces impelling toward catholic unity.' It is arguable that this concern for other Christian churches and communities in the use of 'subsist' was falsely applied to interpret the meaning of other religions in too optimistic a manner.[17]

The rest of the document until paragraph 16 delineates the different types of relation and belonging to the Church, first for Catholics and then for other Christians and then, finally, in section 16 in relation to other religions. Catholics are 'fully incorporated' (*plene incorporantur*) into the Church and catechumens, unbaptized people wishing to join the Church, are 'united' (*coniunguntur*) to the Church in virtue of their desire to join the Church (14). The term *voto* (desire) is used solely for catechumens. Then we have non-Catholic Christians, who are 'joined' (*coniuncti*) to the Church in various ways, but are 'incorporated' (*incorporantur*) into Christ. Finally, in paragraph 16 the Council turns to non-Christian religions and non-religions. The stage is now set for our topic and three points are important.

First, *LG* (14) reiterates the ancient teaching: *extra ecclesiam nulla salus* (there is no salvation outside the church) but with a different phrase: '*Docet autem, sacra scriptura et traditione innixa, Ecclesiam hanc peregrinantem necessariam esse ad salute*' ('Basing itself on scripture and tradition, it teaches that the Church, a pilgrim now on earth, is necessary for salvation').[18] The different Latin phrase outlines an important shift of *emphasis*: the old dogmatic truth is reiterated – that Christ and his Church are necessary for salvation; but that truth is now expressed not in negative relation to others, but as a positive teaching about the Church and its binding force upon those who properly hear its proclamation. Hence, this same section ends: 'Whosoever, therefore, knowing that the Catholic Church was made necessary by Christ, would refuse to enter or to remain in it, could not be saved' (14). What might be negatively employed against non-culpable non-Christians in the past is now turned into a profound call to Catholic Christians and all those who truly hear the Gospel message. But it does not negate the objective claim that the Church is necessary for salvation. Rather there is an acknowledgement that hermeneutically, the way this might apply to different groups, requires contextualizing and further theological reflection.

Before the Council there had already been clarification on *extra ecclesiam nulla salus* when in 1949 the Holy Office, now called the Congregation for the Doctrine of the Faith, condemned the teachings of Leonard Feeney SJ who held a literal interpretation of *extra ecclesiam nulla salus*. Feeney claimed all non-Catholics were damned, including other Christian denominations as well as those in non-Christian religions. The Holy Office issued a letter against Feeney's interpretation making it clear that the teaching did not mean damnation for all those who were not Roman Catholics. The letter stressed that all people who had not explicitly rejected the Gospel (Moses would be a good example) had a possibility of being 'related to the Mystical Body of the Redeemer by a certain unconscious yearning and desire'.[19] Moses denotes uncontroversially those before Christ, but it is now accepted that there are those who like Moses, did not explicitly know of Christ through no fault of their own. This teaching would find different expression in the Council which dropped the notion of 'unconscious desire' and 'Mystical' Body, as the former was just one model of explaining how this might happen and the Council was not keen to close down discussion in this area, but simply offer a general orientation. It thus still insisted on a connection to the Body of Christ, the Church. The Council also reiterated the clear teaching that those who die not knowing Christ on earth, and even those who do not explicitly know God, might still be saved: 'Those also can attain to salvation who through no fault of their own do not know the Gospel of Christ or His Church, yet sincerely seek God and moved by grace strive by their deeds to do His will as it is known to them through the dictates of conscience. (*) Nor does Divine Providence deny the helps necessary for salvation to those who, without blame on their part, have not yet arrived at an explicit knowledge of God and with His grace strive to live a good life' (16). This is not Pelagianism through the back door (salvation by works), but presumes grace for the possibility of the 'good life'. This is important for otherwise the effects of original sin would be gravely undermined.

Here we have Christological, Trinitarian and ecclesiological truths delicately welded together in Catholic theology. Christ, the self-revelation of the triune God, through the power of the Spirit is the source of all salvation. But Christ, through the power of the Spirit founds the Church which is his instrument for salvation to the entire world because the Church is the sacramental body of Christ to the world. Thus all non-Christians who are saved are related to the Church. The relationship of Christ to the Church and precisely how it is to be explained in the context of the salvation of non-Christians is a matter for Catholic theologians to attend to. The Council was simply laying down the legitimate dogmatic parameters for reflection, reiterating the tradition. After the Council there have been significant debates about the two central links in this claim: first, whether and how Christ is the sole constitutive cause of all saving grace; and second, whether and how the Church is the means of salvation to those who die outside its visible boundaries but may nevertheless be saved. What is important right now is to state those claims and note that there has been considerable discussion about them.[20]

Second, *LG* 16 addresses the question of non-Christians (those from other religions and none) and distinguishes their relation to the church not in terms of those 'incorporated', or 'united', or 'joined', but as those 'ordained (*ordinatur* – *) in various ways, to the People of God'. In the footnote to the term *ordinatur*, Aquinas' *Summa Theologiae* III, q. 8, a. 3, ad. 1 is cited. In that section of the *Summa*, Thomas is discussing the headship of Christ both to the Church and to all humans and is answering the objection that the unbaptized have no relation to the head as they are not part of the body (the Church). The answer given by Thomas resists any such decapitation and severance of relation: 'Those who are unbaptized, though not actually in the Church, are in the Church potentially. And this potentiality is rooted in two things – first and principally, in the power of Christ, which is sufficient for the salvation of the whole human race;

secondly, in free-will.' It should be recalled that Aquinas' adoption of Aristotelian terms here require 'potentially' to be understood as referring to something future, which at present exists only as a germ to be evolved. This potentiality has been variously interpreted subsequent to Aquinas as we saw above in Vitoria and Soto, and see recently in the work of Karl Rahner.[21] Pius XII used the term *ordinatur* in *Mystici Corporis* (1943) of those who have not been baptized to say they are 'oriented towards [the Church] by a certain unconscious desire and wish' (*inscio quodam desiderio ac voto ad mysticum Redemptoris corpus ordinari*) (103). Here, Thomas' 'potentiality' is given its future orientation towards *actus* (being fulfilled) in terms of 'unconscious desire'.[22] This matter has been hotly debated since the Council. My own elaboration of the implication of this future actualization of potentiality can be found elsewhere.[23] However, let me make three brief remarks concerning salvation and the eschaton.

First, it is clear that salvation is possible for the non-Christian, yet salvation involves the beatific vision (the direction vision of God as Father, Son and Spirit), then I would argue that salvation for the non-Christian is an eschatological event (as it is for the Christian). It cannot be an event that happens in this life for the non-Christian who dies as a non-Christian, not because they are necessarily lost (which is contrary to Church teaching), or because they lack nobility, holiness and goodness that might put many a Christian to shame, but simply because to posit the beatific vision for such a person would be epistemologically overriding their freedom. Ontologically, in God's eyes so to speak, this person is known to be saved, but the epistemological reality of this is yet to happen. Does this mean that non-Christians are any the less good and noble? Not at all. Does it mean that as human persons they do not show remarkable courage and deep compassion? Not at all. All that is being claimed here is that salvation as the enjoyment of the beatific vision is something that will be enjoyed only after this life. To further contextualize these remarks, it should also be said that apart from Mary the beatific vision will only be enjoyed in the eschaton by Christians. [Most Christians, excluding the saints, while being justified by baptism and faith, will die still lacking purity and perfection which is what will be required for their participation in the beatific vision.] Hence, this sense of seeing the salvation of non-Christians as a future event does not in any way provide a commentary on the individual person. It is clear that their religion cannot be objectively true as such, although it may contain many elements of goodness, truth and beauty as well as reflect the Light that enlightens all men and women and is a preparation for the fullness of that Light.

the 'duration' of this transforming burning in terms of the chronological measurements of this world. The transforming 'moment' of this encounter eludes earthly time . . . it is the heart's time, it is the time of 'passage' to communion with God in the Body of Christ.

To conclude this section let me summarize: God through Christ is the cause of all salvation and the Church is Christ's body on earth, the means by which all grace is mediated. How this grace might be mediated to those outside the Church is an area that is not defined or resolved, but that this grace is mediated to those outside the Church is a certainty. Catholics can be confident that non-Christians might be saved and this is the solemn dogmatic teaching on this matter. There is obviously a lot of work for theologians to do in developing, explicating and defending this teaching, but I would claim that this is the basic teaching of the Catholic Church on these questions. I will return to further Vatican II documents after tracing an interesting dogmatic development that takes place in magisterial teaching after the Council.

The Holy Spirit and the Religions: Magisterial Developments after Vatican II

The Council and John Paul II's papal teachings after the Council have developed Catholic teaching regarding the Holy Spirit (pneumatology) in very interesting ways. I do not have space to pay attention to this chronological process, so will here summarize some important pneumatological points, with minor commentary on some of them.

First, the Holy Spirit is acknowledged to be at work from the time of creation and before Christ's incarnation. The Spirit 'blows where he will' (Jn. 3.8).[25] This is most explicitly found in a passage in John Paul's Encyclical, *On the Holy Spirit in the Life of the Church and the World* (*Dominum et Vivificantem*, 1986), 53:

> [W]e cannot limit ourselves to the two thousand years which have passed since the birth of Christ. We need to go further back, to embrace the whole of the action of the Holy Spirit even before Christ – from the beginning, throughout the world, and especially in the economy of the Old Covenant. For this action has been exercised, in every place and at every time, indeed in every individual, according to the eternal plan of salvation, whereby this action was to be closely linked with the mystery of the Incarnation and Redemption, which in its turn exercised its influence on those who believed in the future coming of Christ. This is attested to especially in the Letter to the Ephesians. (See Eph 1:3–14.) Grace, therefore, bears within itself both a

> Christological aspect and a pneumatological one, which becomes evident above all in those who expressly accept Christ: 'In him [in Christ] you ... were sealed with the promised Holy Spirit, which is the guarantee of our inheritance, until we acquire possession of it.' (Eph 1:13f.) ...
>
> The Second Vatican Council, centred primarily on the theme of the Church, reminds us of the Holy Spirit's activity also 'outside the visible body of the Church.' The Council speaks precisely of 'all people of good will in whose hearts grace works in an unseen way. For, since Christ died for all, and since the ultimate vocation of man is in fact one, and divine, we ought to believe that the Holy Spirit in a manner known only to God offers to every man the possibility of being associated with this Paschal Mystery.' (*GS* 22; *LG*, n. 16)

We have a two fold direction of activity in the Spirit's operation upon which Christology is dependent: (1) in preparing people for Christ before his coming (and perhaps analogically preparing people for Christ after the time of Christ); and (2) in applying the fruits of Christ to people after His coming, both those who have received him in faith and to others retrospectively (the righteous Jews and gentiles) and prospectively (the righteous of the nations and the religions).

Second, we see the Holy Spirit can be found in the hearts of non-Christian people and also in their values, cultures and religions.[26] This is an important move because it allows for both the subjective work of the Holy Spirit in the hearts of women and men as well as the fruits of that activity that is lodged in their cultural institutions, texts, rituals and practices. While these latter are not to be understood sacramentally, in an *ex opere operato* fashion (see below), this does not diminish either the subjective and historical elements of God's grace that may be found in the hearts of persons and in visible elements in their religion. Third, the Holy Spirit within these religions can cause Christians deep shame at their disposition to doubt 'truths revealed by God and proclaimed by the Church'.[27] It would follow that if the Spirit is at work in other religions, it can also call into question false practices and beliefs held by Christians who have failed to grasp their own faith properly, when, for example, the faithfulness in prayer five times a day or fasting at Ramadan in Islam, rightly calls into question the way prayer and fasting are ignored by some Christians. This action of the Spirit will also help a deepening grasp of the truths that have been given to us in revelation. I will return to this theme when I deal with mission and inculturation below. Fourth, the Holy Spirit's work serves as a preparation for the Gospel (*praeparatio evangelica*) and can only be understood in reference to Christ.[28] This latter emphasis is important in countering those pneumatologies that have been employed to bypass what is sometimes called the Christological 'impasse' in the theology of religions,

Second, this individualist manner of speaking about salvation only tells part of the story. Salvation is also a corporate and social event for the body of Christ is not about the salvation of an individual but the salvation of a community. Here Karl Barth's rereading of double predestination is most illuminating. Barth questions Calvin's focus on the individual as the site of predestination, and sees this double predestination concretized in Jesus Christ in two ways: first, as the damned, in so much as Jesus undertakes that which rightly belongs to the damned – death and dereliction; and second, as the redeemed, in so much as Jesus through his resurrection redeems fallen human nature. This latter aspect is developed in a universalist direction. Barth overstepped the mark, at least the Catholic mark, in then arguing from this to a form of universalism (that all men and women will be saved). [Christ's resurrection and transformation of humanity means that all men and women who have not heard the Gospel will have the opportunity to be saved, as taught by Vatican II and the tradition, not that all men and women will actually be saved. Universalism compromises the radical nature of human freedom.]

Third, if we are to uphold Augustine's teaching that conversion cannot happen after death, a teaching that has been upheld by the majority of the tradition since Augustine's days and forms one of the parameters within which we must try and address the question, have we come to a dead end (in a double sense) when dealing with the question of the fate of the non-Christian? Fortunately, there is another route to think through this matter and it is along the route related to the righteous before the coming of Christ. Elements of the tradition teach that Christ descended into hell to save these souls who were destined for paradise but could not yet enter the gates of heaven as they had not yet met Christ. Are there not many millions after Christ who are in an analogous situation? These people have not had the opportunity to hear the Gospel but may, through God's Spirit and thus through the promptings of grace, have followed the dictates of their conscience and the good elements within their religions and thereby sought to follow the good at great personal cost. [This does not mean that they have formally accepted Christ, but rather that they would do if it were an option put to them with maximal clarity (as in Thomas' difference between potentiality and actuality) and in this sense, their future salvation may be construed.]

This analogical application of an ancient doctrine is not without problems, but has the benefit of keeping intact a non-Christian's freedom, allowing for their decisions in this life (potentiality) to bear full fruit (actuality) in the beatific vision. Clearly, there is some continuity and discontinuity involved, but we must assume that only God is the just judge who can adjudicate on such questions and how they might be measured. After all, it took the thief on the cross a single moment of recognition to be assured of future salvation (Lk. 23.39–43). One can imagine that after death he had much inner transformation to undergo before final purification was attained. Augustine argued that he was probably someone who had already been baptized and had fallen away from the church so that his argument about conversion after death was not weakened, but there is little to support such a reading, although there is admittedly little evidence to refute it. Furthermore, it should also be remembered that apart from Mary and the saints, Catholic theology teaches that many who are Christians and are destined for salvation, will nevertheless after death enter into an interim stage of further purification and transformation before enjoying the beatific vision. This is called purgatory. Elsewhere I have related these doctrines of purgatory and the *limbus patrum* (the limbo of the fathers, the place where the righteous before Christ awaited his descent into hell and the opening of the gates of heaven) to provide a solution to an unresolved lacuna in Catholic teaching: how a non-Christian who dies as a non-Christian can be said to be saved, when salvation (as beatific vision of the blessed trinity) entails a state of which they have no conscious awareness in this life.[24] This is a private speculative opinion and an attempt to explain a magisterial teaching that has been explained in other ways.

The metaphoric complexity of both the limbo of the fathers and purgatory should make us wary of pushing these models too far. When writing about the fires of purgatory, Benedict XVI touches on this deepest of mysteries in his Encyclical *Spe Salvi*, 47:

> Some recent theologians are of the opinion that the fire which both burns and saves is Christ himself, the Judge and Saviour. The encounter with him is the decisive act of judgement. Before his gaze all falsehood melts away. This encounter with him, as it burns us, transforms and frees us, allowing us to become truly ourselves. All that we build during our lives can prove to be mere straw, pure bluster, and it collapses. Yet in the pain of this encounter, when the impurity and sickness of our lives become evident to us, there lies salvation. His gaze, the touch of his heart heals us through an undeniably painful transformation 'as through fire'. But it is a blessed pain, in which the holy power of his love sears through us like a flame, enabling us to become totally ourselves and thus totally of God. In this way the inter-relation between justice and grace also becomes clear: the way we live our lives is not immaterial, but our defilement does not stain us for ever if we have at least continued to reach out towards Christ, towards truth and towards love. Indeed, it has already been burned away through Christ's Passion. At the moment of judgement we experience and we absorb the overwhelming power of his love over all the evil in the world and in ourselves. The pain of love becomes our salvation and our joy. It is clear that we cannot calculate

the difficult claims regarding the utter uniqueness of Christ. These revisionist moves end up in danger of being binitarian or very vague about the nature of the Holy Spirit.[29]

Fifth, the Holy Spirit moves every 'authentic prayer' of those from other religions: 'We can indeed maintain that every authentic prayer is called forth by the Holy Spirit, who is mysteriously present in the heart of every person.'[30] This is a profound acknowledgement that when we speak of the Spirit we speak of the deepest longings and desires within a person which are to be found in the 'cave of the heart'. Finally, and related to the discussion above regarding salvation and the eschaton, it is through the Holy Spirit that every person is offered the 'possibility of being associated with this paschal mystery [Christ]' so that all may have the possibility of salvation.[31] These six themes regarding the Holy Spirit will be developed below.

Dialogue and engagement with other religions

What precisely does *LG* say *about* the different non-Christian *religious cultures?* Not much, but what it says is very significant. At this point I will also draw from the Declaration on the Relation of the Church to Non-Christian Religions (*Nostra Aetate* – 1965; subsequently *NA*). A 'declaration' has no dogmatic value but here acts as a phenomenological commentary on the dogmatic claims in *LG* 16. We must recall that Aquinas had already argued that the minimal condition for salvation, following Hebrews 11.6, was faith in a God who rewards good and punishes evil. *Theism* and *morality* are the minimal requirements for saving faith. After all, this had sufficed for Israel before Christ. The Council takes this approach a step forward recognizing the genuine theism (assuming that Jews and Muslims have not knowingly rejected the Gospel) in both Judaism and Islam, while recognizing the *sui generis* relationship with the Jewish people. But it moves beyond this in positively affirming Hinduism and Buddhism (developed in *NA*, but only indirectly in *LG* referring to 'shadows' and 'images') in so much as Hindu and Buddhist beliefs and practices are not in contradiction to the Gospel. First, let me cite the relevant section in *LG* 16 before interlacing *NA* comment on *LG*:

> Finally, those who have not yet received the Gospel are related [*ordinatur*] in various ways to the people of God. (*) In the first place we must recall the people to whom the testament and the promises were given and from whom Christ was born according to the flesh. (See Rom 9: 4–5) On account of their fathers this people remains most dear to God, for God does not repent of the gifts He makes nor of the calls He issues (see Rom 11: 28–9). But the plan of

salvation also includes those who acknowledge the Creator. In the first place amongst these there are the Muslims, who, professing to hold the faith of Abraham, along with us adore the one and merciful God, who on the last day will judge mankind. Nor is God far distant from those who in shadows and images seek the unknown God, for it is He who gives to all men life and breath and all things, (see Acts 17:25–8) and as Saviour wills that all men be saved. (See 1 Tim. 2.4)

Let me address each religion in turn interpolating *NA* into the discussion. In *LG* the Catholic Church provides a particular reading of Romans that marks a real advance in formally accepting that God does not revoke God's covenant with Israel. This excludes the notion that Israel's covenant has come to an end with the coming of Christ. However, contrary to various modern commentaries, I would argue that it cannot be assumed that Israel has been faithful to the covenant without further qualification, or that the covenant can be understood without its necessary fulfilment in Christ.[32] But what is significant here is the recognition that the Jewish covenant (for Jews and for Christians) is God-given and thus genuinely related (*ordinatur*) in terms of potentiality to the Church and Christ. *NA* adds three further important points. First, due to the 'common spiritual heritage', referring back to Paul's reading of Romans and the 'Old Testament', the Council enjoins 'mutual understanding and appreciation' (4.e).[33] Given the years of anti-Semitism among Catholic Christians this is a remarkably important and ground-breaking statement. There is a positive call to learn from and appreciate what is present in Judaism which has flowered in many ways since the Council. Clearly, the Council has no authority over Jews, so this learning can only be seen as an invitation to Jews, but is a duty for Catholics. The foundation of a dicastery in the Vatican related to the Jewish people under the wing of Christian ecumenism compared to the dicastery for non-Christians, which is separate, indicates the serious recognition of Judaism in modern Catholicism.

Second, there is a disavowal of the charge of Jewish deicide that has caused so much Christian anti-Semitism: 'neither all Jews indiscriminately at that time, nor Jews today, can be charged with the crimes committed during [Jesus'] passion' (4.d). Third, the Council actively rebukes any form of 'antisemitism levelled at any time or from any source against the Jews.' It took 35 years and John Paul II to produce a formal repentance for the anti-Semitism within Catholicism expressed in the Liturgy of the Day of Pardon presided over by the Pope on the First Sunday of Lent in the Millennium.

Of Islam there is an acknowledgement of a genuine theism and a genuine basis for morality, for 'along with us they adore [*adorant*] the one merciful God who will judge humanity on the last day' (*LG* 16). This is an important dogmatic point. *NA* adds three further important points. First, it notes the high esteem in which Jesus is held in Islam and also the honour given to the Virgin Mary who is 'at times devoutly invoked' (3.b). Of course, there is also the common root of Abraham 'to whose faith Muslims eagerly link their own'. Notice the phrase does not affirm or deny this claim, but states it as a point of possible contact. As with the mention of Jesus, these commonalities operate within the context of a greater and insuperable difference: 'Although not acknowledging [Jesus] as God' is the rightful beginning of the sentence just quoted above.[34] This allows for possible points of contact, or what the document calls 'what men have in common' (1). Second, there is a qualified approval of selective beliefs and practices, rather than some disembodied notion of Islam. Arising out of Muslim belief and worship of the creator God, the Council notes their 'way of prayer, alms-deeds and fasting' (4.b). Third, as with the Jewish people, the Council tries to move forward from periods of very troubled relations between Islam and the Church. The purpose of this move forward is mutual service to the 'common good', as it is the Church's duty to 'foster unity and charity' among individuals, nations and religions (*NA* 1).

When we turn to the Eastern traditions, *LG* 16 is very thin indeed. It uses Paul's speech to the Areopagus regarding the worship of the 'Unknown God' in 'shadows and images' to suggest the wider connection with non-theistic traditions (Acts 17.22–34). It also cites 1 Timothy 2 verse 4 regarding God's desire to save all peoples. One should recall *LG* is not concerned to flesh out this skeleton, but only indicates its dogmatic existence. The two dogmatic points here are as follows: first, there is an acceptance that non-theistic religions might exemplify a genuine search for God – and in this sense, there is an analogical extension of Aquinas' 'potentiality'; second, there is a further extension to non-religious cultures which can also be 'orientated' towards the Church. The latter is a remarkable move given the Catholic Church's opposition to Communism and secularism, although neither is affirmed *per se*. The Eastern traditions are given a little more flesh in *NA*. In Hinduism, which contains 'theistic' strands, although quite different from Semitic theism,[35] it is acknowledged that there is an exploration of the divine mystery in 'myth' and 'philosophy' (beliefs) – and also in practices. This latter is found in the 'ascetical practices' and 'profound meditation' in the non-theistic traditions, and through 'recourse to God in confidence and love' in the *bhakti* devotional traditions.[36] While any scholar of Hinduism might balk at this thin description, one should instead perhaps marvel and rejoice that any positive description is being made at all. A door is being opened to serious scholarship and indology to theologically flesh out and think through these starting points for engagement towards realising the 'common good'.

Buddhist beliefs and practices are likewise singled out, even though there are no theistic elements within Buddhism, at least in the sense of Abrahamic theism. Nevertheless, in Pure Land and other forms of Buddhism there are emphases upon 'divine' aid. Thus NA affirms the insight regarding the 'inadequacy of the changing world' and the way Buddhists seek 'perfect liberation' and 'supreme illumination' 'either through their own efforts or by the aid of divine help' (2).

I want to use the example of Buddhism to make a subsidiary point. NA is only concerned to encourage positive pastoral orientation. It makes no claims about comprehensive or detailed evaluation of any religious culture. How could it? Hence, it should be no surprise that two intellectually probing popes after the Council have, in their 'private' writings (i.e. writings that have no magisterial authority), made negative judgements about Buddhism. Cardinal Ratzinger, now Benedict XVI, suggested in an interview with a French newspaper that in Buddhism the self-help involved in meditation and release amounted to salvation by one's own efforts and thus might be compared to 'auto-eroticism'. He is reported as saying: 'If Buddhism is attractive, it is because it appears as a possibility of touching the infinite and obtaining happiness without having any concrete religious obligations. A spiritual auto-eroticism of some sort.'[37] Pope John Paul II, in *Crossing the Threshold of Hope* explored the question whether Buddhist meditation and contemplation is the same as mediation and contemplation in orthodox Christianity. Buddhist meditation strives to 'wake' one from existential delusions regarding the status of the world. Christian meditation in the Carmelite tradition begins where the Buddha left off. He continues: 'Christian mysticism . . . is not born of a purely negative "enlightenment." It is not born of an awareness of the evil which exists in man's attachment to the world through the senses, the intellect, and the spirit. Instead, Christian mysticism is born of the Revelation of the living God.'[38] Taking another religion seriously in terms of what it teaches is part of the process of respectful and informed theological engagement. None of these explorations negate the positive outreach towards Buddhism.

Vatican II opened the door to scholarship *about* the religions and theological engagement and reflection *on* the religions. There is thus room here for both a theology of religions (which is concerned primarily with the dogmatic questions of Christology, trinity, Church, grace, salvation, etc.) and a theology in engagement with each particular religion (dealing with the different contexts of engagement and thus with often very particular sets of questions). In this book, uniquely, both come together in the essays that follow.

I should finally note that Vatican II only mentioned some religions. There are many more in the world such as Sikhism, Confucianism, Daoism, folk and tribal religions, and in the West, New Religious Movements. The latter are most important to a Western audience and they are thus included in this book. While the Council could hardly address all these it started a process that would orient Catholic scholarship and practice towards a positive and rigorously critical engagement with these traditions. Catholics may have much to learn from this process about the disciplines and practices that help build up the common good, that help men and women resist evil and despair, and that encourage selflessness and service. But none of these things, however true, good and noble, can displace the necessity of Christ's call to total conversion to the triune God, to rejecting the depths of sin and violence and falling upon his forgiving grace, knowing that only in this grace is there salvation. Nothing allows the Catholic Christian to forego offering that which is the greatest gift that they themselves know: Jesus Christ, the transforming and redeeming relationship between God and his creation. Thus, engagement with other religions is inevitably complex in terms of not only acknowledging and rejoicing in that which is true, good and holy and also the many promptings of the Holy Spirit, but also respectfully questioning and critically engaging with that religion.

The meaning of other religions in God's plan of salvation

What is the theological status of these religions in the light of the two sets of discussions above? There is widespread consensus that Vatican II was silent about the theological status of these religions, neither denying nor affirming that they can be viewed as 'salvific means'.[39] The Council itself does use a group of cognate phrases which indicates a reasonably clear answer. In the most important dogmatic document *LG* 16, we find the significant phrases that these positive elements in the religions and non-religions are 'considered by the church as a preparation for the gospel [*praeparatio evangelica*]'.[40] Eusebius and the tradition after him that employed this phrase did not impute any salvific significance to what was to be found in the traditions, but rather that the truth there at least provided a bridge whereby the Gospel might be understood and error abandoned. The *prisca theologia* (ancient theology) tradition is not invoked, but the *semina verbi* (seeds of the Word) is. In *NA* 2 it says of the religions that while differing from the Catholic Church's teachings they nevertheless 'often reflect a ray of that truth which enlightens all men'. This is also found in *AG* 11, (see note 25) which says that Christians living among non-Christians 'should be familiar with their national and religious traditions and uncover with gladness and respect those seeds of the Word which lie hidden among them'. From Justin Martyr onwards and in the Council, 'seeds' is not used in any way to justify religions *per se* but denotes them as preparatory, like Aquinas' potentiality, for the coming of Christ even while being immersed in error and superstition.[41]

Given the subsequent heated theological debate on this matter after the Council, the magisterium issued a specific clarification on this issue: *On the Unicity and Salvific Universality of Jesus Christ and the Church* (*Dominus Iesus* – 2000, subsequently *DI*). Paragraphs 20–22 address the intention of the Council teachings and also indicate illegitimate explications from the Council documents. *DI* acknowledges that while the religions may contain truth and goodness moved by the Spirit, nevertheless 'it is clear that it would be contrary to the faith to consider the Church as *one way* of salvation alongside those constituted by the other religions, seen as complementary to the Church or substantially equivalent to her, even if these are said to be converging with the Church towards the eschatological kingdom of God.' [This thereby counters any form of pluralism *de iure* (in principle). It also shows why the other religions cannot be understood as a 'means of salvation' as this term is uniquely applied to the Church precisely because of its Christological foundations.] It is for this reason that the document is able to say, despite the many positive teachings which are unhesitatingly repeated, that the other religions *per se* cannot be understood as ways to salvation. Section 21 is important (as are its notes[42]):

> Certainly, the various religious traditions contain and offer religious elements which come from God,[85] and which are part of what 'the Spirit brings about in human hearts and in the history of peoples, in cultures, and religions'.[86] Indeed, some prayers and rituals of the other religions may assume a role of preparation for the Gospel, in that they are occasions or pedagogical helps in which the human heart is prompted to be open to the action of God.[87] One cannot attribute to these, however, a divine origin or an *ex opere operato* salvific efficacy, which is proper to the Christian sacraments.[88] Furthermore, it cannot be overlooked that other rituals, insofar as they depend on superstitions or other errors (cf. *1 Cor* 10:20–21), constitute an obstacle to salvation.[89]

The door is thus closed on trying to establish any form of pluralism *de iure*,[43] but it is kept open to explore how these religions might be forms of 'participated mediation' in so much as their positive elements might actually be part of God's plan to lead all people to Christ. These positive elements cannot be viewed as positive in themselves, but only as some form of *praeparatio*. Such a distinction is crucial. *DI* rightly suggests that this is a question that requires serious theological exploration.

However, it also needs to be said that the 'positive elements' that might act in this fashion are not necessarily how those religions would interpret themselves. In other cases the positive elements will be mutually affirmed by both Christians and the partner, as in alms giving and fasting, valued by both Muslims and Catholics (and affirmed in *NA*). And in some cases the positive elements might cause deep shame, learning and wonder in a Catholic – as when Catholics encounter ritual Muslim prayer and silent Buddhist meditation and non-violent practices in Jainism. Needless to say, these latter also raise many critical questions.

To summarize: while other religions might be affirmed in the way outlined above, they can only be seen as part of God's plan in so much as they provide a *praeparatio* to the Gospel, but not in themselves as a means of salvation. While saying the latter, there is no implication that non-Christians are damned or that genuine holiness and wisdom is absent from non-Christian religions. We see emerging a nuanced and delicate balance between a group of theological principles that uphold both the ancient orthodox faith of the Catholic Church as well as positively engaging with this new context whereby the religions are seen as other than schismatic and heretical cultural configurations. Of course, that they might contain idolatries and heresies of all sorts is also an important continuity in teaching. This point is consistently made in all the documents we have examined.

I have been stressing the positive points of contact, but they cannot be taken seriously and in a balanced manner without fully considering the reality of sin. *LG* 16 adds this ominous and realistic note after the positive appraisal of the religions: 'But often men, deceived by the Evil One, have become vain in their reasonings and have exchanged the truth of God for a lie, serving the creature rather than the Creator. (See Rom. 1.21, 25) Or some there are who, living and dying in this world without God, are exposed to final despair. Wherefore to promote the glory of God and procure the salvation of all of these, and mindful of the command of the Lord, "Preach the Gospel to every creature", (Mk 16.16) the Church fosters the missions with care and attention.'

Mission and inculturation

I have touched on these two themes above, but it is time to be explicit: what does the Council teach about mission? Three things are clear in numerous

Council documents. First, it is the nature of the Church to be a light to all nations, to call all men and women to the good news that Christ has come to bring salvation into the world.[44] There is no exception to the extent of evangelization, for to exclude anyone would be to exclude them from God's great gift to all men and women. Second, while there is a call to universal mission, there is also a call to respect the dignity of every human person and thus their freedom of conscience.[45] [No one should be coerced to follow Christ and mission does not call for disrespect or belittling of other beliefs and practices.] I have also noted how after the Council, the Church has officially recognized that Catholics have not always followed their own teachings. Third, mission means planting Christian communities in every nation so that all cultures and creation can join in a hymn of praise and thanksgiving to the triune God. Mission involves the gradual transformation of the Church through a critically sifted process of inculturation.

This third point is worth dwelling on further, for it raises the important question: what elements from other religions might transform future Christian practices and beliefs? The answer I think is in principle simple: anything that is good, true and holy in the cultures of the world can and should be incorporated into the Church if it is not already there. In practice the answer is far more complex. After the discovery of the 'New World', as it was called, Catholic missionaries engaged with all types of religious cultures, some of which had appalling dark elements and others which elicited high praise and respect. It goes without saying that the same was true for the missionaries' own religious culture. Discerning dark from light is sometimes rather complex and incorporating the good and positive elements likewise. Today, for example, we would not necessarily share the judgement of a Jesuit in India who found in the practice of widow immolation (*sati*) something so noble and dutiful, that it would truly challenge Hindus if Christians could engage in such self-sacrificial martyrdom![46] Staying with India, some Catholic missionaries were perhaps uniquely able to appreciate what some of the Protestant missionaries could only see as Hindu 'idol worship' in the practices of Hindu *pūjā* (those same Protestant missionaries sometimes saw idol worship in the practices of Catholicism!).

Regarding inculturation (the use of cultures to give shape and form to the proclamation of the Gospel) it is a fair generalization to say that within Catholicism the Western Latin tradition dominated for historical and geographical reasons. As Newman has argued, the Latin tradition was a long slow process of critical inculturation of Greek and Roman traditions, practises and conceptualities.[47] The inculturation of 'positive elements' from non-Christian traditions forms the historical explication of 'faith', which as 'faith' cannot be reduced to any single culture. In this sense although these elements might be western in their origins, they have universal patrimony for all Christians if they have been received by the church, for they form that which is called 'tradition', and tradition contains all sorts of normative statements (in Councils, etc.) that are determinative for shaping developments and articulations of the faith in different cultural mediums. With the slow crumbling of European economic and political power this issue will become more and more acute in the Western Latin tradition. In 1659, in the early days of the discovery of the new non-European worlds, the Sacred Congregation for the Propagation of the Faith issued an instruction to new missionaries to China regarding the matter of adapting to local customs and respecting the habits of the countries to be evangelized: 'Do not act with zeal, do not put forward any arguments to convince these peoples to change their rites, their customs or their usages, except if they are evidently contrary to the religion and morality. What would be more absurd than to bring France, Spain, Italy or any other European country to the Chinese? Do not bring to them our countries, but instead bring to them the faith, a faith that does not reject or hurt the rites, nor the usages of any people, provided that these are not distasteful, but that instead keeps and protects them.'[48] It might be said that the famous Chinese rites controversy was not about inculturation, but rather a battle between the Dominicans and Jesuits. The lifting of the ban of 1705 against using local rites in 1939 by Pius XII was in part politically motivated regarding the freeing up of the Catholic Church's operations in China.[49]

LG continues in this tradition of respect for cultures but with a sharp critical eye, recognizing that the process of inculturation will often transform the elements of that which is incorporated: 'Through her work, whatever good is in the minds and hearts of men, whatever good lies latent in the religious practices and cultures of diverse peoples, is not only saved from destruction but is also cleansed, raised up and perfected unto the glory of God, the confusion of the devil and the happiness of man' (17). An example from the Asian Church will be helpful here. Some Catholics employ meditational techniques from the yoga tradition of Hinduism and from Japanese Buddhist practices. Breathing, posture, stillness and concentration, it is sometimes claimed, are immensely helpful ways of stilling the mind to be receptive to God. Examples could be drawn from the French Benedictine Dom Henri Le Saux, later called Swami Abshiktananda, who learnt meditation under a Hindu guru, or the Trappist monk Thomas Merton who found great wisdom in Zen meditation enriching his own contemplative Trappist tradition.[50] Furthermore, some Asian Catholics are trying to think through dogmatics with the aid of Sankara and Ramanuja in the same way that Aquinas employed Aristotle.[51] As *LG* put it, all that is good in people's hearts, rites, cultures will be raised and purified in this transformation into a hymn of praise to God when incorporated into a church which we might find very difficult to recognize.

While there are important and exciting developments, some critical problems should also be registered, for the stream of engagement with other religions and cultures contains complex currents. While legitimately drawing on Sankara, can the Latin heritage simply be seen as 'European' so that the Indian Church is not tied to this Latin tradition as is argued by some radical Indian theologians?[52] John Paul II argued against such a move in his Encyclical *Faith and Reason* (*Fides et Ratio*, 1998), 72: 'the Church cannot abandon what she has gained from her inculturation in the world of Greco-Latin thought. To reject this heritage would be to deny the providential plan of God who guides his Church down the paths of time and history.' This is not to privilege the Greco-Latin heritage, for he then continues: 'This criterion is valid for the Church in every age, even for the Church of the future, who will judge herself enriched by all that comes from today's engagement with Eastern cultures and will find in this inheritance fresh cues for fruitful dialogue with the cultures which will emerge as humanity moves into the future.' What is at stake here is valuing different traditions and allowing fresh formulations to be accountable to the Bible and earlier traditions. The magisterium is the final arbiter when traditions conflict rather than symphonically reflect God's truth.

In the West we have seen this issue arise with the employment of Marx by some (not all) liberation theologians. One must be sensitive to the way some philosophies and practices can contain presuppositions and accompanying world-views which if not challenged and questioned can render 'inculturation' into uncritical assimilation. When this happens, as in the case of some forms of liberation theology, the Church can suddenly be viewed in primarily sociological categories of power rather than in sacramental terms. And with the use of some types of Eastern meditational practices by Christians, this might (but not necessarily) lead to pseudo-Gnosticism which aims to liberate the soul from matter and body into a state of superior knowledge. It might also lead to 'Messalianism', named after the fourth-century charismatics who identified the redeeming grace of the Holy Spirit with the experiences of His sustaining and enlivening presence in the soul. Both errors are in danger of attempting to overcome the distance separating creature from creator and to bypass the humanity of Christ and the sacraments of the Church. These are only dangers, not intrinsic to proper inculturation, but happen when uncritical syncretism or assimilation takes place.[53] To note these dangers is important, but they should in no way inhibit critical inculturation as affirmed in *LG* as the Church's very Catholicity is otherwise compromised.

In the future, who knows what the Indian Catholic church might look like in its customs and rites and theology. And this organic growth, when done under the guidance of the bishops, can be understood as the Holy Spirit's uncovering ever anew the face of Christ. Christ's face is both known and unknown, but never seen in its fullness until we come to see Christ face to face in the eschaton. The Vatican called upon the Benedictine and Cistercian monastic orders, precisely those trained in meditation and prayer, to engage with Eastern religious traditions and communities to further this important quest for both better understanding of the 'Other' as well as deep learning through this process. The Monastic Interreligious Dialogue committee has developed its activities over many years and in many different countries.[54]

Before moving on, I should touch on one last issue: the issue of prayer. If Judaism and Islam are involved with the real and living God, is interfaith prayer possible between Catholics and these religious traditions? Indeed, is interfaith prayer possible between Christianity and other theistic traditions such as Sikhism and strands of Hinduism? The formal teachings on this matter clarify three issues. First, authentic prayer is addressed to God as trinity, is moved by the Holy Spirit, and draws us into an active and real relationship with the living God.[55] Second, the prayers of Israel in the Psalms are seen as authentic, even though they are not addressed explicitly to the Trinitarian God. Third, as we see from point two, while not denying the 'authenticity' of some forms of non-Christian prayer, interfaith prayer is quite problematic because the explicit 'object' of prayer is different (Jews and Muslims, let alone Sikhs, do not pray to Father, Son and Spirit).

This last point is worth dwelling on as the issue is addressed in *Redemptoris Missio* 29. It is said that the prayers from other religions can arise from the movement of the Holy Spirit within a person's heart and be a genuine seeking after God. Pope John Paul II tried to clarify his presuppositions behind the Assisi meeting he convened in 1986 and again in 2002 after substantial concerns were expressed by some of the Roman curia. In an address to the curia the Pope said: 'Every authentic prayer is under the influence of the Spirit "who intercedes insistently for us . . . , because we do not even know how to pray as we ought," but he prays in us "with unutterable groaning" and "the One who searches the heart knows what are the desires of the Spirit." (See Rom. 8:26–7) We can indeed maintain that every authentic prayer is called forth by the Holy Spirit, who is mysteriously present in the heart of every person.'[56] This insight, slightly modified, has subsequently entered into an Encyclical with teaching authority. In *RM* 29 it is said that the 'Church's relationship with other religions is dictated by a twofold respect: "Respect for man in his quest for answers to the deepest questions of his life, and respect for the action of the Spirit in man." (*) Excluding any mistaken interpretation, the interreligious meeting held in Assisi was meant to confirm my conviction that 'every authentic prayer is prompted by the Holy Spirit, who is mysteriously present in every human heart.'[57]

The reality of the action of the Holy Spirit in human hearts and cultures has now been repeated in a number of teaching documents so in one sense, its application to prayer as one element of culture is unsurprising. But these prayers cannot be understood to be a full participation in the life of the triune God, but a form of participation that will find its fulfilment in Trinitarian prayer and praise. Needless to say, the heart of a non-Christian might be more receptive and transformed (and thus their lives) in such prayer, compared to a Christian who prays the Lord's Prayer without receptivity to the Spirit. The objective forms of beauty, reverence and solemnity such as the Muslim call to prayer properly recited, or the ecstatic joy and transformative rhythms of Sufi sung prayer are remarkable. I have met Muslims whose prayer life has caused me to feel shame for the lack of sincerity and regularity of my own. All this is of course a very different act from interfaith prayer, which while possibly legitimate in some very limited cases,[58] cannot be possible as a regular practice given our deep differences in understanding God. I do not want to accentuate the intellectual dimension of prayer, but this aspect cannot be negotiated away either. Cardinal Ratzinger makes a good case for deep respect and reverent witnessing to the prayers of others, but cannot find a strong case for interfaith prayer.[59]

Social justice

As we have seen the relation between religions from a Catholic perspective has been profoundly oriented towards the common good.[60] There are two points to emphasize regarding this issue. First, Catholics are required to work with all people of good will to attain the common good of society, nationally and internationally. Poverty, the environment, the arms race, and the oppression of women and children all over the world are just some of the horrendous crimes that cry out to God. Christians are called to address these problems in every way they can and that includes working with those from other religions to bring about the 'common good'.[61] These alliances can be grass-root communities working to build a well together, or they can be local groups to lobby politicians, or official international bodies coming together, like the Vatican and certain Muslim states working in tandem to put pressure on the United Nations regarding the issues of fertility. Of course, issues of social justice might also entail questioning and challenging religious communities with whom Christians share social space. Hence, the Indian and Pakistani Roman Catholic bishops have repeatedly criticized legislation in those two countries as being anti-Catholic or/and against the common good which requires equal rights for all religious communities. The Vatican has made recent demands for reciprocal rights to be granted to Christians in Muslim countries such that Muslims enjoy in most Western democracies. Clearly, putting the common good at the centre might entail working together with other religions and equally, sometimes working against other religions. [The important point here is that there is no inhibition about social cooperation and mutual political activity between religions.]

Second, while some Catholic theologians have called for a prioritizing of socio-political liberation as the basis of interfaith dialogue, this position is attractive but also has problems.[62] It is attractive because the Gospel is fully oriented to the poor, the outcast, and the marginalized and should rightly be a priority, or as the *Compendium of the Social Doctrine of the Church* puts it: 'The principle of the universal destination of goods requires that the poor, the marginalized and in all cases those whose living conditions interfere with their proper growth should be the focus of particular concern. To this end, the preferential option for the poor should be reaffirmed in all its force' (182). But this very prioritizing, as is argued in the *Compendium*, is based on God's plan for humanity as disclosed in Christ, so that it is impossible to bypass the question of truth and instead prioritize social justice. For social justice is rooted in both Christ and the natural law that is ordered towards him. One can understand that some might be impatient with philosophical and theological argumentation between religions while millions die of poverty, but *if* we are to address the full complexity of the question of the relation between religions, there is no use trying to bypass the central issues of intellectual truth as if they were divorced from practices.

Conclusion

I want to commend the approach I have outlined above because it remains faithful to the ancient dogmatic teachings of the Christian Church, while applying and thinking them through in a very new context. It remains faithful to Christ and the revelation of the triune God, it remains faithful to Christ's founding of the Church as the means of salvation for all people, and yet without compromising these foundational tenets, it reaches out to other religions and their adherents in the spirit of cooperation and friendship. In this reaching out there is a generous and joyful acknowledgement of the work of God in these religious cultures (in differentiated and nuanced ways) and a patient learning from these cultures. There should also be repentance for our many failures in these areas. In this reaching out there is a concern to join together to act for the common good and to help transform society and alleviate the suffering of the poor, to herald in the Kingdom of God. In this meeting the other there should be an acknowledgement that Catholic Christians can only 'reach out' as equals, seeking to learn how to love and serve and not to dominate or denigrate. And in this dialogue, there is finally and foremost a call to be witnesses to Christ, to be missionaries of the Gospel, and to call all peoples to baptism in the threefold name. Mission requires a delicate sensitivity to a plethora of issues, but it cannot be ignored or downplayed. Of course, the planting of church communities is the greatest witness, especially when those communities are marked by charity, love of the poor and serving others out of the endless service of Christ to us. Learning to love involves an activity whereby only by being attentive to the triune God, the forsaken on the cross, can we learn that God's grace and judgement is to be found where we might expect it least.

Notes

1 See Congregation for the Doctrine of the Faith, *Instruction on the Ecclesial Vocation of the Theologian*, 1990 (this and all Vatican documents cited, unless otherwise stated, can be found on www.vatican.va website. All website cited in this essay were checked in November 2009.) I have developed this view of the theologian in *Theology in the Public Square* (Oxford: Blackwell, 2005), 77–111; and see also Joseph Ratzinger, *The Nature and Mission of Theology: Approaches to Understanding Its Role in the Light of Present Controversy* (San Francisco: Ignatius Press, 1995) which acts as a commentary to the *Instruction*.
2 See Alasdair MacIntyre, *Three Rival Versions of Moral Enquiry* (London: Duckworth, 1990).
3 See Paul Griffith's challenging thesis on this matter in *Religious Reading: The Place of Reading in the Practice of Religion* (New York: Oxford, 1999).
4 See Avery Dulles, *Magisterium. Teacher and Guardian of the Faith* (Florida: Sapientia Press, 2007) for a very good discussion of the magisterium and the complex question of establishing the different levels of authority within the magisterium. For a good discussion of contemporary Catholic debates see Jacques Dupuis, *Towards a Christian Theology of Religious Pluralism* (Maryknoll, NY: Orbis, 1997); and for pre-Vatican II debates on this matter, see Maurice Eminyan SJ, *The Theology of Salvation* (Boston: St Pauls, 1960). For a magisterial overall study in this area see Louis Capéran, *Le Salut des*

Infidéles (Paris: Louis Beauchesne, 1912); and in English, the best work is Francis A. Sullivan, *Salvation Outside the Church? Tracing the History of the Catholic Response* (London: Geoffrey Chapman, 1992).

5 For more biblical materials Dupuis, *Towards*, 29–52 presents a very rich Catholic synopsis of biblical materials, as does Gerald O'Collins, *God's Other Peoples: Salvation for All* (Oxford: Oxford University Press, 2008). While their coverage is excellent, I would disagree with both in their exegesis of various texts. For a more balanced picture see Gerald R. McDermott, *God's Rivals. Why Has God Allowed Different Religions? Insights from the Bible and the Early Church* (Illinois: IVP Academic, 2007).

6 The Greek: *katelthonta eis ta katôtata*.

7 *In III Sent.* D.25, q. 2, a. 1, sol. 1, ad. 1; and *De Veritate*, q. 14, a. 11, ad. 1 (Parma edition): 7.272 and 9.246 respectively (1852–1873), reprinted: New York, 1948. Aquinas does seem to have been aware of individual non-Christians but not of nations who had not been evangelized.

8 See William T. Cavanaugh, *Theopolitical Imagination* (Edinburgh: T & T Clark, 2002); and my *Christianity and World Religions. Disputed Questions in the Theology of Religions* (Oxford: Blackwell, 2009), 74–102 for a critique of the 'wars of religion' thesis and a foregrounding of the effects of the emergence of the nation-state that increasingly generated one type of secularism that was inimical and hostile to religion. This form of secularism plays an important part in France and parts of Europe, while secularism in the United States should be understood quite differently.

9 See Stratford Caldecott, *Understanding the New Age Movement* (London: Catholic Truth Society, 2006) and the Pontifical Council for Culture and Pontifical Council for Interreligious Dialogue, *Jesus Christ the Bearer of the Water of Life: A Christian Reflection on the 'New Age'* (London: Catholic Truth Society, 2003).

10 On science see Amos Funkenstein, *Theology and the Scientific Imagination from the Middles Ages to the Seventeenth Century* (Princeton: Princeton University Press, 1986); on the turn to the East see Wilhelm Halbfass, *India and Europe: An Essay in Understanding* (Albany, NY: SUNY Press, 1988).

11 See Edward H. Flannery, *The Anguish of the Jews. Twenty-Three Centuries of Antisemitism* (New Jersey, Paulist Press, 2004), 2nd ed.

12 This trajectory is thoughtfully discussed and contextualized in Tracey Rowland, *Culture and the Thomist Tradition. After Vatican II* (London: Routledge, 2003).

13 For commentaries on the Council see Giuseppe Alberigo, ed., *History of Vatican II*, 5 volumes (Maryknoll, NY: Orbis, 1995, 1997, 2000, 2003, 2006); and Herbert Vorgrimler, ed., *Commentary on the Documents of Vatican II*, 5 volumes (New York: Crossroads, 1967, 1968, 1968, 1969, 1969). For the best single-volume commentary see Matthew L. Lamb and Matthew Levering, eds, *Vatican II: Renewal within Tradition* (Oxford: Oxford University Press, 2008).

14 1994, 388 (http://www.vatican.va/archive/catechism/ccc_toc.htm).

15 When an asterisk is used in a quote within parentheses '(*)', it signifies a note in the original cited text which I have omitted.

16 See, for example, Karl Joseph Becker, 'An Examination of *Subsistit in*: A Profound Theological Perspective', *L'Osservatore Romano*, Weekly English

Edition, 14 December 2005, 11; and Francis Sullivan's response: 'Quaestio disputata: A Response to Karl Becker, SJ, on the meaning of *subsistit in*', *Theological Studies*, 67, 2006, 395–409.

17 See the essays by Ilaria Morali in Morali, Karl Josef Becker with Gavin D'Costa and Maurice Borrmans eds, *Catholic Engagement with World Religions. A Comprehensive Study* (New York: Orbis, 2010), 69–142.

18 The Latin texts are taken from Austin Flannery, ed., *Vatican Council II. The Conciliar and Post Conciliar Documents* (Dublin: Dominican Publications, 1975); and all English translations are taken from the Vatican website – see above.

19 *Letter: The True Sense of the Catholic Doctrine That There is no Salvation Outside the Church* – which can be accessed in English translation on http://www.romancatholicism.org/feeney-condemnations.htm#a2 along with other key texts related to this matter.

20 In *The Meeting*, 99–142, and in *Christianity and World Religions*, 161–211, I have explicated these two claims.

21 See especially his 'Membership of the Church according to the Teaching of Pius XII's Encyclical "Mystici Corporis"', *Theological Investigations*, Volume 2 (London: Darton, Longman & Todd, 1963), 1–88.

22 This is contrary to Dupuis exegesis of the term in *Towards*, 348–349, where he concludes that non-Christians can be saved solely in relation to Christ and not in relation to the Church. Dupuis' conclusion was also called into question by the Congregation of the Doctrine of the Faith, *Notification on the Book Toward a Christian Theology of Religious Pluralism* (Maryknoll, NY: Orbis, 1997) by Father Jacques Dupuis, SJ, 2001: http://www.vatican.va/roman_curia/congregations/cfaith/documents/rc_con_cfaith_doc_20010124_dupuis_en.html. I cite this not to minimize Dupuis contribution to this debate, but simply to indicate inappropriate avenues for further exploration.

23 See *Christianity and World Religions*, 161–211.

24 D'Costa, *Christianity*, 161–211.

25 *Dominium et Vivificantem*, 1986, 53; drawing on Vatican II's Decree on the Church's Missionary Activity (*Ad Gentes*, 1965 – subsequently *AG*), 4, 11.

26 *The Redeemer of Man* (*Redemptor Hominis*, 1979), 6, 11; drawing on Vatican II: *AG*, 11; *LG*, 1964, 17.

27 *Redemptor Hominis*, 6; drawing on the Pastoral Constitution on the Church in the World (*Gaudium et spes, GS*, 1965), 92: 'Our thoughts go out to all who acknowledge God and who preserve precious religious and human elements in their traditions; it is our hope that frank dialogue will spur us all on to receive the impulses of the Spirit with fidelity and act upon them with alacrity.'

28 *RM*, 1991, 29; drawing on *AG* 11.

29 See Amos Yong, *Beyond the Impasse. Toward a Pneumatological Theology of Religions* (Grand Rapids, MI: Baker Academic, 2003), although Yong is guilty of the same weaknesses he identifies in other theologians when their Spirit-approaches bypass Christ.

30 *RM* 29 in which a key address is cited: *Address* to Cardinals and the Roman Curia, 22 December 1986, 11; *Acta Apostolicae Sedis* 79 (1987), 1089, where the Pope explained his Assisi meeting.

31 Second Vatican Council: *GS* 22; *LG* 16.

32 See *NA* 4.d. See further Roy H. Schoeman, *Salvation is From the Jews: The Role of Judaism in Salvation History from Abraham to the Second Coming* (San Francisco: Ignatius Press, 2003).

33 Letters after the section numeral denote the paragraph within the section, that is, a = first, b = second, and so on.

34 See Christian W. Troll, *Dialogue and Difference: Clarity in Christian Muslim Relations* (New York: Orbis, 2009).

35 See, for example, Julius Lipner, 'The Christian and Vedantic Theories of Originative Causality: A Study in Transcendence and Immanence', *Philosophy East and West*, 28, 1, 1978, 53–68.

36 Martin Ganeri, 'Catholic Encounter with Hindus in the Twentieth century: In Search of an Indian Christianity', *New Blackfriars*, 88, 2007, 410–432; and 'Knowledge and Love of God in Ramanuja and Aquinas', *Journal of Hindu-Christian Studies*, 20, 2007, 3–9.

37 See Leo D. Lefebure, 'Cardinal Ratzinger's Comments on Buddhism', *Buddhist-Christian Studies*, 18, 1998, 221–223. The original quote is from *L'Express*, 20 March 1997.

38 *Crossing the Threshold of Hope* (London: Jonathan Cape, 1994), 81; and see further, Paul Williams careful interrogation of Buddhism in 'Aquinas Meets the Buddhists: Prolegomenon to an Authentically Thomist Basis for Dialogue' in Jim Fodor and Frederic Christian Bauerschmidt (eds), *Aquinas in Dialogue: Thomas for the Twenty-First Century* (Oxford: Blackwell, 2004), 87–118, and *The Unexpected Way* (London: Continuum, 2004).

39 For a good discussion of this see Dupuis, *Towards*, 165–170; and in contrast Mikka Ruokanen, *The Catholic Doctrine on Non-Christian Religions According to the Second Vatican Council* (Leiden: Brill, 1992).

40 Citing Eusebius of Caesarea, *Preparation for the Gospel*, 1.1; see also on this matter the very helpful historical contextualization of Eusebius' approach which properly roots it in a biblical historical world-view: Aaron P. Johnson, *Ethnicity and Argument in Eusebius' Praeparatio Evangelica* (Oxford: Oxford University Press, 2006).

41 A good study of Justin's context and intention can be found in Ragnar Holte, 'Logos Spermatikos. Christianity and Ancient Philosophy according to St Justin's Apologies', *Studia Theologica*, 12, 1958, 109–168. The patristic tradition is often viewed overpositively in this regard. For a spirited critique of these readings see Paul Hacker, *Theological Foundations of Evangelisation* (St Augustin: Steyler Verlag, 1980).

42 The sources for the footnotes as given in the document are as following: '(85) These are the seeds of the divine Word (*semina Verbi*), which the Church recognizes with joy and respect (cf. Second Vatican Council, Decree *Ad gentes*, 11; Declaration *Nostra aetate*, 2). (86) JOHN PAUL II, Encyclical Letter *Redemptoris missio*, 29. (87) Cf. ibid.; *Catechism of the Catholic Church*, 843. (88) Cf. COUNCIL OF TRENT, *Decretum de sacramentis*, can. 8, *de sacramentis in genere*: DS 1608. (89) Cf. JOHN PAUL II, Encyclical Letter *Redemptoris missio*, 55.'

43 See my '"Christian Orthodoxy and Religious Pluralism": A Response to Terrence W. Tilley', 23, 3, 2007, *Modern Theology*, 435–446 and the ensuing debate in the same journal on this point.

44 The document most important here is *AG*, but see also *LG* and *NA*.

45 Besides *AG*, the key document here is in fact the *Declaration on Religion Liberty* (*Dignitatis Humanae* – 1965), 3.
46 Catherine Weinberger-Thomas, *Ashes of Immortality: Widow Burning in India* (Chicago: University of Chicago Press, 1999), 18 cites this and other very interesting comparative materials.
47 See John Henry Newman, *An Essay on the Development of Christian Doctrine* (London: Longman, 1890).
48 See *Missions étrangères de Paris. 350 ans au service du Christ* (Paris: Editeurs Malesherbes Publications, 2008), 5. [English and French cited in the entry on Paris Foreign Missions Society: http://wapedia.mobi/en/Paris_Foreign_Missions_Society?t=5.]
49 See George Minamiki, *The Chinese Rites Controversy: From Its Beginning to Modern Times* (Chicago: Loyola University Press, 1985).
50 See Abhishiktananda, *Hindu-Christian Meeting Point* (Bangalore: CISRS, 1969); *Saccidananda: Christian Approach to Advaitic Experiences* (Delhi: Indian Society for Promoting Christian Knowledge, revised edition, 1998). For Merton see *Asian Journal* (New York: W. W. Norton & Co, 1975), and *Zen and the Birds of Appetite* (New York: W. W. Norton & Co, 1968).
51 For an excellent guide to early Indian experiments in the nineteenth and twentieth centuries see Joseph Mattam, *The Land of the Trinity: A Study of Modern Christian Approaches to Hinduism* (Bangalore: Theological Publications in India, 1975).
52 For example, Felix Wilfred, *Sunset in the East. Asian Challenges and Christian Involvement* (Madras: University of Madras Press, 1991).
53 See the Congregation for the Doctrine of the Faith, Letter to the Bishops of the Catholic Church on some Aspects of Christian Meditation, 1989: (http://www.ewtn.com/library/curia/cdfmed.htm). The critical responses to this document sometimes fail to acknowledge that the document never criticizes inculturation, but rather points to dangers in uncritical assimilation.
54 See official website: http://www.mid-gbi.com/index.html
55 See *RM* 29; *The Catechism*, 2596; and my *The Meeting*, 143–171.
56 In *Address* to Cardinals and the Roman Curia, December 22, 1986: published in *Bulletin* (Secretariat for Non-Christians), 64, 22, 1, 1987, 54–62.
57 The text then refers to the earlier papal speech given to the curia – see note 30.
58 Such as a terrible public disaster within a community (like 9/11, or the 2004 Tsunami in East Asia) or more intimately and interpersonally in hospital chaplaincies or interfaith marriages.
59 *Truth and Tolerance. Christian Belief and World Religions* (San Francisco: Ignatius Press, 2004), 106–109.
60 See the *Compendium of the Social Doctrine of the Church* (Vatican: Liberia Editrice Vaticana, 2004) and for the history of the social teaching, see Charles E. Curran, *Catholic Social Teaching 1891–Present: A Historical, Theological and Ethical Analysis* (Washington: Georgetown University Press, 2002).
61 See *Compendium*, paras 164–170.
62 See, for example, Paul Knitter, 'Dialogue and Liberation', *Drew Gateway*, 58, 1, 1987, 1–53; and Aloysius Pieris, *An Asian Theology of Liberation* (New York: Orbis, 1988).

Some Further Readings

Dupuis, Jacques (1997), *Towards a Christian Theology of Religious Pluralism*, Maryknoll, NY: Orbis.

Eminyan, Maurice (1960), *The Theology of Salvation*, Boston: St Pauls.

Griffiths, Paul (1991), *An Apology for Apologetics: Study in the Logic of Interreligious Dialogue*, Maryknoll, NY: Orbis.

Lombardi, Riccardo (1956), *The Salvation of the Unbeliever*, London: Burns & Oates.

Ratzinger, Cardinal Joseph (2004), *Truth and Tolerance. Christian Belief and World Religions*, San Francisco: Ignatius Press.

Ruokanen, Mikka (1992), *The Catholic Doctrine on Non-Christian Religions according the Second Vatican Council*, Leiden: Brill.

Sullivan, Francis (1992), *Salvation Outside the Church? Tracing the History of the Catholic Response*, New York: Paulist Press.

CHAPTER 2

CATHOLICISM AND JUDAISM

Roy H. Schoeman

Overview

The word 'Judaism' has at its root the name 'Judah', from which name 'Jew' is also derived. The Jews are (in principle) the descendants of Abraham through his only legitimate son Isaac and Isaac's chosen heir Jacob, and as such are the inheritors of the promises made by God to Abraham. (The history of Abraham, and the nature of these promises, will be discussed further on.) Jacob's name was changed to Israel after a dramatic encounter with an angel.[1] Jacob had 12 sons among whom he divided his patrimony; they became the forefathers of the 12 tribes of Israel, with the term 'Israel' coming to refer to both the people and the land.

Each tribe occupied a distinct geographic region in Israel. The ten Northern tribes were conquered by Assyria and more or less disappeared, leaving the two Southern tribes of Judah and Benjamin. Since Judah was the tribe from which the kings came, as well as being the larger tribe in terms of numbers, power and territory, the name of that tribe eventually became the root of the names for both the people, 'Jews', and the religion, 'Judaism'.

The relationship between Judaism and Christianity is unique – it is not the normal relationship between two different religions. The sacred scriptures on which Judaism is based are accepted in their entirety as Divine Revelation by Christianity as well as by Judaism. Those scriptures prophesy the future coming of a Messiah who will transform the nature of the world as well as the relationship between God and Man. When Jesus came, claiming to be that long-awaited Messiah, a fork in the road was produced. Those who believed that Jesus was the Messiah, and who after his death followed the new way introduced by him and his disciples, became the first Christians. The word 'Christ' is simply the Greek for the Hebrew word 'Messiah', which means 'anointed one'. The kings in the Old Testament received their office through being anointed; the Messiah was to be the 'anointed one' par excellence.

So Christianity and Judaism can be seen as two branches that fork off of the same trunk, with Judaism being the original trunk in its unchanged state and Christianity its transformation after the coming of the Messiah.

his view of Judaism as the trunk from which the Church, and in fact of of salvation, sprang is described in the documents of Vatican II:

> In carefully planning and preparing the salvation of the whole human race the God of infinite love, by a special dispensation, chose for Himself a people to whom He would entrust His promises. First He entered into a covenant with Abraham and, through Moses, with the people of Israel . . . The plan of salvation foretold by the sacred authors, recounted and explained by them, is found as the true word of God in the books of the Old Testament . . . The principal purpose to which the plan of the old covenant was directed was to prepare for the coming of Christ, the redeemer of all and of the messianic kingdom, to announce this coming by prophecy, and to indicate its meaning through various types . . . God, the inspirer and author of both testaments, wisely arranged that the New Testament be hidden in the Old and the Old be made manifest in the New . . . the books of the Old Testament with all their parts . . . acquire and show forth their full meaning in the New Testament and in turn shed light on it and explain it.[2]
>
> [T]his sacred council remembers the spiritual ties which link the people of the new covenant to the stock of Abraham. The church of Christ acknowledges that in God's plan of salvation the beginnings of its faith and election are to be found in the patriarchs, Moses and the prophets . . . and that the salvation of the church is mystically prefigured in the exodus of God's chosen people from the land of bondage. On this account the church cannot forget that it received the revelation of the Old Testament by way of that people with whom God in his inexpressible mercy established the ancient covenant. Nor can it forget that it draws nourishment from that good olive tree onto which the wild olive branches of the Gentiles have been grafted (see Rom 11:17–24). The church . . . is mindful, moreover, that the apostles, the pillars on which the church stands, are of Jewish descent, as are many of those early disciples who proclaimed the Gospel of Christ to the world . . .[3]

Jesus himself, of course, was a Jew, as was the Holy Family, the 12 apostles, the disciples and almost all of the first wave of Christians. The Church's history, theology, and even liturgy flow from its pre-Messianic, that is its Jewish, roots. For a Christian, Judaism comes alive when seen through the eyes of Christianity, and Christianity takes on even more depth, meaning and beauty when seen in its relationship to Judaism. This is particularly true of Catholic Christianity, which retains many echoes of Judaism in its liturgical and sacramental practices.

The Jewish Religion

To understand Judaism, it is helpful to consider it as a people, as a faith and as covenantal relationship.

As a people

Judaism represents a single people, or tribe – the descendents of Abraham, the father of the Jews, through his son Isaac. Of course, over the 4,000 years since Abraham, there has been conversion into, as well as out of, Judaism, and extensive intermarriage and intermingling of people, but the Jewish people's identity as the 'seed of Abraham' remains as a central theological principle of Judaism.

As a result, Judaism has never considered itself as appropriate for all peoples, and the evangelization of non-Jews has never been a priority. Rather, it represents a covenant made by God to a single people, for the special role that that people were to play among all the nations of the earth. Judaism sees the Jews as having been specially chosen by God to live in a uniquely close relationship with Him, not just for their own sakes, but to intercede for the rest of humanity as a 'priestly people' ('You shall be to me a kingdom of priests and a holy nation' – Exod. 19.4), bringing the knowledge of God, and His blessings, to the whole world ('I have given you as a covenant to the people, a light to the nations' – Isa. 42.6). As a leading rabbi recently wrote:

> The Jew is a creature of heaven and of earth, of a heavenly Divine soul which is truly a part of Godliness clothed in an earthly vessel . . . whose purpose is to realize the transcendence and unity of his nature and of the world in which he lives within the absolute unity of God. The realization of this purpose entails a two-way correlation: one in the direction from above downward to earth; the other, from the earth upward. In fulfillment of the first, man draws holiness from the Divinely given Torah and commandments, to permeate therewith every phase of his daily life and environment; in fulfillment of the second, man draws upon all the resources at this disposal as vehicles for his personal ascendancy and, with him, that of the surrounding world.[4]

This self-understanding as a special people chosen for a special vocation results in Jews often placing a primary emphasis on maintaining their separate identity.

As a covenantal relationship

Judaism originated with a very special and particular covenant that God made with Abraham, and through him with his descendants – the so-called 'Abrahamic Covenant'. The story of this covenant is told in Genesis 12–22. About 2,000 years before Christ, when all the peoples of the earth were pagans, worshiping a host of false gods and idols (which were in fact fallen spirits, or demons – 'the gods of the pagans are demons', Ps. 96.5), the one true God revealed Himself to one of the pagans, Abram (later renamed Abraham) and asked him to travel to a distant land, where God would make him the father of a great people. After Abraham demonstrated his fidelity through a series of tests, culminating in his willingness to sacrifice his only legitimate son to God, God rewarded Abraham with the promise of a special blessing on his seed, and that through them all the peoples of the earth would be blessed: 'I have sworn, says the LORD, because you have done this, and have not withheld your son, your only son, I will indeed bless you, and I will multiply your descendants as the stars of heaven and as the sand which is on the seashore. And your descendants shall possess the gate of their enemies, and by your descendants shall all the nations of the earth be blessed, because you have obeyed my voice' (Gen. 22.16–18). This was the origin of the Jewish people, of their special election or 'chosenness' by God, and of God's promise to one day send, through them, the Messiah to establish God's reign on earth.

About 500 years later, when Moses was leading the Jewish people out of Egypt and through the desert to the Promised Land, God established a second covenant with the Jewish people – the 'Mosaic Covenant'. This second covenant laid out an elaborate sacramental system through which the Jewish people could attain, maintain and restore a state of ritual purity and obtain the forgiveness of their sins. This sacramental system involved a hereditary ritual priesthood, animal sacrifice and a host of laws regulating behaviour in areas including, but not restricted to, the food they could eat, the clothes they could wear, sexual behaviour and the observance of festivals. In fact, the bulk of the second through fifth books of the Old Testament (Exodus through Deuteronomy) is dedicated to describing the details of this 'Mosaic Covenant'. Later, in considering how the coming of Christ transformed the relationship between God and Man, it will be important to keep in mind this distinction between the Abrahamic and the Mosaic covenants.

As a faith

The Jewish scriptures
God continued His special relationship with Abraham's son, Isaac, Isaac's son Jacob (later renamed Israel) and Jacob's sons, who became the patriarchs of the 12 tribes of Israel. During a time of famine, Jacob and his sons moved to Egypt, where their descendants were later made slaves.

One of them, Moses, was appointed by God to be their liberator. Moses led the Jews out of their captivity in Egypt and through the desert to the 'promised land', then called Canaan, later called Israel. During the journey through the Sinai, God appeared to Moses on Mount Sinai and gave him the first five books of the Bible. These are called in Judaism the 'Torah', or 'Law'. The Torah became the cornerstone of the Jewish faith. Over the succeeding centuries, revelations made to other Jewish prophets were accepted as of Divine Origin and added to the original Torah to make up the Old Testament, which Jews call the 'Tanakh'. Tanakh is a Hebrew word made up of the initial consonants of the three words: 'Torah', or 'law', the five books revealed to Moses on Mount Sinai; 'Nevi'im', or 'prophets', referring to the revelations given to the prophets; and 'K'tuvim', or 'writings', which refers to the wisdom literature such as the books of Psalms, Proverbs, and so on. The Jewish Old Testament in its entirety is accepted as Divine Revelation by the Catholic Church.

The Jewish canon of scripture – that is, the exact collection of books to be considered Sacred Scripture and included in the Tanakh – has varied from century to century and place to place. A few hundred years before Christ, a compilation of such writings were collected and translated into Greek for use by the Jews, many of whom no longer understood Hebrew. This Greek language version of the Jewish Old Testament is known as the Septuagint.

Later, however, a number of books contained in the Septuagint were eliminated from the Jewish canon. When the Temple in Jerusalem was destroyed in 70 AD and the Jews expelled from that city, the leading rabbis regrouped in the town of Jamnia, which became the centre of Jewish learning. There, in the beginning of the second century AD, it was decided that the more recently written books of the Septuagint should be excluded from the canon. The reason for this is unclear. Since it was done at the same council at which the New Testament was condemned, some think that it was done to purify Judaism from the taint of Christianity.

The Catholic canon of the Old Testament includes those books dropped from the Jewish canon at Jamnia, while the Protestant canon of the Old Testament rejects them. It is hard to see why a decision made by Jewish authorities decades after the Church was formed should be considered relevant for the Church, especially when made by the same authorities who anathematized Christians and condemned the writings of the New Testament.

The final stage in the development of the Jewish scriptures took place between the third and the fifth century AD, when Jewish authorities wrote down the oral tradition that had developed within Judaism. This became known as the Talmud, or 'teaching'. It is the record of discussions and exegesis by leading rabbis over the generations, and is granted an authority within Judaism comparable to that of the Old Testament.

A Jewish creed
The closest that Judaism comes to an official creed is the 'Thirteen Principles of Faith' of Moses Maimonides (1135–1204), the primary Jewish sage of the Middle Ages. They serve as a good introduction to the central tenets of the Jewish faith.

The first five of the principles revolve around the heart of the Jewish faith – the belief in, and fidelity to, the one true, uncreated, creator God (in particular contrast to the polytheistic pagan idol worship of those around them in the times of the Old Testament). They are as follows:

1. God is the Creator and Ruler of all things. He alone has made, does make and will make all things.
2. God is One. There is no unity that is in any way like His. He alone is our God He was, He is and He will be.
3. God does not have a body. Physical concepts do not apply to Him. There is nothing whatsoever that resembles Him at all.
4. God is first and last.
5. One may only pray to God. One may not pray to anyone or anything else.

The next four of the principles assert the truth, divine origin and immutability of the Jewish scriptures:

6. All the words of the prophets are true.
7. The prophecy of Moses is absolutely true. He was the chief of all prophets, both before and after Him.
8. The entire Torah that we now have is that which was given to Moses.
9. This Torah will not be changed, and there will never be another given by God.

The next two are:

10. God knows all of man's deeds and thoughts. It is thus written (Ps. 33.15), 'He has molded every heart together, He understands what each one does.'
11. God rewards those who keep His commandments, and punishes those who transgress Him.

These reflect the belief in God's absolute sovereignty, omniscience and omnipotence, which is central to Judaism. He knows and sees all things ('Thou knowest when I sit down and when I rise up; thou discernest my thoughts from afar' Ps. 139). He has given the Jewish people, as his special priestly people, an extensive body of law, much of which applies only to them, that will be a source of peace, happiness and blessing to them if they obey it. If they fail to, they will be punished.

Judaism expects, in general, that the reward or punishment for good or bad behaviour will occur in this life, as well as in the next. The central prayer of Judaism, recited three times a day, is the 'Shema', drawn from Deuteronomy 11 verses 13–17, which promises temporal good fortune as a reward for obedience to God:

> If you obey My commandments that I command you . . . then will I send the rain for your land in its season . . . And I will provide grass in your field for your cattle, and you shall eat and be sated. Be careful that your heart be not tempted and you turn away to serve other gods and bow to them. For then God will be furious with you and will block the heavens and there will be no rain and the land will not yield its produce, and you will perish quickly from the good land that God gives you.[5]

Of course, Judaism also recognizes a mystery behind suffering, and that at times the good suffer too (e.g. the story of Job). But there is no well-developed theology of the redemptive value of suffering in Judaism (or in the Old Testament) comparable to what is found in Christianity. This is only logical, from a Christian viewpoint, since it was only with the coming of Christ that suffering took on its ultimate redemptive value, thorough ones uniting it with the suffering of Christ.

The next of Maimonides' principles reflects the Jewish faith in the coming of the promised Messiah, who will establish God's reign on earth:

12. The Messiah will come. However long it takes, I will await His coming every day.

The belief in the coming of the Messiah is absolutely central to traditional Judaism (although in recent times the more modern forms of Judaism have moved away from the belief). The Old Testament contains hundreds of prophecies relating to the Messiah which detail who he will be, of what lineage, where and when he will be born, what he will do, how he will transform the world, and so forth.[6] Many of them are, however, somewhat mysterious or veiled in nature.

There is also some apparent contradiction between them – in particular, some seem to predict a Messiah who will come to suffer and die in atonement for the sins of the people (e.g. the 'suffering servant' passage in Isaiah 53), while others portray a Messiah who will come in victory to restore the glory of the Israel and establish a kingdom of peace and prosperity on earth (e.g. Isa.11 and 25).

This apparent contradiction is the topic of extensive discussion in the Talmud, which concludes that there will be, in fact, two Messiahs, one who will come to suffer and die (referred to in the Talmud as 'Messiah son of Joseph'), and one who will come in victory ('Messiah son of David'). This mirrors quite closely the Christian resolution of the same apparent contradiction, which recognizes some of the Messianic prophecies as referring to Christ's First Coming (to suffer and die), and others to his return in glory at the Second Coming. And the names given to the two Messiahs in the Talmud appear deeply prophetic to a Christian, for in the Gospels Jesus was identified as the son of Joseph when his human nature, in which he was to suffer and die, was being emphasized (e.g. in Mt. 13.54–55), and as the son of David when his divine nature was being pointed to (e.g. in Mt. 21.9–11).

The traditional Jewish liturgy contains prayers for the coming of the Messiah during daily morning, afternoon and evening prayers.

The final principle of faith is:

13. The dead will be brought back to life when God wills it to happen.

Judaism has a much less developed theology of the afterlife than does Christianity, as this principle reflects. The general sense in the Old Testament (typified in the book of Job) is that there is an eternal life which entails reward and punishment, but the details are best left in the hands of God. (This uncertainty in Judaism about the afterlife is reflected in the New Testament in the disputes between the Pharisees and the Sadducees on just this issue – Matthew 22, Mark 12, Luke 20, Acts 23.) Although there is discussion of both heaven and hell in the Talmud, it leaves room for a variety of opinions on heaven, hell, the resurrection, and even reincarnation.

From a Christian perspective it makes sense that the Jewish scriptures – revelations made to man before Christ – should be vague about the afterlife, since according to Christianity before Christ descended to the dead after the crucifixion, there *were* no human souls in heaven. Rather, the souls of the just were consigned to a shadowy underworld, the 'limbo of the fathers', awaiting His coming to open the gates of Heaven.[7]

Jewish Laws

One distinguishing characteristic of Judaism is its emphasis on following a wide range of ritual laws. Traditional Judaism identifies 613 commandments in the Old Testament, which in aggregate dictate ones behaviour in almost every aspect of life. Many of these laws require further elucidation and specification – for instance, what constitutes the sort of 'work' that is prohibited on the Sabbath? This elucidation is provided, sometimes at great length, in the Talmud.

From a Jewish perspective, this ritual law is natural and intrinsic to the role of the Jews as a 'priestly nation'. It is natural that as such, every aspect of their lives is to be consecrated to God. A Catholic can see this as roughly analogous to the difference in the manner of life of an ordinary Christian, versus one in religious life, that is, a monk or nun. It is as though every Jew is called to follow the sort of strict regime of laws that characterizes Catholic religious life, especially as it was in past centuries, when almost every aspect of how a religious ate, dressed, behaved, spoke, slept, worked and prayed was dictated by a rule. The rule was a way for the religious to consecrate every aspect of his life to God. That is how Jewish ritual observance, which permeates every aspect of the religious Jew's life, is best understood.

In the realm of eating, the laws define the foods one is, or is not, allowed to eat; how the animal must be slaughtered; what foods may not be eaten together; and how one is to purify oneself prior to eating. They define how one is to dress, the wearing of special clothing with ritual significance (e.g. a head covering at all times, and the *tzitzit*, or fringes, on the corners of the garment[8]), and what fabrics can be worn and in what combination. They define various aspects of personal grooming, forbidding men from shaving or cutting the hair on their temples (hence the traditional beards and earlocks of strictly observant Jews[9]). They define whom one is or is not allowed to touch, how the Sabbath and festivals are to be observed, how and when one is to pray, and so forth.

Many of these laws may appear arbitrary, foolish or rude to non-Jews. Yet most come directly from the Old Testament and so the Christian must recognize them as having been commanded of the Jews by God. It was only when Christ came that these laws were lifted from the Jews – they were never commanded of the Gentiles – as described in the New Testament (e.g. Matthew 15, Acts 10, Romans 14). Of course, since Judaism rejects the authority of the New Testament, it considers these laws still binding.

Rabbinic and Temple Judaism

There are nonetheless great differences between today's Judaism and the Judaism that is presented in the Old Testament, especially around the role of animal sacrifice. These changes were necessitated by the destruction of the Temple in Jerusalem in 70 AD. The sacramental system prescribed for the Jews in the Old Testament required animal sacrifice which had to be performed in one place, the Temple in Jerusalem. Animals were to be sacrificed daily – for the remission of sins, for purification, for atonement and as thanksgiving. After the Temple was destroyed and those sacrifices were no longer possible, the leading rabbis of the day gathered in Jamnia, which at the time served as the seat of Jewish learning (the Jews had been expelled from Jerusalem under pain of death by the Romans), and developed as an alternative the current system, known as 'Rabbinic' Judaism (as opposed to the earlier form, 'Temple' Judaism), in which prayers, almsgivings and good deeds are substituted for the no longer possible animal sacrifice.

The Jewish Liturgical Year

Judaism strives to consecrate every aspect of the Jew's life to God – through obedience to the laws, through prayer and through the observance of the Jewish liturgical year. Home observances, as opposed to sacraments that take place outside the home, are the heart and soul of Jewish religious life. These observances are driven by the regular cycles of the Jewish liturgical year.

The Weekly Sabbath

The basic rhythm of Jewish religious life is set by the weekly Sabbath. The Sabbath begins shortly before sundown on Friday, and ends with nightfall the next day. During that period, all 'work' is forbidden, which for observant Jews includes riding in a car or other vehicle, buying or selling, lighting a fire, turning on electric lights or appliances (hence no television, radio, etc.), walking any significant distance, carrying anything, sports activities, writing, cooking, gardening, or doing any secular work.

Sabbath observance traditionally starts with the woman of the house lighting the Sabbath candles shortly before sundown on Friday, followed by an elaborate meal that is accompanied with special prayers and blessings. The following day is devoted to synagogue worship, religious study, and family activities. The religious and family orientation of the day is ensured by the Sabbath observance laws, which prohibit most of the activities which might tend to draw family members apart, or to inject a worldly element into the day. The Sabbath is so observed in fulfilment of the commandment found in Exodus 20 verses 8–11:

> Remember the Sabbath day, to keep it holy. Six days you shall labor, and do all your work; but the seventh day is a Sabbath to the LORD your God; in it you shall not do any work . . . for in six days the LORD made heaven and earth, the sea, and all that is in them, and rested the seventh day; therefore the LORD blessed the Sabbath day and made it holy.

Sabbath ends at nightfall on Saturday evening with the *havdala* ceremony which makes use of a special multi-wicked candle, a spice box and wine, along with special prayers and blessings, to conclude the Sabbath.

The Festivals

Most of the Jewish festivals share the same restrictions on 'work' as the Sabbath, and much of their celebration and observance takes place in the home, often accompanied with special foods, objects or activities unique to the feast. A brief description of some of the major holidays follows:

Rosh Hashanah *('New Year')* and Yom Kippur *('Day of Atonement')*

These two holidays are separated by ten days, and usually fall in September or October.[10] Rosh Hashanah is considered the anniversary of God's creation of the world, and it is the day that God looks at the deeds of each individual to determine their destiny for the coming year. This sobering prospect is reflected in a central prayer of Rosh Hashanah, the *U'Netaneh Tokef* ('How utterly holy this day is'):

> All will pass before You like members of the flock. Like a shepherd pasturing his flock, making sheep pass under his staff, so shall You cause to pass, count, calculate, and consider the soul of all the living; and You shall apportion the fixed needs of all Your creatures and inscribe their verdict.
> On Rosh Hashanah will be inscribed and on Yom Kippur will be sealed how many will pass from the earth and how many will be created; who will live and who will die; who will die at his predestined time and who before his time; who by water and who by fire, who by sword, who by beast, who

by famine, who by thirst, who by storm, who by plague, who by strangulation, and who by stoning. Who will rest and who will wander, who will live in harmony and who will be harried, who will enjoy tranquility and who will suffer, who will be impoverished and who will be enriched, who will be degraded and who will be exalted.

Since the verdict will be inscribed on Rosh Hashanah and sealed on Yom Kippur, the ten days between the two holidays are an intense time of prayer, almsgiving and reconciliation aimed at averting the 'severe decree' before it is too late. They are known as the 'ten days of Repentance'.

Yom Kippur serves as the climax of this period of repentance. It is observed as a strict fast day, with no food or water being taken from sundown the evening before to nightfall of the day itself (in addition to fasting, also prohibited are wearing leather shoes, bathing or washing, anointing oneself with oil and marital relations). Most of the day is spent in the synagogue praying the most solemn liturgy of the year. When the Temple still stood in Jerusalem (it was destroyed for the final time in 70 AD), Yom Kippur was the one and only day of the year that the High Priest entered the Holy of Holies, making atonement for the sins of the Jewish nation as well as his own. Today's Yom Kippur liturgy still reflects that unique solemnity.

Sukkot

Sukkot (or 'booths') falls four days after Yom Kippur and lasts one week. It is one of the most joyful holidays of the year. It celebrates the harvest, and also commemorates the 40-year period during which the Jews wandered in the desert following the Exodus from Egypt, living in temporary shelters. In observance of this, during Sukkot observant Jews live in temporary shelters ('Sukkot', or 'booths') outside the home, and work is prohibited on the first and second days. The observance of the holiday was directly commanded by God in the Old Testament (Leviticus 23).

Hanukkah

The eight-day festival of Hanukkah begins on the 25th of the month of *Kislev* on the Jewish calendar, which usually falls around Christmas. Although theologically not a holiday of primary importance, it has assumed a greater weight because of its proximity to Christmas, and the alternative it provides. The holiday is mentioned in 1 and 2 Maccabees. It celebrates the victory of the Maccabees against the Emperor Antiochus who, after coming to power over the Jews, forced them to follow pagan practices, and desecrated the Temple. When the Maccabees defeated Antiochus, they recaptured and rededicated the Temple, enabling the resumption of the sacrifices so central to the Jewish sacramental system.

As soon as they reconsecrated the Temple, the Maccabees relit the multibranched lamp (*menorah*) which was to burn uninterruptedly in the Temple. However, due to the just-ended war, only enough oil for a single day could be obtained. Miraculously, the oil lasted for eight days, until a new supply could be found. In commemoration, Hanukkah lasts for eight days, and a menorah[11] with eight branches is lit each evening – one candle the first night, two the second, and so forth, until on the last night all eight are lit. There are special prayers and songs for the lighting of the menorah, and it is customary for children to receive gifts each night. There are also traditional foods and children's' games associated with the holiday.

Passover

The Jews' 'Exodus', their being freed from slavery to the Pharaoh in Egypt, is commemorated by an eight-day feast called 'Passover'. Passover is inaugurated by the Passover Seder, a festive meal in the home replete with special ritual foods, extensive prayers and narrative thanking God for freeing the Jewish nation from slavery in Egypt. Before the destruction of the Temple, the Passover meal included a lamb sacrificed in the Temple in commemoration of the lambs killed by the Jews just before their flight from Egypt, the blood of which was daubed on the doorposts of their houses to tell the angel of death to 'pass over' the house[12] – the 'Passover' lamb, hence 'Passover'. On the first and last days of the feast no work is to be done, and during the entire eight-day period no leavened bread, or any forms of leavening, are to be eaten.

Shavuot (Pentecost)

Shavuot falls on the fiftieth day after Passover. The name 'Shavuot' literally means 'sevens', for it falls seven weeks after Passover. It commemorates the giving of the Law to Moses on Mount Sinai; therefore many religious Jews observe the holiday by spending the entire night in Torah study, either at home or in synagogue.

Judaism Today

There are currently about 14 million Jews in the world today, or about two-tenths of 1 per cent of the world population. Of these, about 6 million live in North America, 5 million in Israel, and 1.5 million in Europe.[13] Their prominence is far disproportionate to their numbers. For instance, since the Nobel Prize was founded in 1901, over 20 per cent of its winners (between 158 and 173, depending on the definition of being Jewish, out of 758) have been Jewish – in the sciences, almost 30 per cent.[14] Within the Jewish community can be found a wide range of beliefs and practices.

'Orthodox' Judaism

Only a minority of Jews today attempt to follow the full range of Jewish law and observance, adhering to a strict interpretation of Jewish law and practices as they appear in the Old Testament and the Talmud. These are generally referred to as 'Orthodox Jews', and account for about 10 per cent of the Jews in the United States, 17 per cent of those in Israel.[15] In practice, Orthodox Jews, with the exception of the 'ultra-Orthodox', described below, often live and work among non-Jews, but distinguish themselves by an observance of Jewish laws which set them apart. These laws include the following:

- a strict prohibition against working – which is defined as including driving, turning on an electric device, lighting a stove, and so on – on the Jewish Sabbath, which begins at sundown Friday and ends sundown Saturday
- the requirement for men to keep their heads covered (and hence the wearing of skullcaps)
- a prohibition against men shaving (although some interpret the law to allow electric shavers)
- strict dietary laws, such as the prohibition against eating any milk products and any meat products at the same meal, eating any unclean animal (defined in Leviticus 11 as including shellfish, pork, etc.) or any animal not properly slaughtered according to Jewish law (based on the rules found in Leviticus 17).

The orthodox subscribe to the Jewish faith as described in the 'Thirteen Principles', including the belief in the coming of a Messiah, the rebuilding of the Temple in Jerusalem, and the resurrection of the dead. Their liturgy and religious study are conducted almost exclusively in Hebrew.

Within the orthodox is found smaller, even more observant, subgroup, known as Hasidim (3 per cent of US Jews, 5 per cent of Jews living in Israel). They were founded in Poland in the mid-eighteenth century by Rabbi Israel ben Eliezer, known as the Baal Shem Tov ('Master of the Good Name'), who wished to put love of God at the centre of Judaism, rather than the dry legalism that he saw around him. As he said, 'I have come into this world to teach how to live by three precepts: love of God, love of Israel, and love of the Torah.' Hasidic Judaism is characterized by a charismatic element. Their worship often involves joyful chanting, or even dancing, and some of their rabbis are famous for such charismatic gifts as the reading of souls, foreknowledge of events and miracle working. Hasidic Jews follow a strict interpretation of traditional Jewish law, often living apart in separate communities under the authority of a rabbi. The strictness of their religious observance can limit their interaction with the outside world. Nonetheless, their numbers have doubled in the past 20 years, as a result both of their high birthrate and successful evangelization of non-Hasidic Jews, making them one of the fastest growing groups within Judaism.

'Reform' Judaism

Following the emancipation of the Jews in Germany in the nineteenth century, when for the first time Jews were granted full civil rights, including the right to live and operate freely in the non-Jewish community, a liberalizing trend that came to be known as 'Reform' Judaism emerged and soon spread throughout in Western Europe and America. Its aim was to modernize Judaism by replacing the traditional Hebrew liturgy with one in the vernacular, allowing the individual to decide for himself what laws to follow, applying modern 'higher criticism' to the understanding of scripture, replacing the tradition of Jewish emphasis on ritual observance and worship with a concern for social justice, and embracing the customs, mores, and dress of modern culture. It represents about 35 per cent of US Jews.

'Conservative' Judaism

In the late nineteenth century in Germany a countervailing movement emerged among Jews who wanted to participate fully in the modern world, and rejected the literal interpretation of Jewish scriptures and law, yet still wanted to conserve more of the Jewish tradition than the 'Reform' movement did. Hence it came to be known as the 'Conservative' movement. It falls in a middle ground between orthodox and Reform Judaism, mixing both Hebrew and the vernacular in the liturgy; adopting a historical-critical method in the interpretation of Jewish scripture and law; and adopting a positive attitude towards modern society. It accounts for about 26 per cent of US Jews.

Mystical Judaism/Kabbalah

The esoteric, occult, or mystical stream within Judaism is known as *Kabbalah*. Until recently, interest in the *Kabbalah* was restricted to a small segment within the ultra-orthodox or Hasidic communities, but in recent decades interest in it has spread to both less religious (or even non-religious Jews) and to the wider 'New Age' or occult communities. It is essentially the repository of mystical or occult knowledge within Judaism, fulfilling the role in Judaism that Sufism does in Islam and Gnosticism or Hermeticism[16] does in Christianity.

Kabbalah comprises a set of esoteric teachings and techniques. The teachings purport to explain the relationship between the infinite, unknowable Creator (or creative forces of the universe) and the created world, shedding light on the nature of the universe, of man, the meaning of existence and various other ontological questions. They also claim to reveal the inner significance of the *Tanach* and Jewish ritual observance.

The techniques purport to enable the practitioner to achieve higher levels of consciousness in which he or she can directly gain knowledge of the higher worlds, and communicate with (and even control) spiritual beings.

The foundational text for *Kabbalah* is the *Zohar*. It was introduced to the world in the late thirteenth century by a Jewish rabbi in Spain, Moses De Leon, who claimed that it was a text by the second-century Rabbi Simeon bar Yochai that he had discovered. Most modern Jewish academic scholars believe that it was written by De Leon himself; Kabbalists tend to accept De Leon's claim as to its origin.

Messianic' Jews/Jewish converts[17]

Another, somewhat controversial, group to consider is Jews who recognize Jesus as the Jewish Messiah. Although most of them still consider themselves

Jewish – often more so than ever, since now they follow the Jewish Messiah – usually the rest of the Jewish community does not. Some enter the Catholic Church or one of the conventional Protestant denominations; others remain separate in distinct 'Messianic Jewish' congregations which maintain some of the traditional Jewish liturgical practices.

This group is large, and growing – there may be more Jewish conversion to Christianity underway today than at any time since the early days of the Church. Most of the statistics which exist are of Messianic Jewish congregations; their numbers may serve as a proxy for overall Jewish conversion. Before 1967, there were at most 4 or 5 Messianic Jewish synagogues in the United States[18] – today there are over 150. By the mid-1970s, *Time* magazine placed the number of Messianic Jews in the United States at over 50,000; by 1993 this number had grown to 160,000 in the United States[19] and over 350,000 worldwide. There are currently over 400 Messianic synagogues worldwide, including at least 150 in the United States.

Of particular interest is the spread of Messianic Judaism in Israel itself. Despite opposition by the Israel government, there is now hardly a town or city in Israel without a Messianic Jewish congregation. One recent estimate places the number of Messianic Jews in Israel today at 15,000.[20] This cannot help but call to mind the prophecy that Jesus made when he sent his apostles out on their mission to evangelize (Mt. 10.6–7, 23):

> [Go] to the lost sheep of the house of Israel. And preach as you go, saying, 'The kingdom of heaven is at hand' . . . When they persecute you in one town, flee to the next; for truly, I say to you, you will not have gone through all the towns of Israel, before the Son of man comes.

Unaffiliated Jews

The final group is that of Jews who do not identify with any of these forms of Judaism, holding a variety of religious beliefs or none, yet still consider themselves Jewish. They account for about 29 per cent of Jews in the United States.

Judaism from a Catholic Perspective

The rest of this chapter will be a discussion of the theological import of Judaism from a purely Catholic perspective.

The Jews' role prior to the First Coming of Christ

As mentioned at the outset, according to the Catholic faith Judaism has played an absolutely central role in bringing about the salvation of all mankind. It was Jesus himself who said, 'salvation is from the Jews' (Jn 4.22).

The role Judaism played over the first phase of salvation history, from the creation of man until the incarnation, is actually quite straightforward. When man was first created, he was to live in a state of uninterrupted bliss and intimacy with God for all eternity. When Adam sinned, that initial state was shattered, and from that very moment – actually, even before then, since God is outside time – God knew that He would someday restore man to an even higher state through the future incarnation of the Second Person of the most Holy Trinity as a man. If the Second Person of the most Holy Trinity was to incarnate as a man, it would be at a particular point in time and among a particular, 'chosen' people. That people have to be prepared over many centuries. First, they would have to be separated from all of the other tribes around them who worshiped fallen spirits – that is, demons – masquerading as gods ('The gods of the gentiles are demons' – Ps. 96). They would have to learn about and worship the one true God, the uncreated Creator of all that is. They would have to be taught about the creation and fall of man, the seriousness of sin, the need for redemption and the coming of a Redeemer. They would have to be taught to adhere to a sufficiently high moral code that the incarnation itself would not be a sacrilege. They would have to be given sufficient divine revelation to be able to recognize the Redeemer when he came, and to be able to spread knowledge of his redemption to the rest of the world after he died. Finally, they would have to prepare, over the generations, a virgin of such purity and holiness that she could give her flesh and blood to be the flesh and blood of the God-man (the Blessed Virgin Mary). That was the role for which the Jews were chosen, and at which they succeeded, despite their widespread failure to follow him. They were chosen to bring about the coming of the Redeemer, and he came, and they were chosen to spread the Gospel to the four corners of the earth, and it has been spread. There could hardly be about 2 billion Christians in the world (of which about 1 billion are Catholics), had they failed.

Why the Jews?

Why did God choose the Jews for this special role, the most important role ever given to any one people? There are many answers to this question.

One is that He had to choose somebody, and whoever that was, we would now be asking why He chose *them*. Another is that God seems to like to choose the weakest and most insignificant for His special missions, precisely to make it apparent that God is behind all that is happening, not the individuals involved. For instance, St Bernadette, the illiterate peasant girl who received the apparitions of the Blessed Virgin Mary at Lourdes, said 'The Holy Virgin chose me because I was the most ignorant of creatures. If she had found anyone more ignorant than myself, she would have chosen her instead.'[21] And when Jesus appeared to St Margaret Mary Alacoque, the nun chosen to receive the Sacred Heart apparitions, he explicitly told her 'I have chosen you as an abyss of unworthiness and ignorance for this great design, so that everything may be done by me.'[22] The fact God's choice of the Jews was related to their insignificance and unworthiness is explicit in the Old Testament:

> Thus says the Lord God to Jerusalem . . . On the day you were born, your naval string was not cut, nor were you washed with water to cleanse you nor rubbed with salt nor swathed with bands . . . And when I passed you by, and saw you weltering in your blood, I said to you in your blood, live! . . . Then I bathed you with water and washed off your blood, and anointed you with oil. I clothed you with embroidered cloth and shod you with leather. I swathed you with fine linen and covered you with silk . . . And your renown went forth among the nations because of your beauty, for it was perfect through the splendor which I had bestowed upon you, says the Lord God. (Ezek. 16.3–14, extracts)

Yet there is also a positive reason why God chose the Jews. He chose the Jews in part to reward Abraham for the extraordinary fidelity he showed in his willingness to sacrifice his son Isaac on Mount Moriah. The story is told in the book of Genesis:

> After these things God tested Abraham, and said to him, 'Abraham! . . .' And he said, 'Here am I.' He said, 'Take your son, your only son Isaac, whom you love, and go to the land of Moriah, and offer him there as a burnt offering upon one of the mountains of which I shall tell you.' So Abraham rose early in the morning, and took his son Isaac, and went to the place of which God had told him. And Abraham took the wood of the burnt offering, and laid it on Isaac his son; and he took in his hand the fire and the knife. So they went both of them together. And Isaac said to his father Abraham, 'I see the fire and the wood; but where is the lamb for a burnt offering?' Abraham said, 'God will himself provide the lamb for the sacrifice, my son.' When they came to the place of which God had told him, Abraham built an altar there, and laid the wood in order, and bound Isaac his son, and laid him on the altar, upon the wood. Then Abraham put forth his hand, and took the knife to slay his son. But the angel of the LORD called to him from heaven, and said, 'Abraham, Abraham!' And he said, 'Here am I.' He said, 'Do not lay

your hand on the lad or do anything to him; for now I know that you fear God, seeing you have not withheld your son, your only son, from me.'

And Abraham lifted up his eyes and saw a ram, caught in a thicket by his horns; and Abraham went and took the ram, and offered it up as a burnt offering instead of his son. So Abraham called the name of that place 'the LORD will provide'. And the angel of the LORD called to Abraham a second time from heaven, and said, 'Because you have done this, and have not withheld your son, your only son, I will indeed bless you, and I will multiply your descendants as the stars of heaven and as the sand which is on the seashore. And your seed shall possess the gate of their enemies, and in your seed shall all the nations of the earth be blessed, because you have obeyed my voice.' (Gen. 22.1–18, condensed)

The Christological import of this story can hardly be overstated. Abraham's willingness to sacrifice Isaac was intimately linked to, one could even say reciprocated by, God's willingness, 2,000 years later, to sacrifice *His* only-begotten Son on the very same mountain, just a few hundred yards away, at the spot known as 'Calvary'. The very circumstances of Abraham's act foreshadowed, that is reflected in advance, the ultimate fulfilment 2,000 years later. 'Take your son, your only son, whom you love' (Gen. 22.2) was echoed 2,000 years later in 'For God so loved the world that he gave his only Son . . . [His] beloved Son' (Jn 3.16, Mt. 3.17). As the son of Abraham climbed the mount with the wood on his shoulders for his own execution, so too did the Son of God. Abraham's utterance 'God himself will provide the lamb for a burnt offering' (Gen. 22.8) was prophetic far beyond anything he could have known, referring not only to the provision of the ram 'provided' by the Lord, but far more profoundly to the only truly acceptable sacrifice, the 'Lamb of God, who took away the sins of the world' (Jn 1), God's own Son offered on the altar of Calvary.

The transformation of Judaism with the coming of Christ

The relationship between Judaism and Christianity may be a somewhat arcane topic today, but that was hardly the case in the early days of the Church. The origin of the Church in Judaism and the need to understand how Judaism was transformed by the coming of Christ were at the centre of the Church's early self-understanding. The Letter to the Hebrews is largely an explanation of that transformation. The Church Fathers wrote extensively on the transformation and the Christological meanings hidden in Judaism that were only brought to light with the coming of Christ. The story of Abraham's near sacrifice of Isaac was one example of such Old Testament prefigurement. Others abound.[23] Perhaps the ultimate example is that of the transformation of the Passover Seder into the Catholic Mass at the Last Supper.

The Last Supper

As is clear from the Gospels, the Last Supper was a Passover Seder.[24] The Exodus from Egypt[25] is absolutely central in the theological history of the Jews, and the Passover celebration which commemorates it central to Jewish liturgical life. The Church Fathers saw the entire story of the Exodus as a prefigurement of man's true liberation with the coming of Christ. St Cyril of Jerusalem, a Church Father, catechized candidates for baptism with an account of the Christological meaning of the Exodus:

> Let us now teach you the effect wrought upon you on that evening of your baptism ... When Pharaoh, that most bitter and cruel tyrant, was oppressing the free and highborn people of the Hebrews, God sent Moses to bring them out of the evil bondage of the Egyptians. Then the door posts were anointed with the blood of a lamb, that the destroyer might flee from the houses which had the sign of the blood; and the Hebrew people was marvelously delivered. The enemy, however, after their rescue, pursued after them, and saw the sea wondrously parted for them; nevertheless he went on, following close in their footsteps, and was all at once overwhelmed and engulfed in the Red Sea.
>
> Now turn from the old to the new, from the figure to the reality. There we have Moses sent from God to Egypt; here, Christ, sent forth from His Father into the world: there, that Moses might lead forth an afflicted people out of Egypt; here, that Christ might rescue those who are oppressed in the world under sin: there, the blood of a lamb was the spell against the destroyer; here, the blood of the Lamb without blemish Jesus Christ is made the charm to scare evil spirits: there, the tyrant was pursuing that ancient people even to the sea; and here the daring and shameless spirit, the author of evil, was following thee even to the very streams of salvation. The tyrant of old was drowned in the sea; and this present one disappears in the water of salvation.[26]

Thus we see that the crossing of the Red Sea to pass from slavery to freedom prefigured the Christian's baptism freeing him from original sin; the Blood of the Lamb on the doorpost turning away the avenging angel and sparing the Jews from death prefigured the Blood of Christ on the Cross turning away God's condemnation to eternal death; the 40-years journey in the wilderness until reaching the 'promised Land' was a 'type' of one's lifetime on earth until reaching the true 'Promised Land', the 'Heavenly Jerusalem'; and the manna with which God miraculously fed the Jews in the desert prefigured the true bread of life, the Eucharist, the heavenly food which nourishes the faithful during their pilgrimage on earth. Jesus himself drew the parallel: (Jn 6.48–49, 51):

> I am the bread of life. Your fathers ate the manna in the wilderness, and they died ... I am the living bread which came down from heaven; if any one eats

of this bread, he will live for ever; and the bread which I shall give for the life of the world is my flesh.

And the Paschal lamb, sacrificed on that first Passover night in Egypt, was but a figure of the true Paschal Lamb, Jesus sacrificed on Calvary. As St Augustine said (in *Contra Faustum Manichaeum*):

> [What was thus prefigured in] the feast of the paschal lamb . . . has been fulfilled in the sufferings of Christ, the Lamb without spot . . . In the gospel we have the true Lamb, not in shadow, but in substance; and instead of prefiguring the death, we commemorate it daily [in the holy sacrifice of the Mass].[27]

It is worth dwelling on this for a moment. Abraham's willingness to sacrifice his beloved son Isaac was reciprocated by God's willingness to sacrifice his only beloved son, Jesus, 2,000 years later on the very same mountain. In Jewish thought, it was Abraham's fidelity which earned the grace of the Messiah being sent. The Bible explicitly states that 'because you have done this' in your seed 'all the nations of the earth will be blessed'; this was always understood in Judaism to be a reference to the fact that the Messiah was to be born of the seed of Abraham. Isaac was replaced at the last moment by a ram caught by its horn in a thicket, miraculously provided by God. The sacrificial lambs used by the Jews in the intervening 2,000 years harkened back to that original lamb of sacrifice. The blowing of a ram's horn (the *shofar*) in Jewish liturgies is a reference to that original ram, caught by its horn in a thicket, a reminder to God of his promise to send the Messiah, for whom the sacrificial lambs were simply placeholders.

When Jesus appeared, John the Baptist recognized him as the fulfilment of that promise, as the true lamb of sacrifice: 'Behold, the Lamb of God, who takes away the sin of the world!' (Jn 1.29). Jesus' sacrifice took place at Passover: 'My time is at hand; I will keep the Passover at your house with my disciples' (Jesus' words in Mt. 26.18). The crucifixion took place on the eve of Passover, at the very moment that lambs for the Passover sacrifice were being slaughtered in the Temple, a short distance away. The Last Supper, at which Jesus instituted the Eucharist, and which was therefore the first Catholic Mass, was a Passover Seder. The bread that he consecrated was unleavened Passover Matzo, which is why the Roman rite to this day permits only unleavened bread for the Eucharist. One may easily conclude that the Last Supper was simultaneously the last sacramental Passover Seder and the first Catholic Mass. The prefigurement was transformed into the realization; Judaism was transformed into the Church; and the Old Covenant[28] was transformed into the New Covenant at the very moment that Jesus elevated the unleavened bread at the Last Supper and turned it into the first Eucharist with the words: 'This is my body which is given for you. Do this in remembrance of me' (Lk. 22.19).

Other Liturgical Parallels

Because Judaism was the precursor to the Catholic Church, foreshadowing it in many ways, there are many resonances between Jewish and Catholic liturgical practices. For instance:

> *Ritual Immersion*: In Judaism immersion in a ritual bath, or *mikvah*, is required to establish ritual purity in many circumstances. In fact, Jewish law requires that a *mikvah* be constructed before a synagogue may be built. In the days of the Temple, the priests had to immerse themselves in the *mikvah* prior to participation in the Temple liturgies. To this day, any prospective convert to Judaism must undergo immersion in the *mikvah*, as must Jewish women to restore ritual purity after menstruation. The baptism practiced by John the Baptist would have been seen at the time as naturally fitting into the Judaism of the day. The use of Holy Water in the Catholic Church, as a sacramental for ritual purification and a reminder of baptism, may also be seen as resonating with this practice.
>
> *Shavuot/Pentecost*: The Jewish feast of *Shavuot*, which falls seven weeks (or on the fiftieth day) after Passover, commemorates the giving of the Law to Moses on Mount Sinai. Pentecost, which falls fifty days after Easter (of which Passover was the foretype) commemorates the falling of the Holy Spirit – the new law written on men's hearts rather than on tablets of stone (cf. 2 Cor. 3.3) – on the disciples.
>
> *The Torah/The Eucharist*: The Torah is the 'word of God'; Jesus of course is the 'word' incarnate (Jn 1.1). The Torah is the holiest object available to Judaism, and the respect shown to it echoes the respect due to the Eucharist. The Torah scrolls in a synagogue are kept in an ornamented case (the 'Ark') on the altar, on the centreline of the synagogue (the place of greatest honour and prominence) – the same as the traditional placement of the Tabernacle in a Catholic Church. A lamp is to be kept perpetually burning in front of the Ark, as one is kept by the Tabernacle.[29] If a Torah scroll is dropped, all present are to fast to make atonement for the sacrilege. The Torah scroll is to be treated with such reverence that until recently women were prohibited from touching it

(because of possible ritual impurity associated with menstruation), and when it was read from, a silver pointer was used to follow the words to avoid the reader touching it with his finger. This reminds one of how, until recently, only the anointed hands of a priest or deacon were permitted to touch the Eucharist. When a Torah scroll is too worn out to be used any longer, it must not be thrown away, but rather it is given a burial similar to that of a human being, echoing how when any particles of consecrated host must be disposed of, they must go directly into the ground (for which sacristies have a special sink, or *sacrarium*).

Jewish-Christian relations

As Pope Benedict XVI said, 'The history of relations between the Jewish and Christian communities has been complex and often painful.'[30] For the first few decades after the death of Jesus, Christianity was seen as a new sect within Judaism, one that comprised those Jews who believed Jesus to have been the Messiah. This would make it no anomaly at the time – every few years a new pretender to the title of Messiah would emerge with his group of followers. As such the early Christians, almost all of whom were Jews by origin, were seen as 'apostate' Jews and subject to punishment by the Jewish authorities as heretics. And they themselves, too, still saw themselves as Jews, albeit ones who followed the new 'way' that was introduced by the Jewish Messiah, Jesus. Hence the Jewish-Christians continued to participate in many Jewish practices, including synagogue and Temple worship. This only ended definitively around 132 AD, with the emergence of another claimant to the title of Messiah, Bar Kochba. When Bar Kochba called on the Jews to take up arms and violently overthrow their Roman oppressors, virtually all of the Jews in Jerusalem and the surrounding region joined the revolt,[31] except for one group – the Christian Jews. They could not participate without implicitly acknowledging the Messianic claims of Bar Kochba, which would be unfaithful to their belief in Christ. It was their refusal to participate in the Bar Kochba revolt (which resulted in the final dispersion of Jews from the Jerusalem and the surrounding region) that led to the definitive separation between the Jewish-Christians and the rest of the Jewish community. Thus, ironically, Jewish-Christians were excommunicated from the synagogue not for following a 'false' Messiah, but for refusing to do so.[32]

The early centuries of the Church were characterized by a harshly polemical stance between the Jewish and Christian communities, and many early Christian theologians, including among the Church Fathers, made extremely critical statements about Jews and Judaism. In some cases these were motivated by a desire to eradicate a particular heresy, known as 'judaizing', which was held by some early Jewish-Christians – that Jewish ritual law must be followed by Jews even after they enter the Church. In other cases these statements were apparently motivated by animosity, a polemical spirit or misguided theology. The statements of three such Church Fathers are given below. Although it is unpleasant to bring up such citations, it is necessary to know of them in order to understand the dynamics of the relationship between the two communities over the past two millennia, and to understand just how dramatic the recent change in the Church's attitude is.

> St Cyprian (d. 258): 'The Bible itself says that the Jews are an accursed people ... the devil is the father of the Jews.'[33]
>
> St John Chrysostom (347–407): 'Although such beasts are unfit for work, they are fit for killing. And this is what happened to the Jews: while they were making themselves unfit for work, they grew fit for slaughter.' This is why Christ said: 'But as for these my enemies, who did not want me to be king over them, bring them here and slay them'.[34] '[T]he synagogue is ... a brothel ... a den of robbers and a lodging for wild beasts ... When God forsakes a place, that place becomes the dwelling of demons.'[35] 'They live for their bellies ... their condition is not better than that of pigs or goats ... They know but one thing: to fill their bellies and be drunk.'[36] '[D]emons inhabit the ... synagogue ... the Jews themselves are demons ... In their synagogue stands an invisible altar of deceit on which they sacrifice not sheep and calves but the souls of men ... I am talking about the ungodliness and present madness of the Jews ... [D]emons dwell in the synagogue, not only in the place itself but also in the souls of the Jews ... Do you not shudder to come into the same place with men possessed, who have so many unclean spirits, who have been reared amid slaughter and bloodshed? ... Must you not turn away from them since they are the common disgrace and infection of the whole world? Have they not come to every form of wickedness? ... what manner of lawlessness have they not eclipsed by their blood-guiltiness? They sacrificed their own sons and daughters to demons. They ... became more savage than any wild beast ... they slew their own children with their own hands to pay honor to the avenging demons, the foes of our life.'[37] 'I hate the Jews[38] ... I hate the Synagogue and abhor it.'[39]
>
> St Ambrose of Milan (338–397) took credit for burning down a synagogue in his city: 'I declare that I set fire to the synagogue, or at least that I ordered those who did it, that there might not be a place where Christ was denied.'[40]

On the other side of the polemical coin, it is true that the Talmud contains some extremely disparaging and blasphemous statements about Jesus and the Blessed Virgin Mary. These cast aspersions on Jesus' mother's purity, characterize Jesus as a Messianic pretender who used magical arts to lead Jews into apostasy, and conclude that as a result he was rightfully condemned to death by the Jewish authorities and is now suffering the torments of hell.[41]

There was a political dimension, too, to the early conflict. The Jewish community had finally achieved a workable relationship with the Roman authorities under whom they lived, and feared that the new Christians – who were perceived by the Roman authorities as another type of Jew – would endanger that relationship. For in their favourable treatment of slaves and the poor, the Christians were seen as a threat to the prevailing social order.

With rare exceptions, a contentious relationship between the Jewish and Christian communities continued throughout most of ensuing centuries. The causes for the tension included social, economic, theological, political and spiritual ones. Jews were visibly outsiders, a separateness emphasized by their distinctive dress and customs, and the dietary and religious practices dictated by Jewish law, and their continued visible existence, given their rejection of Christ, seemed to be an insult to the truth of Christianity.

Social and economic factors also contributed to the tension. In many Christian countries Jews were forbidden from owning land or engaging in trades, leaving them little alternative than to support themselves by buying and selling. As such, they were seen as making a parasitic living off the productive work of others. Since Christian religious principles were generally seen as prohibiting Christians from lending money at interest, banking activities fell to the Jews, which also led to resentment. When the Jews became a powerful economic force, it would often be to the political or economic advantage of the secular leaders to incite animosity, or even violence, against them.

At times Church actions, too, worsened the situation of the Jews, placing onerous restrictions on the activities permitted to Jews and on interactions between them and Christians. For instance, the Council of Elvira in 306 AD forbad clergy to eat with Jews, a ban extended by the 325 Council of Nicaea to any conversation or fellowship with Jews by the clergy. The 1050 Synod of Narbonne prohibited Christians from living in Jewish homes. In 1215, the Fourth Lateran Council required Jews to wear distinctive clothing. The 1267 Synod of Breslau established compulsory ghettos for Jews, and the 1279 Synod of Ofen banned Christians from selling or renting real estate to Jews. The 1415 bull *Etsi doctoribus genium* was a collection of anti-Jewish laws, and the 1555 bull *Cum nimis absurdum* restricted Jews to living in the ghetto in Rome, a restriction later extended to Tuscany, Padua, Verona and Manua. The same bull also forbad contact between Jews and Christians, required Jews to wear distinctive dress, and limited their economic activities to lending money and selling second-hand items. In 1456 Pope Callistus III banned all social communication between Christians and Jews; in 1566 Pope Pius IV expelled Jews from all the cities of the Papal States except the port of Ancona, and in 1826 Pope Leo XII decreed that Jews were to be confined to ghettos and their property confiscated.

Although these attitudes and actions waxed and waned over the centuries, it was not until the twentieth century that a final fundamental change in the Church's statements and teachings about the Jews was seen. This sea change can be considered to have been inaugurated with the famous statement Pius XI made to a group of Belgian pilgrims in 1938, when he said, 'Whenever I read the words [in the canon of the Mass]: "the sacrifice of our Father Abraham," I cannot help being deeply moved. Mark well, we call Abraham our Patriarch, our ancestor. Anti-Semitism is irreconcilable with this lofty thought . . . Anti-Semitism is inadmissible; spiritually, we are all Semites'.[42]

Subsequent Popes, as well as the Second Vatican Council, further developed this trend towards what might be called philo-Semitism. When the future Pope John XXIII (while still Papal Nuncio in Paris) saw newsreel footage of the Auschwitz liberation, he exclaimed: 'There is the mystical body of Christ!'[43] Later, as Pope, he expressed contrition for previous Christian hostility towards the Jews:

> We are conscious today that many, many centuries of blindness have cloaked our eyes, so that we can no longer see the beauty of Thy Chosen People, nor recognize in their faces our privileged brethren. Forgive us for the curse we falsely attached to their name as Jews. Forgive us for crucifying Thee a second time in their flesh. For we knew not what we did.[44]

Vatican II repeated this positive attitude towards the Jews and denunciation of anti-Semitism in the document 'Nostra Aetate', when it stated:

> The Church, therefore, cannot forget that she received the revelation of the Old Testament through the people with whom God in His inexpressible mercy concluded the Ancient Covenant. Nor can she forget that she draws sustenance from the root of that well-cultivated olive tree onto which have been grafted the wild shoots, the Gentiles . . .
>
> . . . She also recalls that the Apostles . . . as well as most of the early disciples who proclaimed Christ's Gospel to the world, sprang from the Jewish people . . . God holds the Jews most dear for the sake of their Fathers; He does not repent of the gifts He makes or of the calls He issues . . . What

happened in His passion cannot be charged against all the Jews, without distinction, then alive, nor against the Jews of today ... The Jews should not be presented as rejected or accursed by God, as if this followed from the Holy Scriptures ... The Church, mindful of the patrimony she shares with the Jews, decries hatred, persecutions, displays of anti-Semitism, directed against Jews at any time and by anyone.[45]

John Paul II continued this trajectory. On 17 November 1980, in an address to the Jewish community of Mainz, he declared, 'Whoever meets Jesus Christ meets Judaism'.[46] On 13 April 1986, he visited the Great Synagogue of Rome, the first visit by a pope to a synagogue since Peter. During the visit he said,

The Jewish religion is not 'extrinsic' to us, but in a certain way is 'intrinsic' to our own religion. With Judaism, therefore, we have a relationship which we do not have with any other religion. You are our dearly beloved brothers and, in a certain way, it could be said that you are our elder brothers.[47]

On 26 March 2000, during his pilgrimage to Israel, he placed a prayer of contrition for historical anti-Semitism in the Western Wall,

God of our fathers, you chose Abraham and his descendants to bring Your name to the nations: we are deeply saddened by the behavior of those who in the course of history have caused these children of Yours to suffer and asking Your forgiveness we wish to commit ourselves to genuine brotherhood with the people of the Covenant.[48]

Pope Benedict XVI (before his election to the papacy) went even further, making a number of statements that explicitly confirmed the continuing special role of the Jewish people in salvation history:

The mission of Jesus consists in leading the histories of the nations in the community of the history of Abraham, in the history of Israel ... All nations, *without the abolishment of the special mission of Israel*, become brothers and receivers of the promises of the chosen people.[49] (emphasis added)

That the Jews are connected with God in a special way and that God does not allow that bond to fail is entirely obvious. We wait for the instant in which Israel will say yes to Christ, but we know that it has a special mission in history now ... which is significant for the world.[50]

The way that this tiny people, who no longer have any country, no longer any independent existence, but lead their life scattered throughout the world ... keep their own identity; ... the way the Jews are still Jews and are still a people, even during the two thousand years when they had no country, this is an absolute riddle. This phenomenon in itself shows us that something else is at work here ... You can see, in this way, that there is something more

> than mere historical chance at work. The great powers of that period have all disappeared. Ancient Egypt and Babylon and Assyria no longer exist. Israel remains – and shows us something of the steadfastness of God, something indeed of his mystery.[51]
>
> ... Israel still has a mission to accomplish today. We are in fact waiting for the moment when Israel, too, will say Yes to Christ, but we also know that while history still runs its course, even this standing at the door fulfills a mission, one that is important for the world.[52]
>
> God ... has obviously entrusted Israel with a distinctive mission in the 'time of the Gentiles.'[53]

When contrasted with the earlier, negative attitude towards the Jews reflected by the Church Fathers, this new positive attitude is nothing less than revolutionary, and may itself be a 'sign of the times'. As will be further discussed in the final section of this chapter, Church teaching holds that a unification of Jew and Gentile, and a wholesale entry of Jews into the Church, will shortly precede the Second Coming. One may suspect that this new positive teaching coming from the highest authorities in the Church may itself be a part of that process.

Evangelizing the Jews

This recent emphasis in Church teaching on the positive value of Judaism has led some to fall into an unfortunate theological error known as the 'dual-covenant theory', which has had a negative effect on efforts aimed at evangelizing the Jews. This theory holds that, since '"God does not take back the gifts he bestowed or the choice he made" ... Jews are "the people of God of the Old Covenant, never revoked by God ... partners in a covenant of eternal love which was never revoked"'.[54] In other words, the Jews do not need to be evangelized because they already partake in their original, saving covenant with God.

This confusion is quickly cleared up and the error goes away when one makes the necessary distinction, discussed earlier, between the 'Abrahamic Covenant' that established God's special predilection for and promises to the Jewish people, and the 'Mosaic Covenant', that established an elaborate system for ritual purity and sanctification, involving animal sacrifices and a wide range of ritual prohibitions (such as the Jewish dietary laws). Although the latter was abrogated, the former was not.[55]

The 'dual-covenant theory' is clearly irreconcilable with both the Gospels and Catholic dogma. The Gospels make abundantly clear that Jesus came *first* for the Jews (Mt. 15.24 'I was sent only to the lost sheep of the house of Israel'). It was to Jews that Jesus said, 'unless one is born of water and the Spirit, he cannot enter the kingdom of God' (Jn 2.5), and 'unless you eat the flesh of the Son of man and drink his blood, you have no life in you' (Jn 6.53). Jesus spent his entire life evangelizing Jews, not Gentiles, and was crucified for evangelizing Jews, not Gentiles. St Peter, the first pope, was known as the 'apostle to the Jews'. St Paul in his letters discusses at length the need that Jews have for Christianity; there are also the examples of his own conversion and his repeated near-martyrdom for evangelizing Jews. There is no way to read the New Testament and maintain that Christianity was intended only for Gentiles, not Jews.

Nevertheless, this theory unfortunately resulted in the Church reducing its efforts to evangelize Jews, by missionary activity and even by prayer. Such a failure to evangelize the Jews is a disservice to the truths of the Catholic Faith; a disservice to the Jews, to whom the rest of the world owes the infinite gift of Jesus and His Church; and a disservice to Jesus Himself, in that it denies Him the joy of receiving His own especially beloved Jewish people into His Church. Finally, it is a disservice to both God and the world in that such a failure constitutes an impediment to the Second Coming itself. As CCC states in paragraph 674:

> The glorious Messiah's coming is suspended at every moment of history until his recognition by 'all Israel', for 'a hardening has come upon part of Israel' in their 'unbelief' toward Jesus [Rom. 11.20–26; cf. Mt. 23.39] . . . The 'full inclusion' of the Jews in the Messiah's salvation, in the wake of 'the full number of the Gentiles' will enable the People of God to achieve 'the measure of the stature of the fullness of Christ' [Rom. 11.12, 25; cf. Lk. 21.24] . . .

In other words, the catechism explicitly states that the Second Coming cannot take place until there is a widespread conversion of the Jews. The final section of this chapter will be an exploration of this mystery, in the light shed on it by St Paul in his Letter to the Romans.[56]

Paul's Letter to the Romans, Chapter 11

> 1–2: I ask, then, has God rejected his people? By no means! . . . God has not rejected his people whom he foreknew . . .

A flat assertion that despite the Jews' rejection of Jesus, they have not been rejected by God. This letter was written, of course, well after the crucifixion, and after the Jews stubbornly resisted the Gospel. As St Paul adds later in the chapter verses 28–29, 'As regards the gospel they are enemies of

God, for your sake; but as regards election they are beloved for the sake of their forefathers. For the gifts and the call of God are irrevocable.' Hence the election of the Jews continues, in at least some way, despite their rejection of Jesus.

> 7–8: What then? Israel failed to obtain what it sought. The elect obtained it, but the rest were hardened, as it is written, 'God gave them a spirit of stupor, eyes that should not see and ears that should not hear, down to this very day . . . '

Here St Paul is asserting that God actually veiled the eyes of at least some of the Jews so that they would not recognize Jesus, 'down to this very day'. What could the reason be? Paul provides the answer:

> 11–12: Have they stumbled so as to fall? By no means! But through their trespass salvation has come to the Gentiles, so as to make Israel jealous. Now if their trespass means riches for the world, and if their failure means riches for the Gentiles, how much more will their full inclusion mean!

Paul is suggesting that the failure of the Jews to recognize Christ was necessary in order for Christianity to spread throughout the Gentile world, and that after that has taken place, it will make the Jews jealous, resulting in them too recognizing Christ. (We see this same idea, that the Jews' failure to recognize Christ was in order to enable Christianity to spread to the Gentiles, in verse 28: 'As regards the gospel they are enemies of God, for your sake.')

Paul seems to be alluding to the fact that if large numbers of Jews had accepted Jesus, Christianity would have been seen as a sect within Judaism intended primarily for Jews, resulting in a serious impediment to the spread of Christianity. This was an early danger in the Church. Acts 15 recounts that the first Church Council, called about 18 years after the crucifixion, was convened precisely to determine whether Gentiles should be permitted to become Christians without first becoming Jews – in other words, whether Christianity was for everyone, or just for Jews. This danger was greatly lessened by the Jews' widespread failure to respond to the Gospel. Hence 'their failure', to recognize Christ, meant 'riches for the Gentiles', that is, facilitated the spread of Christianity to the Gentiles.

Yet St Paul immediately continues with the suggestion that this failure will not be permanent, and that when the Jews do enter the Church, they will bring a special blessing to it: 12–15 '. . . if their failure means riches for the Gentiles, how much more will their full inclusion mean! . . . For if their rejection means the reconciliation of the world, what will their acceptance mean but life from the dead?'

He then continues (16–24):

> If the dough offered as first fruits is holy, so is the whole lump; and if the root is holy, so are the branches. But if some of the branches were broken off, and you, a wild olive shoot, were grafted in their place to share the richness of the olive tree, do not boast over the branches. Remember it is not you that support the root, but the root that supports you. You will say, 'Branches were broken off so that I might be grafted in.' That is true. [But] even the others, if they do not persist in their unbelief, will be grafted in, for God has the power to graft them in again. For if you have been cut from what is by nature a wild olive tree, and grafted, contrary to nature, into a cultivated olive tree, how much more will these natural branches be grafted back into their own olive tree.

Here Paul is reminding his Gentile listeners not to feel superior to the Jews on the basis of their failure to recognize Christ. The Jews were the natural branches growing on the olive tree of salvation; some were broken off – the Jews who rejected Jesus – to make room for the grafting in of wild olive branches – the Gentiles – but that is no reason for the grafted-in wild branches to boast. For later, when the cultivated branches – the Jews – will be grafted back in, they will be even better suited to the tree – salvation through Christ – than the Gentiles, for they had originally been a part of it. When will this happen?

> 25–26: I want you to understand this mystery, brethren: a hardening has come upon part of Israel, until the full number of the Gentiles come in, and so all Israel will be saved.

After 'the full number of the Gentiles' has come in, the veil that has been cast over the eyes of the Jews will be lifted, and they too will recognize Christ. What does that refer to? This idea of the 'times of the Gentiles' which ends only after the 'full number of the Gentiles come in' appears in a prophecy made by Jesus himself, shortly before the crucifixion, in which he said:

> They [the Jews] will fall by the edge of the sword and be led captive among all nations, and Jerusalem will be trodden down by the Gentiles, until the times of the Gentiles are fulfilled, and there will be signs in sun and moon and stars and upon the earth distress of nations and perplexity of roaring of the sea and the waves, men fainting with fear and with foreboding of what is coming on the world, for the powers of the Heavens will be shaken, and then they will see the Son of Man coming in a cloud with great Glory. (Lk. 21.24–27)

The Jews literally fell by the edge of the sword and were led captive among all nations when Jerusalem fell to the Romans, first in 70 AD and then for the final time in 135 AD. From that point on Jerusalem was 'trodden down by the Gentiles', that is, in Gentile hands, until 1967 AD, at which point the old city of Jerusalem returned to Jewish hands for the first time in almost 2,000 years. Jesus' prophecy then continues with a vivid description of the Second Coming. Thus the 'times of the Gentiles' seems to refer to the period between the First Coming of Christ, and a time shortly preceding the Second Coming. During this epoch the Jews will, by and large, reject Jesus as the Messiah, leaving the way open for the Gentiles to enter, and predominate in the Church. Once the 'full number of the gentiles' has come in, the veil will be lifted from the eyes of the Jews, and they too will recognize Jesus, entering the Church in great numbers. In so doing, their 'full inclusion' will mean 'great riches' for the Church, 'bringing life from the dead'. Shortly thereafter (as we saw in the earlier citation of CCC para. 674), Christ will return in glory, to a Church now completed by the [re]entry of the Jews, who were the original olive branches which were broken off to make room to graft in the wild olive branches, the Gentiles.

Given this glorious future for the Church, Jew and Gentile, one can do no better than to conclude with the words with which St Paul closes Romans 11:

> Just as you [the Gentiles] were once disobedient to God but now have received mercy because of their [the Jews'] disobedience, so they [the Jews] have now been disobedient in order that by the mercy shown to you they also may receive mercy. For God has consigned all men to disobedience, that he may have mercy upon all.
> O the depth of the riches and wisdom and knowledge of God! How unsearchable are his judgments and how inscrutable his ways! 'For who has known the mind of the Lord, or who has been his counselor? Or who has given a gift to him that he might be repaid?' For from him and through him and to him are all things. To him be glory forever. Amen. (Rom. 11.33–36)

Notes

1 This encounter, and Jacob's name change to Israel, is described in Genesis 32.
2 Pope Paul VI, Dogmatic Constitution on Divine Revelation *Dei Verbum* (18 November 1965). The translation here and following are from the official Vatican website www.vatican.va
3 Second Vatican Council, *NA*, para. 4 (1965).
4 From Rabbi Schneerson's introduction to Schneur Zalman of Liadi's *Tanya*, English translation (Brooklyn, NY: Kehot Publication Society, 1962), vii.
5 This translation from *Weekday Prayer Book* (New York City, NY: Rabbinical Assembly of America, 1962), 47–48.

6   For example, Daniel 9.24–27; Genesis 49.10; Isaiah 6.9–10, 7.14, 9.1–6, 11.1–4, 35.4–7, 40.3–5, 53.1–12, 61.1–2; Jeremiah 23.5; Malachi 3.1; Micah 5.2; Numbers 24.17; Psalm 22, 34, 72.1–11; 2 Samuel 7.12–13; Wisdom 2.12–24; Zechariah 9.9, 12.10.
7   Cf. CCC, para. 633. This and all quotes from the Catechism are from the Vatican website www.vatican.va
8   The *tzitzit* come from Numbers 15.38–40 'Speak to the people of Israel, and bid them to make tassels on the corners of their garments throughout their generations, and to put upon the tassel of each corner a cord of blue; and it shall be to you a tassel to look upon and remember all the commandments of the LORD, to do them, not to follow after your own heart and your own eyes, which you are inclined to go after wantonly. So you shall remember and do all my commandments, and be holy to your God.'
9   The wearing of beards and earlocks is based on the law found in Leviticus 19.27: 'You shall not round off the hair on your temples or mar the edges of your beard.'
10 Our calendar is a 'solar' calendar. It maintains a precise synchronization with the earth's orbit around the sun, but ignores the moon's orbit around the earth; as a consequence, the new moon may fall on any day of the month. By contrast, the Jewish calendar is a 'solar-lunar' calendar, based both on the earth's orbit around the sun and on the moon's rotation around the earth, such that every month begins with a new moon. In order to achieve this, the number of days in the year varies slightly from year to year. Because of this, from year to year Jewish festivals fall on different days of the Western calendar.
11 Technically an eight-branched menorah is a *hannukiah*, but the term menorah is more generally used.
12 Exodus 12.13; the overall story of Passover is told in Exodus 2–15.
13 'World Jewish population grows by 70,000', *Jerusalem Post*, Jerusalem, Israel, 25 September 2008.
14 Tallies vary because of varying definitions of who is a Jew (one parent, both parents, etc.). Sources include *Israel Science and Technology Directory* 2010 and the *Jewish Virtual Library* 2010 (a division of the American-Israeli Cooperative Enterprise).
15 The statistics in this section are compiled from various studies conducted, in the United States and Israel, by the World Jewish Congress (1998), the American Jewish Committee (2000) and Israel's Central Bureau of Statistics and Ministry of Immigrant Absorption. The US figures may be roughly representative of the Jewish population in the United Kingdom and Western Europe, too.
16 Named after 'Hermes Trismegistus' ('thrice great Hermes'), a combination of the Greek god Hermes and the Egyptian god Thoth.
17 Many Jews who come to faith in Christ do not consider that they have 'converted' at all, but rather feel they remain as Jewish as ever – or more so, since now they are followers of the Jewish Messiah. The term is adopted here for ease of use.
18 Dan Cohn-Sherbok, ed., *Voices of Messianic Judaism* (Baltimore, MD: Lederer Books, 2001), 12ff.
19 Sheri Ross Gordon, 'Inside Jews for Jesus', *Reform Judaism*, 22 (Winter 1993), 24.
20 Mike Decker, 'Messianic Jews and the Law of Return', *Israel Today*, 24 September 2007.

21 Spoken to her superior, Mother Marie-Therese Bordenave. *Some of Bernadette's Sayings* (Nevers, France: St Gildard's Convent, 1978), 68.
22 *Thoughts and Sayings of Saint Margaret Mary* (Rockford, IL: Tan Books, 1935), 4.
23 Examples include Judith's cutting off the head of the enemy leader Holofernes (book of Judith) was as a picture of the Blessed Virgin Mary crushing the head of the serpent and Esther's intercession to save the Jewish people before the throne of King Ahasuerus (book of Esther) as a prefiguration of the intercessory role of the Blessed Virgin Mary with God. See, for example, St John Chrysostom *Catechesis*, St Irenaeus of Lyons *Against Heresies* and St Cyril of Jerusalem *Mystagogical Catecheses*.
24 Although this is explicit in the synoptic accounts (cf. Mt. 26; Mk 14; Lk. 22), there is some ambiguity about whether it was celebrated a day earlier than one would normally expect (Jn 18).
25 Recounted in the book of Exodus.
26 St Cyril of Jerusalem, 'First Lecture on the Mysteries', *Nicene and Post-Nicene Fathers*, Second Series, Vol. 7. Edited by Philip Schaff and Henry Wace (Peabody, MA: Hendrikson, 1995), 144–145.
27 St Augustine, 'Contra Faustum Manichaeum, Book XXXII', *Nicene and Post-Nicene Fathers*, First Series, Vol. 4, 144–145, 335.
28 'Old Covenant' here refers to the sacramental salvific system introduced by Moses (the 'Mosaic covenant') rather than the special election of the Jews inaugurated at the time of Abraham (the 'Abrahamic covenant').
29 'A special lamp to indicate and honor the presence of Christ is to burn at all times before the tabernacle in which the Most Holy Eucharist is reserved' – Canon 940, *Code of Canon Law* (Washington, DC: Canon Law Society of America, 1995), 349.
30 Spoken during his August 2005 visit to the synagogue in Cologne, Germany; quoted in *Catholic World Report* March 2010, 19.
31 This unanimous support was not entirely voluntary; Bar Kochba killed those who refused to join the revolt. Cf. Edward Flannery, *The Anguish of the Jews* (Mahwah, NJ: Paulist Press, 1985), 36.
32 See, for instance, Ray Pritz, *Nazarene Jewish Christianity: From the End of the New Testament Period until Its Disappearances in the Fourth Century* (Jerusalem, Israel: Hebrew University Magnes Press, 1988), 59; 'It was his [Rabbi Akiva's] endorsement of a false messiah (and for Jewish-Christians a rival messiah) which was the last straw which broke the ties of the notzrim [Nazarenes] with rabbinic Judaism.' Other scholars hold differing views.
33 Pinchas Lapide, *Three Popes and the Jews* (New York: Hawthorn Books, 1967), 39.
34 St John Chrysostom: Homily 1, section II, para. 6. Translation here and following are from *Internet Medieval Sourcebook*, ed. Paul Halsall (New York: Fordham University Center for Medieval Studies, 2006).
35 St John Chrysostom: Homily 1, section III, para. 1.
36 Ibid., section IV, para. 1.
37 St John Chrysostom: Homily 1 on the Judaizers, section VI, paras 2–8.
38 St John Chrysostom, Homily 6 on the Judaizers, section VI, para. 9.
39 St John Chrysostom: Homily 1 on the Judaizers, section V, para. 2.
40 St Ambrose 'Letter XL: To Emperor Theodosius', para. 8; *Nicene and Post-Nicene Fathers*, Second Series, Vol. 10, 441.

41 See, for instance, R. Travers Herford, *Christianity in Talmud and Midrash* (New York: KTAV Publishing House 1975), 35ff.
42 Lapide, *Three Popes and the Jews*, 114.
43 Ibid., 315.
44 *Catholic Herald* 14 May 1965, cited ibid., 318.
45 *NA*, para. 4 (1965).
46 John Paul II, *On Jews and Judaism* (Washington, DC: U.S. Catholic Conference, Inc. 1987), 33–34.
47 Ibid., 82.
48 Text from Vatican website http://www.vatican.va/holy_father/john_paul_ii/travels/documents/hf_jp-ii_spe_20000326_jerusalem-prayer_en.html
49 Cardinal Joseph Ratzinger, 'Reconciling Gospel and Torah: The Catechism' (an address given at the International Jewish-Christian Conference in Jerusalem in 1994). Later included in Joseph Cardinal Ratzinger *Many Religions: One Covenant* (San Francisco: Ignatius Press 1999) under the title: 'Israel, The Church, and The World: Their Relation and Mission', 21ff.
50 From the article 'Ratzinger Speaks Out in New Book', *National Catholic Reporter*, 6 October 2000.
51 Cardinal Joseph Ratzinger, *God and The World* (San Francisco: Ignatius Press 2002), 148.
52 Ibid., 149–150.
53 Joseph Cardinal Ratzinger, 'Interreligious Dialogue and Jewish-Christian Relations', *Communio* 25, 1 (1998). This article is reprinted in *Many Religions, One Covenant* (San Francisco: Ignatius Press, 1999), where the citation appears on page 104.
54 Quote is from the document 'Reflections on Covenant and Mission' of the Bishops Committee for Ecumenical and Interreligious Affairs of the United States Catholic Conference of Bishops (USCCB) on 12 August 2002, as it appeared on the USCCB website www.usccb.org. It was later retracted, and a corrective document, 'A Note on Ambiguities Contained in Reflections on Covenant and Mission', was issued by the USCCB on 18 June 2009.
55 It is worth noting that even if the Mosaic covenant had not been abrogated, the Jews have been unable to fulfil their end of it since 70 AD when the Temple in Jerusalem was destroyed and all animal sacrifice ceased in Judaism.
56 A far fuller discussion of the role that the Jews have to play between the First and Second Comings of Christ can be found in the author's book *Salvation is from the Jews: The Role of Judaism in Salvation History from Abraham to the Second Coming* (San Francisco: Ignatius Press, 2003), which is devoted to addressing the issue in depth.

Further Reading

Titles on Judaism

Buber, Martin (1948), *Tales of the Hasidim*, New York: Schoken Books.
Flanner, Edward (1985), *The Anguish of the Jews*, New York: Paulist Press.
Hertzberg, Arthur (1991), *Judaism*, New York: Simon and Schuster.

Neusner, Jacob (1984), *Invitation to the Talmud*, San Francisco: Harper Collins.
Peters, Joan (2000), *From Time Immemorial*, Chicago, Illinois: JKAP Publishers.
Telushkin, Joseph (1991), *Jewish Literacy*, New York: William Morrow.
Twersky, Isadore (1972), *A Maimonides Reader*, New York: Behrman House.

On Catholicism and Judaism

Bea, Augustin Cardinal (1966), *The Church and the Jewish People*, London: Geoffrey Chapman.
Cervin, Ronda (1994), *Bread from Heaven*, New Hope, KY: Remnant of Israel.
Isaac, Jules (1954), *The Teaching of Contempt*, New York: Holt, Rinehart & Winston.
Klyber, Arthur (2000), *The One Who is to Come*, New Hope, KY: Remnant of Israel.
Lapide, Pinchas (1967), *Three Popes and the Jews*, New York: Hawthorn Books.
Lustiger, Cardinal Jean-Marie (2007), *The Promise*, Grand Rapids, MI: Eerdmans.
Oesterreicher, John (1952), *Walls are Crumbing*, New York: Devin-Adair.
Rich, Charles (1990), *Autobiography*, Pertersham, MA: St Bede's Publications.
Simon, Raphael (1986), *The Glory of Thy People*, Pertersham, MA: St Bede's Publications.
Stern, Karl (2000), *The Pillar of Fire*, New Hope, KY: Remnant of Israel.
Zolli, Eugenio (2008), *Before the Dawn*, San Francisco, CA: Ignatius Press.

Chapter 3

Catholicism and Islam

Christian W. Troll SJ

Section 1: What is Islam?

Islam: Submission to God in Faith

Islam, the system of faith and practice, propagated as the final, divinely revealed religion by Muhammad, entered history in the seventh century AD. Like Christianity, Islam professes a universal truth claim. It addresses potentially every human being. Today both religions have become world religions and they challenge one another globally. The Qur'an, believed by Muslims to contain the definite guidance from God for all times, portrays Muhammad as the last in a long chain of prophets, all of whom preached *al-islam*, the unconditional submission to God. Muhammad's preaching as documented in the Qur'an and the reliable Hadiths[1] was addressed to all women and men. However, Jews and Christians received special attention.

Christianity and Islam, as will be shown in more detail in the following pages, contain both common as well as opposing elements.[2] When dealing with these, in the context of a largely 'creedal' approach to the subject, it would seem to be of paramount importance to discern the core belief of both religions and especially what each religion teaches about God. Only in this way is it possible to assess correctly the specific nature as well as the relative significance of the particular teachings of each tradition. As Christians, when we encounter Muslims, we are expected to know and to understand the basic Islamic beliefs. The effort to understand Islamic beliefs will lead to a sharper and deeper apprehension of our own Christian beliefs. Muslim faith and practice are articulated in the Qur'an and Hadith. They have been expressed in further detail in the works of jurisprudence (*fiqh*) and systematic theology (*kalam*). The Qur'an itself lists the truths that have to be accepted in faith: God, the Angels, the Scriptures, the Prophets and the Last Day (see Qur'an, sura 4.136; subsequently references to the Qur'an will be given in the short form: Q. 4.136).[3] The earliest theological tradition adds 'Predeterminism' (*qadar*) to these five 'articles of faith'. The *shahada*: 'I testify that there is no god except God and I testify that Muhammad is the messenger of God', constitutes the first and basic prescribed act of a Muslim. Its profession before the prescribed witnesses suffices for officially becoming Muslim.

God is the first and fundamental object of Muslim belief and, ultimately, its only one. In other words, Islam is radically centred upon God. Muhammad figures as its second object, since he was sent to convey the authentic and final revelation of God's guidance. The total ordering of the human being towards God expresses itself in the attitudes of adoration, submission to his will and respect of the 'rights of God'. The Muslim is first and foremost a servant-worshipper, *'abd*, and Muhammad is precisely in this regard 'an excellent model' (Q. 33.21) for the believers. Obedience in faith is essential for Muslims, so that their actions may be in total correspondence with the will of God. This precisely is *al-islam*: the act of total surrender to the one God and to his revealed will. The word 'Muslim' derives from the same root S L M as 'Islam'. Muslim is the one 'who has submitted or who submits to God'.

Sunni Muslims and Shia Muslims (also known as Shiites) comprise the two main groupings within Islam. Sunni Muslims today constitute 85–90 per cent of the total Muslim world population. Sunni and Shia identities first formed around a dispute over leadership succession soon after the death of the Prophet Muhammad in 632 AD. Over time, however, the political divide between the two groups broadened to include theological distinctions and differences in religious practices as well.

The Sources of Islam as Faith and Legal Order

The foundation of Islam as faith and jurisprudence is the Qur'an. The word *Qur'ān* literally means 'recitation', 'public [liturgical] reading', and so is first of all recited lesson, recitation. According to Islamic conviction, the Qur'an contains the revealed statements of God himself, exactly as they were communicated to Muhammad through the agency of the angel Gabriel (*Jibril*) (see Q. 69.38–46). According to Islamic belief, the Qur'an was not revealed all at once but rather in the course of 23 years and always in the context of specific 'occasions'. These Qur'anic revelations, Muslims believe, have been preserved letter for letter to this day, without any change whatsoever.

The Qur'an contains many ethical norms, cultic prescriptions and also a number of legal rulings. In interpreting these Qur'anic norms, the Hadiths are taken into consideration as exemplifications, especially in cases where there is a perceived lack of clarity, and finally also in formulating additional rules of conduct. The Sunna: customary practice or lived example of the prophet Muhammad designates the body of information and teaching about how he put Islam into practice (Islam). The life and action of Muhammad function as the chief hermeneutic principle of the Qur'an.

If on a certain matter of faith and practice, on which neither the Qur'an nor the Sunna provide clear guidance, there existed in earliest times a consensus (*ijma'*) of the Companions of the Prophet or even of very early jurists, then this consensus constitutes an abiding source of Islamic Law for later times. Otherwise, through analogical reasoning (*qiyas*) a 'link' can be established between the new case and an earlier legal ruling. This presupposes that there is a correspondence between the two legal issues. However, the schools of legal interpretation are not unanimous as to whether the application of *qiyas* in a given case is licit or not. The Hanbalites[4] have a negative view of the ability of human reason to apply the revealed texts to new situations' (*ijtihad*) and may, therefore, be regarded as the 'ancestors' of today's Islamic fundamentalists. Since they are afraid that regular application of analogical reasoning in jurisprudence may lead to falsification of the divinely revealed law, they reject analogical reasoning.

'Aqa'id: The Doctrines of Islam

Islamic faith is not genuine without effective recognition of the 'articles of the faith'. The firm conviction of the absolute binding nature of these articles of faith is the basis on which, alone, the genuine religious attitude can develop. The articles of faith consist of the following: (1) belief in Allah, the one God; (2) belief in His angels; (3) belief in His books; (4) belief in His messengers; (5) belief in the Day of Judgement; (6) (and) belief in predeterminism. The six articles of faith form an indivisible unity. It is commonly understood that if one does not accept one of these articles of faith, one implicitly denies the others as well.

Belief in Allah, the one God

The 'fundamental statement' of belief in Islam is, as we have stated earlier, the *shahada*. Making a statement of the unity of God (= *tawhid*) in the first part of the shahada is the source of all Islamic principles. The truth of 'pure', undiluted monotheism has absolute primacy in the structure of Islamic belief and imprints its stamp on the entire structure of Islamic thought and life.

The word Allah consists of the definite article 'al' and the word 'ilah', which signifies god or deity. Thus Allah is *the* God, the one and unique Deity, the God of *Ibrahim* (Abraham), of *Musa* (Moses), of *'Isa* (Jesus) and of Muhammad.

The order and perfection of creation and the excellence of the human spirit, whose limits at the same time are obvious, as well as the mystery of life and death – all these phenomena point towards the existence of the Creator God (see Q. 112.1–4). The Qur'an teaches that God is the totally Other, who resembles none of his creatures. He not only transcends any imperfection but rather is himself perfect in every sense. He transcends everything and is not perceivable by the senses. And yet, despite being the Transcendent God, He does not remain aloof from mankind. He can and wishes to be approached by His servants. Q. 50.16 states: 'We created man – we know what his soul whispers to him: We are closer to him than his jugular vein –'

The human person, limited as she is as far as thought and imagination are concerned, cannot properly know the qualities of the almighty Creator, except when God Himself makes them known to her. The oft-repeated phrase *Allahu akbar* means: God is always greater than whatever can be grasped by human intelligence. God is the Almighty, the All-knowing, and His power is at work incessantly. Only He grants life and takes it back. From Him we all come, and to Him we all return. He sustains and nourishes us and takes care of us. He is the All-just, the All-gracious and the All-merciful (see also Q. 2.255, known as 'the verse of the throne).

Jesus and the Triune God
The Qur'an states in various places that God has neither a female consort nor a son. To have a female consort or a son would contradict His uniqueness (see Q. 6.100–103). The teaching of the Qur'an vehemently opposes the idea that *'Isa* (Jesus) is the Son of God. But Muslims honour and respect Jesus as one of the great prophets of God (see Q. 19.27–35).

The Qur'an objects to the idea of Jesus as the son of God, that is, in a biological sense rather than to the theological/biblical title Son of God which it seems to ignore. In Q. 5.116 God asks Jesus in heaven: '[. . .] Jesus, son of Mary, did you say to people, "Take me and my mother as two gods alongside God"?' Christian belief, according to this verse, seems to conceive of three gods or at least a tripartite god. In any case, the Qur'an clearly rejects any notion of 'threeness' in God and exhorts Christians as follows: 'So believe in God and His messengers and do not speak of a "Trinity" [literally: "and do not say: Three"] – stop [this] that is better for you – God is only one God, He is far above having a son . . .' (Q. 4.171).

The Qur'an, furthermore, threatens those who persist in saying 'that God is the third of three' (Q. 5.73) with 'painful punishment'. Indeed, at face value, for Muslims to believe in a triune God amounts to *shirk*, the sin of association.

Two further basic differences between the Islamic and the Christian doctrine should be mentioned here. First of all, Islam, throughout all its various interpretations, rejects the idea that God decided to become human in Jesus, the Messiah, so that through the person of Jesus Christ God is revealed to us. In the Islamic view, the human person can get to know God adequately by simply becoming acquainted with His attributes and by experiencing His power in the grandeur and splendour of His creation. And humans can come closer to God by obeying faithfully His commands and observing his prohibitions, that is, by professing the Islamic creed and implementing all its prescriptions meticulously.

Secondly, Islam also rejects the idea of redemption. Nobody can bear the sin of another human being or take on his responsibility, because to let an innocent pay for the sins of another would contradict the justice of God. Thus Q. 17.15 states: 'Whoever accepts guidance does so for his own good; whoever strays does so at his own peril. No soul will bear another's burden, nor do We punish until We have sent a messenger.' Hence, the idea that one person should have died in order to atone for the sins of mankind is alien to Muslims, at least to Sunni Muslims.[5]

The only sin God does not forgive is the sin of associating others with God (*shirk*). Regarding this to be the gravest of sins, the Qur'an says in Q. 4.116: 'God does not forgive the worship of others beside Him – though He does forgive whoever He will for lesser sins – for whoever does this has gone far, far astray.' Any 'deification' of a human being of the kind Christians, in the eyes of Muslims, practise with regard to the prophet *'Isa*, is irreconcilable with Islam. The Qur'an commands Muhammad to warn believers not to attribute to him or to any human being more than human qualities. Thus Q. 18.110 tells Muhammad to proclaim as follows: 'Say, "I am only a human being, like you, to whom it has been revealed that your God is One." Anyone who fears the Last Day should do good deeds and give no one a share in the worship due to his Lord.'

Belief in His angels

The Qur'an speaks repeatedly of angels. Their service consists above all in worshipping and glorifying God night and day (see Q. 21.19–20). With the permission of God, the angels may intercede for human beings and ask on their behalf for mercy and forgiveness, especially on the Day of Judgment (Q. 42.5). The angels are servants and messengers of God, acting 'according to His command' (Q. 21.26; 22.75; 35.1). One of the foremost tasks God entrusts to angels is conveying the revelation faithfully to the prophets and messengers (Q. 16.2). This service is generally considered to be the special task of the angel Gabriel (*Jibril*), especially with regard to the Prophet Muhammad (Q. 2.97). The angels are also charged with protecting men and women and supporting them, especially in difficult situations (Q. 50.17–18; 66.4). On the Last Day, they will execute the Judgment of God (see Q. 41.30–32).

Satan (*Iblis*) and his followers fell from paradise due to their pride and disobedience. In primordial times, at God's command, all angels bowed down to show respect to Adam, except *Iblis* (see Q. 2.24; 7.11–18; 15.26–43).[6] The divine command to believe in angels is a touchstone for the sincerity of one's faith in the authenticity of the divine revelation and the prophethood of Muhammad. After their fall from paradise, the devil and his helpers became occupied with mankind, trying to seduce them and lead them into disaster. Thus the devil is the 'sworn enemy' of the human beings (Q. 2.168; 35.6).

Belief in His 'Books'

God sent down his holy scriptures as a guiding light for humankind. Through these scriptures, God asked men and women to believe in him, the one God and to serve Him alone. To those who profess God and follow His commandments, He promises well-being here and in the next life. However, in case they turn from Him in disbelief and disregard His commandments, heavy punishment awaits them. According to Islam, *taurat* (Torah), *zabur* (Psalms), *injil* (Gospel) and the Qur'an all are revealed scriptures. These were sent down as literal verbal revelations to Moses, David, Jesus and Muhammad. The 'belief in the Books' relates in fact to their original versions. In the meantime, however, the Qur'an teaches, Jews have 'falsified' (*harrafa*) the text (Q. 2.75) of the original Torah or 'concealed' (*katama*) some of its passages (Q. 2.159), and 'those who were given the Scriptures', that is: both, Jews and Christians 'concealed' the passages in their scriptures which contained evidence of the truth of Muhammad's mission (Q. 2.146; 3.71). Today, almost all Muslims are convinced that the Holy scriptures of the Jews and of the Christians are extant only in unreliable, falsified versions. For them, only the book revealed to Muhammad, namely, the Qur'an, represents the original text of the divine revelation, exactly as it was transmitted word for word to the prophet (see also Q. 5.15–16).

Belief in His messengers

God chose certain human beings to be His messengers and prophets. He entrusted them with the task to communicate to others the revelations He sent down upon them and to teach them how to lead lives fully pleasing to God. Only through these messengers were human beings able to obtain some clarity about the attributes of God, about His will and about life after death. The first human being, Adam, is believed to have been the first prophet. God revealed to him the names of all things. However, in the course of human history, pure monotheism was abandoned again and again and polytheism took on many different forms. Hence, God in His mercy began sending further prophets, who would remind people of the one God and of His right to be worshiped alone. Thus, prophets appeared in many countries and among many tribes and peoples. They all preached the unconditional surrender to the will of the one God that is: *al-islam*.

For the Qur'an, the last of all the prophets was Muhammad. His mission was to teach the religion of Islam not only to his own people, the Arabs, but to the whole of humankind, a mission that he faithfully fulfilled. God has brought Islam to its perfect and final conclusion (see Q. 5.3) with the Qur'an and Muhammad, who is the final Messenger and 'an excellent model for those of you who put their hope in God and the Last Day [. . .]' (Q. 33.21). (God has brought Islam to its perfect and definite conclusion (see Q. 5.3).)

Muhammad – the 'seal of the prophets' (Q. 33.40)
According to the traditional sources, Muhammad was born in Mecca 570 years after Christ. When he was 40-years-old, this successful merchant received revelations urging him to go forth as a prophet and to proclaim afresh the will of the one God. His words, understood as direct revelations from the 'preserved tablet' in heaven, were gathered together in the Qur'an. In 622, Muhammad escaped from persecution by the Meccans through the *hijra*, the emigration from Mecca to Yathrib (later called *Madinat an-Nabi*, the 'City of the Prophet!' or Medina). There he was able to exercise successfully his religio-political mission, uniting all Muslims in the faith in the one God and bringing them together into one community (*umma*), which transcended all tribal divisions. Despite some setbacks, the community of Muslim believers with Muhammad as its chief steadily grew in power.

At this early stage of his public career, Islam was revealed to him and he presented it to Jews and Christians as the pure monotheism of Abraham and thus as the original truth of both the Jewish and the Christian faith. He hoped Jews and Christians would adhere to this message and to his claim to be its divinely appointed messenger. However, this hope was not realized. Matters came to a breaking point when, 16 months after the *hijra*, Muhammad, in obedience to the command of the Qur'an (Q. 2.144), changed the direction for prayer from Jerusalem to 'the Sacred Mosque' (i.e. the Kaaba in Mecca). The Qur'an declared the Kaaba to have been built by Abraham, the supreme model of the pure monotheistic faith, *al-islam*. In 630, Muhammad destroyed the idols, paintings and religious symbols in the Kaaba and two years later Mecca was the destination of the first great pilgrimage, led by Muhammad himself. This established the tradition of the annual *hajj*. Muhammad died in 632.

Besides the Qur'an, Muhammad's life and pattern of behaviour provide a unique model for Muslims. The Prophet was 25-years-old at the time of marrying Khadija, a 40-year-old, wealthy widow whose caravans Muhammad had supervised before they were married. Khadija was the first wife of the Prophet and, during her lifetime, the only one. In the following years, he contracted 12 marriages with women from various Arab clans. According to Islamic Tradition, Muhammad was illiterate, which serves to underline the fact that he owed his teaching entirely to revelation, without any contribution from himself.

It is noteworthy that the outline of many of the lives of prophets in the Qur'an fully corresponds with the life of Muhammad. A prophet is chosen by God from his own people; the prophet speaks his people's language; he proclaims that there is only one God (the same message that all the prophets have taught); he experiences hostility on the part of his own people, who even threaten him with death; however, God saves the one whom He has sent and punishes the unbelieving people. The Qur'anic Jesus, like Muhammad, is a preacher of monotheism and, quite consistently rejects the idea, put into his mouth by others, that he and his mother are 'two gods alongside God' (see Q. 5.116).

In Medina, after the *hijra*, Muhammad encountered hostility from local Jewish tribes. He saw himself and his community as the only true followers of Abraham and rejected the claims of the Jews and Christians to stand in the tradition of Abraham, who was 'neither a Jew nor a Christian'. Rather, Abraham was the supreme model of the 'undiluted' monotheism, which he, Muhammad, had now been sent to renew and restore (see Q. 2.135, 140), not only by preaching the message of the Qur'an but also by translating it effectively into social and political reality. Further, Muhammad saw himself as the heir to a genuine prophetic tradition, which in him, the 'seal of the prophets', found its high point and fulfilment. The Qur'an, the message entrusted to him, was thus the criterion for measuring all previous Holy scriptures.

Muslims firmly believe that Islam, as it was revealed to the prophet Muhammad, will retain its validity forever. The teaching of Islam is suitable for the needs and circumstances of all human beings everywhere at all time. Muslims affirm the veracity of all the true messengers of God. However, it is by the Qur'an as transmitted through Muhammad that all prophetic messages have to be evaluated. The Qur'an is the final and definitive criterion (*furqan*) of the truth.

Belief in the Last Judgement

Belief in the Last Judgment and in life after death means that life in this world will end on a day appointed by God, the day of the Last Judgment. On that day, all human beings that have ever lived on earth will be raised up to new life and will have to give to God an account of their life here on earth. God will judge everyone according to His mercy, justice and wisdom.

Those who have believed in God and his prophet will be rewarded and enter paradise where they will continue to live forever in perfect bliss. Those who offended against His commands will not have been abandoned but will have received God's mercy. Thus, many sinners sincerely will have repented of their errors and will have resolved to avoid them in the future (see Q. 4.110). God will punish with the torments of hell those who have disregarded His commands and have failed to return to Him. There is only one sin that God does not forgive, namely in Arabic *shirk*, that is, to prefer other gods besides God. This means to give something or someone an importance which detracts from one's obedience to God alone. It can also mean to become addicted to something (see Q. 4.48, 116; 39.65).

But what fate awaits the virtuous non-Muslim? The Qur'an affirms that 'the deeds' of persons who have not professed (Muslim) monotheism will 'come to nothing' (Q. 6.88; 18.103–105). The vast majority of the theologians of the various schools of Islam do not hesitate to assign all non-Muslims to hell, whatever may be the value of their works. But there are exceptions among the theologians which are not well known. For instance, the great al-Ghazali (d. 1111), who developed a Muslim theology of the 'unbeliever of good faith' which was taken up by the influential reform theologian Muhammad 'Abduh (d. 1905). Popular opinion prefers a simple solution, namely, that all Muslims go to paradise and all non-Muslims go to hell. Yet, the general view of most of the educated, 'modern' Muslims would be that every person will be judged according to his works, whatever his official faith allegiance may be.

Belief in predestination

A Muslim believer affirms that God, the all-knowing and almighty, knows his creation in every detail; that He has the power to put into practice the decisions which, in His infinite knowledge, He comprehends and approves; that He administers His reign with divine perfection and, finally, that no power could escape His will. Nothing can happen against God's will, and everything that happens is with His permission. Human freedom of choice does not stand in opposition to this. God has given human beings free will and has enabled them to choose and act freely. Hence, it is within God's justice to call mankind to account on the Last Day. The belief in divine providence, in the Muslim view, does in no way condone passivity or fatalism. Mankind is obligated to tackle and to manage the problems of everyday life effectively. God alone determines whether he reaches the goal he aspires to. God will arrange the consequences of human actions in the way He deems right. Belief in Divine Providence, trust in Him alone will give a deep meaning to life, will preserve the believer from despair and will give calm and inner peace (see the prayer of Q. 3.26–27).

Shari'a: The Law of Islam

Genuine belief will result in works of service. Islam means to obey God as His servant, to do His will. Every good deed is an act of obedience. In Islam, all acts of obedience are fundamentally 'acts of worship' ('*ibadat*) insofar as they correspond to the will of God.

The means by which one can organize all areas of life according to the divine will, as revealed in the Qur'an and in the reliable Hadiths, is the Islamic Law, which, including its application, is called the Shari'a. The Shari'a classifies all human actions according to their merit in the eyes of God and regulates them by commands and prohibitions. In this way, the Shari'a gives a legal shape to the injunctions revealed by God to order the life of the individual and the community according to God's will. The Shari'a, ideally speaking, comprises the whole of life with all its social and political relations.

A special method is applied to those questions which are not covered by the Qur'an or Hadith, nor by established precedent (*taqlid*) or by direct analogy (*qiyas*) from known laws. This method is called *ijtihad* and it consists in the effort to evolve new legal judgements directly from the sources of Islamic Law. Only the legal scholars were equipped with the authority to apply this method in the Sunni world up to the tenth century AD. The first rank among them was held by the founders of the four still operative Schools of Law. Although the possibility of a legal scholar appearing who would be equipped to practice *ijtihad* today is recognized by Sunnis in theory, the necessary qualifications expected of him would be tantamount to perfect knowledge of all the laws expounded in past history, which would surely be an impossible expectation to fulfil. Therefore it is usually understood that 'the door of *ijtihad* has been closed' for the past 900 years. In fact, during these last centuries, the tendency of Islamic jurisprudence (*fiqh*) has been to produce only commentaries upon commentaries and marginalia. Naturally this has made Islamic Law a thoroughly conservative force. Only since the late eighteenth century AD, with the growing impact of Western institutions and ideas in the Sunni Muslim world, have reformers who wanted to develop law by means of independent legal thinking and decision-making, gained a measure of support among Muslim intellectuals. Looking at the contemporary scene it would be fair to say that most of the Shiites, individual orthodox Sunni jurists and most modern Muslims consider the 'opening of the doors of *ijtihad*' necessary, so that the modernization of Islamic law may exert its influence on the formation of contemporary society.

The five most important categories by which the legal systems classify human actions are the strictly obligatory (*wajib* or *fard*) actions, the recommended (*mandub*) actions, actions for which neither reward nor punishment is to be expected but which are permissible (*mubah*), actions that are reprehensible (*makruh*) and finally actions that are forbidden (*haram*). *Haram* indicates anything that God has strictly prohibited. Food that is lawful, particularly meat from animals that have been ritually slaughtered, is considered to be *halal*.

The practical application of Islamic law in life is the responsibility of the individual as well as of the community. Judges, as well as other recognized leaders of the community have the duty to care for the application of the law *ex officio*. They are assisted by the counsel of the doctors of the law, the *fuqaha*, and by the formal legal opinions delivered in answer to cases put to them, the *fatwa-s*.

Ethics, understood as the derivation of abstract principles of right behaviour, has not developed greatly in Islamic history because what is good and what is bad, according to traditional Sunni understanding, cannot be known by any inner quality of a given human action or by norms based on rational insight. It can be known only by means of the revealed will of God. God, in His absolute freedom, determines the norms of good and bad. Moral teaching, therefore, like all other Islamic stipulation, is part of the Shariʻa. The responsibility of human beings consists in adhering unconditionally to the will of God.

The determination of moral norms by God's will does not, according to Muslims, diminish human freedom in any way. God's revealed will, rather, is considered a welcome support and orientation for human beings to find and to keep to the right path (see Q. 7.43). The history of humankind is marred by recurrent disobedience against the will of God. However, not all sins count as equally grave – there are great sins and smaller misdeeds (Q. 4.31). The greatest sins are those against God and the faith, and the sins of association (*shirk*), of unbelief and the deliberate rejection of Islam. If people do not repent of them, they put themselves outside the range of God's mercy (Q. 4.116, 137, 168). Not even the intercession of Muhammad can prevail on God to forgive unbelief (Q. 9.80). Other sins are those which are directed against the life of human beings or which encroach upon the property or the good name of others. Such sins can be forgiven.

Forgiveness of sins is granted on the basis of faith in God (Q. 46.31) or because of the faithful following of Muhammad (Q. 3.31) or the faithful fulfilling of religious duties. God forgives the truly repentant sinner (Q. 4.17). Islamic moral teaching contains commandments and prohibitions that are comparable to the biblical Decalogue (see Q. 6.151–152; 17.22–39; 60.12).

The 'Pillars of Islam'

Muslims speak of their religion as the 'house of Islam'. According to this image, the prescribed acts of worship are designated the 'pillars of Islam'. They are: *shahada*, to profess the principal creed of Islam; *salah*, to practice regularly the prescribed ritual prayer; *zakah*, to purify one's economic life by paying the prescribed alms; *siyam*, to fast during the month of Ramadan; *hajj*, to make the annual pilgrimage to Mecca once in one's lifetime.

(1) *Shahada*, literally: 'testimony, witness' refers to the public witness to God's oneness and to Muhammad's prophethood, as has been explained above. To be a Muslim essentially means to give witness to 'God and His messenger' before one's fellow believers as well as the whole world.

(2) After the *shahada*, formal prayer (*salah* in Arabic; *namaz* in Turkish, Persian and Urdu) is the most important duty of a Muslim. We are speaking here about the prescribed ritual prayer, which corresponds roughly to what Christians would term liturgical prayer. It is regulated down to the smallest detail and must be performed five times every day, at fixed times regulated by the passage of the sun and therefore varying with the changes of the calendar year and the geographical location of the worshipper. Moreover, an important non-formal, spontaneous prayer is, for instance, *du'a*: invocation or bidding prayer. Besides *du'a*, Muslims practise many other kinds of spontaneous prayer. The practice of 'remembrance [of God]' (*dhikr Allah*), of which the Qur'an speaks frequently (see Q. 2.152; 29.45; 73.8), refers to invocation of the Divine Name, or to litanies and has a certain resemblance with the old Christian practice of 'the prayer of the heart'.

The formal prayer is essentially an act of adoration and praise of God, performed in the precise manner, which God Himself has prescribed. In their prayer, Muslims express not only their veneration of God but also their willingness to obey a regular and demanding duty imposed by God through the all-comprehensive Shari'a law. With regard to formal prayer, Muslims like to point out that God remains the absolutely Independent. In no way whatsoever does He need our prayers and our obedience. The importance of prayer is understood as a need experienced by the human person since prayer is a source of strength and direction and a bulwark in the face of life's difficulties.

(3) Every Muslim is obligated to pay a certain annual alms-tax fixed by the Shari'a, the *Zakah* according to the value of their property above a certain minimum. Some scholars of the Law, in the light of the conditions of modern life and economy, have pressed for a standardization of these legal prescriptions. The tax is given to the poor or used in any way that serves the common good. Renouncing a small part of one's material possessions helps Muslims to remember that needy people have a right to be assisted by those whom God has granted a more favourable material position. The respect for social justice, which finds expression in this 'pillar', not only constitutes a central theme of dialogue but can lead to greater collaboration of Christians and Muslims in the service of contemporary society.

(4) *Siyam*, or fasting, as prescribed during the month of Ramadan, means that the believer, from dawn until sunset, abstains from all food, drink and sexual activities. By fasting, a Muslim testifies that God's laws have priority over human urges. The real objective of fasting, therefore, is obedience to God. Moreover, fasting has many other uses.

For instance, it teaches self-control, arouses compassion for those who daily experience hunger and thirst and it also helps to develop inner strength. Young, old, insane, chronically ill persons as well as women during pregnancy, breastfeeding and menses are exempted from fasting. Whoever, because of illness or travel or for any other serious reason, cannot keep this obligation during Ramadan, is required to make up for the lost time later.

(5) To perform the *hajj* ('the greater pilgrimage' to Mecca) once in a life time is obligatory for those whose health and means permit it and who, by doing so, do not compromise their responsibilities towards their families. The 'journey to the House of God' takes place once a year and lasts five days and follows closely prescribed rites and formulated prayers attributed to Muhammad himself. The prayers during the *hajj* constantly mention Abraham, whose example of perfect obedience in faith provides the spiritual basis for the *hajj* ritual as a whole. During the pilgrimage, Muslims meet with sisters and brothers in faith from every continent and experience the spiritual energy of the global community of Muslims as well as the summons to transcend divisions within the Muslim community (*umma*).

Jihad

Jihad means 'struggle' (the Qur'an frequently terms it *jihad fi sabil Allah*: 'struggle on the path of God'), and not necessarily military fighting. It is the struggle against our own waywardness and against those who would spread corruption on the earth.[7] The Arabic designation *jihad* belongs to the same linguistic family as the verb *jahada*, 'to struggle (for a cause)'. The active participle *mujahid* designates the fighter ('on the path of God'). The *Shiite* branch of Islam and some of the Islamist movements consider *jihad* the 'sixth pillar' of Islam. For all Muslim believers, *jihad* counts as a meritorious work for which the Qur'an promises the reward of paradise (see Q. 3.163; 4.76, also 2.86–89, 212–213, also 8.40; 9.29 and 61.4).

Early Muslim jurisprudence developed a general theory of *jihad*. Its basic features can be summarized as follows. The world is divided into two parts that are inimical to one another. There are territories that comprise the 'house of Islam' and there are certain areas of the world that are still under non-Muslim rule. These latter are designated as the 'house of war'. This part of the world falls under the banner of Islamic *jihad* until Muslims can implement the Shari'a in these areas as well. *Jihad* must be practised whenever unbelievers attack Islamic territory or hinder Muslims in practising the 'pillars of Islam', or whenever they actually hinder the preaching of Islam. In these cases, *jihad* counts as defensive war. According to pre-modern Islamic political doctrine *jihad* has to be waged until the whole world finds itself under Islamic rule, that is, until the end of the world. However, to engage in this expansionistic *jihad* is not a duty binding on each Muslim individual. It suffices that the political rulers of a given territory are committed to pursue it.

In historical reality, the principle that aggressive war against non-Muslims is demanded by divine law on a permanent basis was not put into practice. There have been long periods of history during which Muslim-ruled and non-Muslim-ruled states lived in peaceful coexistence and engaged in substantial economic and cultural exchange.

For states with which the Muslims engaged in relations based on treaties, the Islamic tradition of law used the collective term *dar al-'ahd* (house of treaty). However, such contractual relations were usually considered a provisional state of affairs, which would ultimately be overcome by Islamic rule all over the world. Whereas many Muslims continue to consider such contractual solutions effective for our times and to be applicable to modern state relations, some advocate abandoning the traditional idea of dividing the world in different 'abodes' and propose instead to consider the whole world as one 'abode of witness' (*dar as-shahada*) or one 'abode of invitation to Islam' (*dar ad-da'wa*).

Today Muslims normally portray Islam as a religion that is peaceful by its very nature. They assert that being Muslim is equivalent to promoting peace. Islam and *salam* are understood to be identical. Proof of this, these Muslims point out, is that Islam describes the struggle against unbelievers as the 'lesser' jihad, whereas the struggle of each believer against selfish desires is understood to be the 'greater' jihad. This view, although it is based on a Hadith which never made it into the six canonical collections of Hadith the Sunnis consider reliable, has been influential throughout the centuries and remains so to this day.

In contrast to strenuous attempts by Muslims in past and present to explain *jihad* as a largely non-violent, ethical and ascetical effort, the extreme Islamists[8] have been promoting for some time the idea of a militant, aggressive *jihad*. According to Sayyid Qutb (1906–1966), for instance, a prominent Islamist ideologue, influential up to the present time, the construction of an international order of peace will be possible only after the Muslim community has conquered the world by means of a well-planned and executed *jihad*. He describes the Muslim duty of *jihad* as a revolutionary process of liberation, which will benefit all humankind.

The ideology inspiring and motivating such extreme groups and movements is often the result of political, social and psychological causes as much as of religious ones. Many Muslim majority countries are suffering from the effects of mass poverty and other acute social circumstances caused by a repressive way of governance, maladministration and the corruption of local political leaders. These circumstances are often perceived to be the consequence of an economic global order that favours the affluent industrial nations and a rate of population growth which cannot be catered for by national economic resources.

Tafarruq: Diversity in Islam

Sunni and Shia Muslims

Disagreement about the succession of the Prophet in the early years of Islam caused an argument between 'Sunnite' majority Islam and the 'party' (*shi'a*) of 'Ali ibn 'Ali Talib, the cousin and fourth successor of the Prophet regarding who should be caliph. Today most Muslims are Sunni (87–90 per cent), while the vast majority of the remainder (10–13 per cent) are Shi'a. The majority of the Shiites belong to the so-called Twelver-Shi'a (*ithna-ash'ariyya*). They live mainly in Iran, Iraq and South Asia but are numerous also in Turkey, Yemen, Azerbaijan, Lebanon and Bahrain. 'Ali is considered by all Muslims to have been outstanding in piety, wisdom and courage. The division that initially had been purely political subsequently generated serious theological differences.

Shi'a Islam differs from Sunni Islam in that it does not recognize the authority of the first three caliphs, not even as authentic transmitters of Tradition. It believes 12 successors and blood relations of Muhammad, the so-called Shiite 'imams', to be infallible in their teaching and to be exclusively gifted with a deeper understanding of the Qur'an. They expect that Imam Muhammad al-Muntazar who is believed to have disappeared as a boy in the year 874 AD to return from his seclusion (*ghayba*) at the appointed time. The Shi'a Muslims attribute to 'Ali as 'friend of God' (*Wali Allah*) a higher status than to all other caliphs and continuously mourn Husain, the grandchild of the Prophet, killed during a massacre near Karbala in Iraq (680 AD). Shi'a Islam is marked by the stress it puts on notions such a martyrdom, redemptive suffering and a sense of Islam's integral mysticism (*'irfan*).[9]

In spite of the above-mentioned differences, the Twelver Shiites fulfil all the conditions for being genuine Muslims that have been mentioned earlier and they, therefore, understand themselves as forming part of the Muslim community. The same is to be said of the Zaidiyya in Yemen and the Ibadites in Oman. This cannot be said, however with the same degree of certitude of all groups belonging to the esoteric Sevener Shia, which recognizes only seven Imams and tries to keep their doctrines secret. The most famous among these are the Isma'ilis. The convictions of the Lebanese Druzes and the Turkish Alevites would not seem to be compatible with the self-definition of either Sunni or Shi'a Islam. Since the proselytizing Ahmadiyya profess their founder, Mirza Ghulam Ahmad (d. 1908), to have received a direct revelation from God, they have been excluded by Sunni authorities from the *umma*, the worldwide community of Muslims.

Popular religion

Even from the earliest days of Islamic history we find two main reactions to the sober outlook of the jurists and the restrictive nature of the Law, namely, popular Islam and Islamic mysticism. The term 'popular Islam' designates the Islam of simple believers who could not relate to the abstract nature of the Islamic concept of God and the absence of mediating factors. The human need to make contact with the holy and the need for persons who could mediate between God and the everyday world led to a kind of Muslim folk religion that consisted of practices like the veneration of saints and their tombs, black magic, fortune-telling, drug-induced ecstasy and belief in miracles. Educated and reformed Muslims tended to censure such aspects of popular Muslim piety as 'heterodox'. However, whether Muslims formed the majority or the minority within a given society, there has always been a wide range of opinions among them as to what was to be considered 'orthodox' and what was to be considered 'heterodox' Islam. In Muslim cultures there has always been considerable variety, even within one and the same country.

Sufism

Islamic mysticism or Sufism emerged as a movement of piety which gave precedence to the love of God over the fear of God and which led to an internalization of the doctrines of the faith. In this sense, Muhammad himself, who spent long hours of the night in prayer, was a 'Sufi'. Soon there were others like him, for example, Hassan (d. 728 AD) and Rabi'a al-Adawiyya (d. 801 AD), both of Basra in Iraq. They were consumed with the 'desire for the face of God' (Q. 13.22). Most of the Sufis did not consider themselves entitled to dispense themselves from the prescriptions of the Shari'a. Instead, the observation of the Law formed the basis of their faith. Qur'anic verses, as for instance the 'Light Verse' (Q. 24.25), have inspired Sufi contemplation. In a later phase, especially between the eleventh and the fifteenth centuries AD, a more philosophical trend appeared among Sufis. They were influenced by neo-Platonic and Gnostic ideas and made union with God the aim of their mystical striving. At the same time, the 'path' to perfection was systematized by means of the organization of Sufi brotherhoods (*turuq*) as well as through Sufi doctrine (*ma'rifa*).

Two Sufis were especially well known among Muslims as well as non-Muslims. They were Hussain Mansur al-Hallaj (857–922 AD), who claimed to be 'one with God' (*ana al-haqq*, that is, 'I am the truth/reality') and Shihab al-Din Suhrawardi (1155–1191 AD), founder of a speculative light mysticism. These two Sufis were executed as blasphemers or heretics. However, indisputably the 'greatest of all masters' (*shaykh al-akbar*) of Islamic mysticism was the Andalusian Muhy al-Din Ibn 'Arabi (1165–1240 AD), whose esoteric interpretation of the Qur'an (*ta'wil*) and orthodoxy remain in dispute to this day.

Like many other Sufis, Ibn 'Arabi was also accused by certain Muslims of a number of faults. These include the arrogance of the elite and metaphysical speculation, of reinterpreting the Qur'an by means of neo-Platonic, Gnostic and ultimately pantheistic categories. Underpinning Ibn 'Arabi's influential thought lies his doctrine of the unity of being (*wahdat al-wujud*), according to which all of reality is a manifestation of the unknowable Absolute. For Ibn 'Arabi, the world is ultimately only an idea without real existence in itself. He explains and justifies his teaching with reference to the Islamic doctrine of the Unity of God (*tawhid*). Distinguishing the created world from God will ultimately lead to dualism (*thanawiyya*). Traditional-minded Muslims see in Ibn'Arabi two main dangers. If God is not a distinct Other, prayer and moral responsibility both become meaningless. Eventually, Ahmad al-Sirhindi (1564–1624 AD) argued against Ibn'Arabi's intellectual theory with his own teaching on the 'unity of vision' (*wahdat al-shuhud*). According to his thinking, the unity which Sufis experience belongs only to the level of visionary experience. It does not belong to ontological reality.

Chief Trends in Contemporary Islam

Surveying the contemporary Islamic world, we can, broadly speaking, identify three main trends in religious thought and practice: (1) a cultural, moderate Islam influenced by the authority of the four classical Law schools; (2) a Qur'an-centred hermeneutics that would emphasize the interpretation of the Qur'an according to the first generations (*salaf*) of Muslims and hence could be termed *Salafi*. The political side of this trend would be identified as Islamism; and (3) an Islam undergoing radical reinterpretation through either an emphasis on the text and the ethics of the Qur'an or an emphasis on the philosophical implications of the Qur'anic message. As a fourth trend one could mention the on-going influence of folk-style Islamic revivalism.

The distinguishing features of contemporary Islamism are, first, a longing to recreate the society and religion of 'Medina' in today's world. In this effort to return to the situation of 'Medina', Islamists strive to reintroduce Shari'a as comprehensively as possible and, wherever possible, to re-establish the Islamic state. The second aspect of contemporary Islamism is a rejection of essential aspects of modern civilization as not having emerged from Islamic cultural tradition. A third aspect of Islamism is a great variety of strategies to strengthen Islam's power and influence. These various types of Islamism can be distinguished from the answer given to the question regarding the legitimate or prescribed methods that would be used to establish the rule of Shari'a and the Islamic social system demanded by an Islamic state. All branches of Islamism concur in their rejection of both Sufism and the religious speculation of Ibn 'Arabi. They would consider the former to be irrational and the latter to be alien to the mind of the Qur'an.

Section 2: Catholic Approaches to Islam

The Basic Challenge and Question

The existence of Islam constitutes a particular challenge to Christians and their understanding of Christian faith and practice. For centuries the Church almost 'naturally' assumed itself to be the only final and true religion. The divine plan of salvation appeared to Christians as an upward progression of the history of religions, with Christianity as its apex. However, we know that Christianity, chronologically speaking, is not the last world religion. Centuries after the birth of the Church another religion entered the stage of world history, namely, Islam, which was able, within a short time, to conquer vast territories and gradually became the culturally and religiously dominant power in these territories and far beyond. The 'community of the Prophet' (*ummat al-nabi*), like the Church, claims to be instituted by God to give 'witness of the truth' (*shahadat al-haqq*). It sees itself as a community of believers, divinely commissioned to invite each and every human being to 'the religion of the truth' (*din al-haqq*), Islam. Furthermore, it understands itself as divinely commissioned to establish, already here on earth, the rule of God and His Law.

How does Catholic faith and theology respond to the spectacular rise and permanence of a post-Christian, and thus post-biblical, religious-political community that claims to be founded by God himself as the true, perfect and final religion and political order for all humankind? Our answer begins with the teaching on Muslims and Islam. This teaching, first, states the Catholic doctrines shared by Christians and Muslims and then discusses those Catholic teachings which Islam criticizes, questions radically or even completely rejects as contrary to reason and sound religion. As a result, the Catholic faith emerges in a clearer way. Also, we shall spell out the conditions without which a peaceful living together of Christians and Muslims at various levels would seem to be impossible. Finally, we shall ask what place Catholic faith and theology assign, within the history of salvation, to Islam and its essential claims and teachings.

The Second Vatican Council and Islam

The Second Vatican Council constitutes, not least with regard to the relations of the Roman Catholic Church with Islam, an event of extraordinary importance. The statements of the Council carry the authority of an official declaration emanating from the highest teaching authority of the Catholic Church, an Ecumenical Council. The first of the two directly relevant texts, in paragraph 16 of the *Dogmatic Constitution on the Church* (*Lumen Gentium* = *LG*), situates Islam as the first of the great non-biblical monotheistic religions.

> But the plan of salvation also includes those who acknowledge the Creator, in the first place amongst whom are the Muslims: these profess to hold the faith of Abraham, and together with us, they adore the one, merciful God, mankind's judge on the last day. (trans. Flannery. Vatican II documents will be quoted from his translation.)

The second text, which is paragraph 3 of *NA*, the *Declaration on the Relations of the Church to the Non-Christian Religions*, is longer and more detailed.

> The Church has also a high regard for the Muslims. They worship God, who is one, living and subsistent, merciful and almighty, the Creator of heaven

and earth, who has also spoken to men. They strive to submit themselves without reserve to the hidden decrees of God just as Abraham submitted himself to God's plan, to whose faith Muslims eagerly link their own. Although not acknowledging him as God, they venerate Jesus as a prophet, his virgin Mother they also honor, and even at times devoutly invoke. Further, they await the Day of Judgment and the reward of God following the resurrection of the dead. For this reason they highly esteem an upright life and worship God, especially by way of prayer, alms-deeds and fasting.

Over the centuries many quarrels and dissensions have arisen between Christians and Muslims. The Sacred Council now pleads with all to forget the past, and urges that a sincere effort be made to achieve mutual understanding; for the benefit of all men, let them together preserve and promote peace, liberty, social justice and moral values.

Two characteristics of this second text will be noticed immediately. Aspects of Muslim faith and practice are named that elicit an unqualified positive echo on the Catholic side. Other elements for one reason or another are not mentioned, for instance, the *hajj*, *jihad* or the veneration of Muhammad. At the same time the fundamental difference between Muslim veneration of Jesus as prophet and the Christian faith in the divine sonship of Jesus is highlighted. The text of the Council opens up the possibility of collaboration between the two religions in the service of a just and peaceful coexistence.

In the opening sentence of this text, we find what may appear to us as an almost worn-out formula: 'The Church has also a high regard for the Muslims. They worship God, who is one, living and subsistent, merciful and almighty, the Creator of heaven and earth, who has also spoken to men.' Yet, in the light of the history of Catholic-Muslim relations throughout the centuries, it must be considered as an utterly new beginning. It is remarkable that the Council does not only invite us 'to forget the past',[10] but rather also asks Christians and Muslims to collaborate 'for the benefit of all men'.

Theological Criteria for Discernment

Vatican II left to post-conciliar theological reflection the inevitable task of assessing Islam as a normative system of beliefs. It is difficult to make such an assessment because of the many substantial commonalities between the teachings of Christianity and of Islam. Not a few terms Christians and Muslims share, quite often conceal deeper divergences. Single biblical and Qur'anic statements have to be understood in the light of the central creedal position of the Qur'an. We shall try to demonstrate this point with regard, first of all, to the attitude and act of faith (*fides qua*), which is central to the teaching of both religions and then with regard to the important other more themes of Islam and the Catholic faith.

The act of faith

The orientation of the whole human person on God finds expression in a life shaped by visible acts of worship, submission to His will and respect for 'the rights of God'. Muslim believers define themselves fundamentally as *'ibad* (sing. *'abd*), that is, servants – worshippers of God. To be Muslim means to believe that God is the only Deity.[11]

The formula: 'I believe that there is no god but God' or, in other words, that God is unique, that God is the one and only Deity, paradoxically gives Muslim theological discourse about faith an 'intellectual' character. And indeed, in the Qur'an and consequently, in Muslim theology, the exactness of the formulation of the object of faith is of paramount importance. And yet, the most commonly used formula among Muslims is: 'to believe in God', and the faith of the common Muslim believer is little concerned with elaborate theological definitions. True, both Islamic theology and ordinary Muslim belief are extremely sensitive when it comes to the language of *union* of God with the human person because all Muslims are alert to the danger of falling into 'the root sin' of *shirk* (association). But it must be remembered that for Islamic as for Christian faith the *union of the human with the divine will*, in perfect surrender to God and in obedience to His commands, is of central importance. Christians pray for this in the *Pater Noster* which includes the words: 'Thy will be done.'

Another noteworthy point is that Muslims believe in God and in His absolute authority not solely on the basis of rational insight. The believer does not develop an image of God on the basis of reason. The existence of God and His being without any rival may be evident to reason. But, the Muslim believer adheres to belief in God and in Muhammad as his final prophet ultimately because God himself has witnessed to this truth in His revealed Word, the Qur'an. This allegiance of faith has, according to Christian theology, a supernatural quality. *It is this characteristic attitude of faith* (fides qua) *common to Muslims and Christians which forms the basis for a theological affinity between the two religions.*[12] *This affinity remains in place despite the fundamental divergences with regard to the object of faith* (fides quae).

Qur'an and Islamic theology both agree that faith is reasonable. However, faith can never be rational in the sense of being a logical conclusion or deduction. Islam considers faith to be at one and the same time the gift of God and an invitation into His mystery. Such faith disposes the believer to accept God and to lead a life conformed to God's will, even when God's designs seem to militate against reason and human desires. The understanding of the nature of faith allows the Catholic Church to affirm that a Muslim believer's faith can lead him or her to salvation.[13]

One cannot fail to notice evidence of a strong faith in God in the lives of Muslims as well as in Muslim societies. One is also struck, and at times shocked, by the all-encompassing nature of their faith commitment. The faith of contemporary Christians, on the other hand, would seem to be characterized by more questioning and searching. Christians and Muslims would do well to cherish both the certitude of faith, which is a gift of God received in prayer and humility and the need for faith to grow and mature by ever new questions of a theological nature.

The Concept of God in Christianity and Islam

The belief in the one God, almighty and merciful Creator, Lord and Judge, is of fundamental importance for Christians and Muslims as, of course also for Jews. In the shared profession of this faith, Christians, Muslims and Jews all share in a common search for the will of God. Differences continue to exist, however, precisely with regard to the concept of God. These differences manifest themselves most clearly in the utter rejection on the part of Islam of the Trinitarian concept of God, the incarnation of the Word of God in Jesus of Nazareth and the salvation of humankind through Jesus Christ. In these Christian doctrines Muslims see a likely return to polytheism and the tendency to idolatry in the sense of attributing absolute value to contingent realities. Islam stresses that the one God is totally 'beyond' any created reality. True, Muslims argue, God communicates to human beings. He manifests His will, and in His goodness and mercy he directs the fortunes of men. But in no way does He communicate his own self, because this would be incompatible with His transcendence. The God of Islamic faith is 'the Lord of Mercy, the Giver of Mercy' (*al-rahman al-rahim*), as every chapter/*sura* of the Qur'an (except one, namely *sura* nine), states at the beginning. However, the God of Muslim faith cannot, without thereby denying His own nature, elevate the human person into communion with Himself. God does not reveal Himself and the mystery of His own life but rather He reveals the mystery of his action towards the created world.

In contrast to Islam's emphasis on God's otherness, Christian faith holds that the one, transcendent God has communicated Himself to men and women. God has offered human beings access (see Eph. 3.12; Rom. 5.2) to Himself. Vatican II states in section 2 of the *Dogmatic Constitution on Divine Revelation*:

> It pleased God, in his goodness and wisdom, to reveal Himself and to make known the mystery of His will (cf. Eph. 1:9). His will was that men should have access to the Father, through Christ, the Word made flesh, in the Holy Spirit, and thus become sharers in the divine nature (cf. Eph. 2:18; 2 Pet. 1:4). By this revelation, then, the invisible God (cf. Col. 1:15; 1 Tim.1:17), from the fullness of His love, addresses men as His friends (cf. Ex. 33:11; Jn. 15:14–15) and moves among them (cf. Bar. 3:38), in order to invite and receive them into His own company.

As the Hebrew scriptures testify, the creator God from the beginning wished to encounter His creatures and to dwell among them. He concluded a covenant with a particular People, namely the Jews, in order ultimately to call all human beings into communion with Himself. He accompanied His people on their march through history. God is profoundly affected by the unfaithfulness of this People and by the sins of some of its members. However, God remains true to His promises and is ever ready to forgive their sin and to remove their guilt. He invites to repentance and reconciliation so that their lives may become whole again. God's invitation to form a community becomes effective in the life of His People when God calls them personally to accept His call in trust and obedience. God makes Himself known as Liberator and Saviour (see Ps. 77.14–21) through Moses, who leads and accompanies God's People to freedom. True, God remains totally beyond human calculation and maintains His own divine freedom (see, for example, Exod. 33.18–33), yet He is present in the foundation of history and in its fulfilment. Thus God reveals Himself in the course of history among His chosen People and makes available to them the richness of His unfathomable love.

God's Self-Revelation in Jesus of Nazareth

As a Jew, Jesus of Nazareth also participates in this history of God with His chosen People. Jesus is fully human, 'in all equal to us, except sin' (see Heb. 2.17, 4.15). He knows that he is totally dependent on God. He suffers mortal anguish and cries to God (see Heb. 5.7). Formed by the faith of his people he trusts God completely as his loving Father, hopes for the coming of God's kingdom and stands in solidarity with his fellow human beings, especially the poor, sick, marginalized and sinners. In all this Jesus is conscious of himself as coming from God and as being loved by God in a unique way. He points away from himself to God his Father as the origin of his life and of all his actions (see Mt. 112.28; Mk 10.18; Lk. 17.18).

Jesus' life reaches its climax in his suffering and death. Although he feels abandoned, he puts himself completely into the hands of God, his Father. When he reaches the end of his human frailty, he trusts that God, through the action of His Spirit, will bring about the expected 'Reign of God'. Although people have rejected Jesus, he neither rejects nor hates them. Rather he prays in loving concern for all, even for those who crucify him (Lk. 23.34). After his death his disciples in faith recognize that in him, the crucified and risen Lord, God is present in an unparalleled way. The first Christian martyr Stephen, 'filled with the Holy Spirit, gazed into heaven and saw the glory of God, and Jesus standing at God's right hand. "Look! I can see heaven thrown open, he said, and the Son of man standing at the right hand of God"' (Acts 7.55–57). It is this witness to Jesus of Nazareth as Son of God that is acceptable neither by Muslim nor by Jewish faith.

In a deeply divided and wounded world, the Christian believer comes to see that, in Jesus' offering of himself for his fellow human beings, God offers himself for all humans in order to reconcile them with Himself and with one another. In Jesus, God has in fact 'reconciled the world to Himself' (see 2 Cor. 5.19). Such offering of self for others is unsurpassable because it is not possible for anyone to give more than oneself, not even to God. In Jesus, God has revealed His true nature as self-giving and forgiving love. The New Testament states unambiguously, thus pointing to God's very essence: 'God is love' (1 Jn 4.8, 16). And Jesus, in whom this 'essential nature' of God is perfectly reflected, is described as 'the image of the unseen God' (Col. 1.15). Jesus' 'love to the end' (Jn 13.1) corresponds to what God is in Himself. So John's Gospel can declare: 'Anyone who has seen me has seen the Father' (Jn 14.9) and: 'The Father and I are one' (Jn 10.30).

The later Christological confessions express this truth in all its depth. Hence, when it is said that Jesus is true God and true man, one must not lose sight of the 'point of reference' of all these statements: Jesus of Nazareth, son of Mary, who was obedient to God his Father even 'to accepting death, death on a cross' (Phil. 2.8) and who by his obedience has lived love in a perfect way. Precisely because Jesus in his obedience and love points away from himself towards God, Jesus *is* the revelation of God, in which God fully expresses Himself.

God, the Triune

The encounter with Jesus the crucified, who in the Easter experience is present with his disciples in a new way, beyond the limits of space and time, is the point of departure for the Trinitarian concept of God. Belief in the triune God in no way removes or even lessens the belief in His oneness and uniqueness. Jesus himself confessed that God is One (see Mk 10.18, 12.29–30; Jn 17.3), and the Christian creed has always professed the unity of God (see Gal. 2.19; Rom. 3.30; Jer. 2.19). From the time of the apostles onwards many Christians witnessed to the one God with their own blood and they are venerated as martyrs.

However, the one God of the Christian faith has revealed and communicated Himself as love. In the relation between Jesus and his Father in the Holy Spirit, who communicates the self-offering of Jesus to his human brothers and sisters in the world, Christian faith recognizes the presence and activity of the one God, for God reveals Himself as differentiated love. No one can comprehend the mystery of God. And yet, the apostles and disciples of Christ, all faithful heirs of Jewish monotheism, in their contemplation of the relationship between Jesus, the Messiah, with his Father and the self-offering of Jesus communicated by the Holy Spirit, recognized that God must be affirmed as one differentiated love. It became evident to them and thus to the Church, that the unity of the one God consisted of a triune unity of self-giving love. The Christian confession of the one God as Trinitarian forms a profound contrast to the Islamic conception of monotheism, which categorically rejects the incarnation and excludes participation in divine life offered to men and women in Jesus Christ.

Muhammad and the Catholic Faith

Vatican II did not mention Muhammad by name nor did it make any statement on him and his claim to be the final messenger of God. However, by challenging Christians to esteem Muslims as monotheistic believers (see *NA* para. 3), the Council implicitly abandoned all polemical and negative assertions about Muhammad, which had been made about him in the past. For, he is the founder of this community and its 'excellent model [of conduct]', as the Qur'an says. The essential difference between Catholic faith and Islam is that, for Muslims prophetic revelation reaches its peak in the Qur'an as it is believed to have been faithfully transmitted and exemplified in the life and career of Muhammad, 'the seal of the prophets', whereas, for the Catholic believer, revelation reaches its fullness (*pleroma* Col. 1.19, 2.9) in Jesus Christ, the Word of God become flesh, who rejected violence and suffered, died on a cross and rose from the dead.[14]

However, the fact that the Catholic faith recognizes the fullness of revelation in Jesus does not prevent Catholics from acknowledging that

God has also made himself [partially] known to humanity in other ways and in other places, both before and after Jesus Christ. Catholic believers will also readily acknowledge that the Qur'an's unambiguous proclamation of the one transcendent God is reminiscent of an essential element in the message of Jesus Christ himself. Thus Christians may be challenged in response to the message of the Qur'an to live more authentically as faithful disciples of Jesus Christ.

The concept 'prophet', as understood in the Islamic sense, refers to a person, whose words when spoken in the name of God, are endowed with divine authority and hence should be obeyed unconditionally. Understood in this way, the title 'prophet' cannot be ascribed to Muhammad by Catholic believers because, if they obeyed Muhammad unconditionally, they would be negating certain key tenets of the Christian faith. Catholics will accept some of Muhammad's teachings and reject others but it is not possible for Catholics to believe in Muhammad and obey him in every way. It would clearly be unacceptable for Muslims to take such a selective approach to Muhammad, whom they regard as a true prophet and indeed the last of the true prophets. Hence it would be preferable for Catholics to take another perspective on Muhammad, namely, to discern whatever is true, good and beautiful in the message of Islam and to respect the spiritual path followed by Muslims; Catholic believers should acknowledge that Muhammad was a religious and political genius and should also be prepared to admit that through God's grace, countless believers have been inspired by the Qur'an and the life of the Prophet Muhammad to live their lives in a genuine relationship with God.

Sin and Redemption

The Bible and the Qur'an emphasize that it is the will of God that we believe in Him and live according to His commandments. All human beings are responsible to God and by transgressing His commandments men and women are in need of God's mercy and forgiveness. The Bible and the Qur'an both refer to eternal salvation as well as to eternal punishment.

The Qur'an teaches that Adam and Eve transgressed the command of God and lost paradise. This transgression, however, has not affected their relationship with Him irreparably (see Q. 2.35–39). The Qur'an rejects the idea of 'original sin' and does not attribute to the Fall the lasting negative impact on relationships between God and human beings and on human beings among themselves, which the Catholic faith attributes to it. Death, according to Qur'anic teaching, is not the consequence of sin but is grounded in the will of God. According to Catholic teaching, on the other hand, the human person in consequence of the Fall is not evil through and through, yet human persons and societies have imbibed a deep-seated inclination to sin against God and against their fellow human beings (see Rom. 3.10–11). The sins of mankind are directed not only against themselves and their fellow human beings, but ultimately against God Himself (see Ps. 51.6). Human beings cannot free themselves from the inclination to sin by their own accord nor can they restore the injustice caused by sin. Any self-reliant effort to restore the damage caused by sin will lead to pride vis-à-vis God (Eph. 2.9) and thus to even greater transgression.

In contrast Muslims believe that the human person is capable of doing good at any time. If believers are taught the divine law (*shari'a*) sufficiently well, they can observe it and in this way gain the favour of God and a rich recompense. The sin of man cannot do any harm to God because it does not 'touch' God in a personal way. For Catholic believers justification and salvation are the fruits of God's gratuitous action through Jesus Christ, made visible and effective through the Church.

The Church: 'Sign and Instrument' of God's Saving Presence in the World

According to Christian faith, God has made known once and for all times the fullness of the mystery of his healing and saving love in the person of Jesus Christ. The members of the Church, by listening to God's word and by celebration of the holy sacraments are forgiven their sins, made pleasing to God and are taken into his mystery. They are enabled to proclaim God's forgiving love in public and witness to it through works of charity. The Church as the community of the believers functions as 'sign and instrument' (*LG* 1) of God's saving presence in the world. Catholic spirituality and mysticism, exemplified in a remarkable cloud of saintly witnesses, matures by listening profoundly to the Word of God, by sincere participation in the celebration of the Liturgy and by more intimate encounter with God in Christ by the regular practice of the Sacraments.

Because of its brokenness and its sinfulness, the Church needs constant conversion and reconciliation with God. Although they have no reason to feel superior to others, Christian believers have been commissioned by God to give witness in deed and word to their fellow human beings, including the Muslims, and to invite them in Jesus' name to be converted to faith in Jesus as the Son of God, to receive Baptism and thus become members of his Body, the Church.

Catholic Church and the Political Community

In the New Testament there is no basis for the formation of a 'Christian state'. Jesus neither founded a state nor established a Christian society to compete with other political societies. A Christian is a citizen endowed with the same rights and duties as any other citizen, even when the ruling elite of a particular state might happen to be unbelievers (see Rom. 13.1–7; 1 Tim. 1.1–2; Tit. 3.1; 1 Pet. 2.13–15). However, from the time of Emperors Constantine and Theodosius I in the fourth century AD, the Church became the state religion for many centuries. In some societies it had held this status, in a diminished form, until about the middle of the nineteenth century. The vacuum in the political structures during the final stages of the Roman Empire led the Papacy to acquire worldly power and this was the origin of the Papal States. Since practically all its inhabitants at the time were Christians, 'the theory of two swords' was developed by which the Pope, who held both swords, was authorized to appoint kings and emperors. The unification of both powers in one institution made it possible for the Church to sanction and even to execute policies that clearly contradicted the spirit of the Gospel, for example, discrimination against non-Christian minorities, the Crusades, the Inquisition and the support of imperial and colonial powers.

With Vatican II the Church made a decision to recover the spirit of the Gospel. This became especially clear in the *Declaration of Religious Freedom: Dignitatis Humanae*, paragraph 12, where it is acknowledged that 'in the life of the people of God in its pilgrimage through the vicissitudes of human history there at times appeared a form of behaviour which was hardly in keeping with the spirit of the Gospel and was even opposed to it'.

Given the broad range of Muslim views concerning relations with non-Muslims, Catholic believers, wherever they live together with Muslims in one country, will have to establish in each concrete case to what extent the fundamental outlook of any particular Muslim movement, organization, party or government is compatible with harmonious and respectful coexistence within a given society. The relevant Council documents (see especially *DH*, paras 2–8 and *GS*, para. 76) teach that only on the basis of respect for human rights can a just and harmonious society be developed that respects cultural and religious diversity. Christians and Muslims, both separately and together, ought to give critical consideration to their relationship with political and military power in past and present. Christians and Muslims both need to make an intelligent critique of their shared history.

Islam as a Way to Salvation?

When Vatican II spoke positively about aspects of Islam which the Holy Spirit can use to bring people closer to God, it did not thereby deny the significance of the differences between its own faith and Islam nor deny the need to proclaim to Muslims, too, the Gospel of salvation. Hence, the following question cannot remain unanswered: What positive role ought we to ascribe to Islam as a religious way of life? To what extent can Islam, from the point of view of Catholic faith and theology, lead its adherents to salvation and in what ways should Islam be considered an obstacle on the way to salvation?

We can distinguish *negative and positive elements in Islam. Positive elements* would include, for example, the sense of God as transcendent and absolute, hidden and mysterious, as well as the radical distinction between the creator and the creation and the fact that created beings owe everything to God. We have pointed out earlier how Islam, inspired by the example of the figure of Abraham as portrayed in the Qur'an, demands an attitude of total submission to the revealed Word of God. After Vatican II, Catholics also appreciate Islamic teaching about the worship and service of God, and the ritual practice in prayer, fasting and almsgiving. Also positive is the Islamic view of humankind as God's representatives or vicegerents on earth and, in the ethical sphere, the 'golden rule' as well as the aspiration to imitate the divine attributes, especially God's mercy.

On the *negative side*, with Farahian and van Nispen[15] we distinguish between, on the one hand, *explicitly negative elements* and, on the other hand, *areas of ambiguity*. In the first category a decisive point is that the God of the Qur'an does not seek to cross the chasm between Creator and humankind by becoming incarnate and thus, as an expression of the freedom of His love, becoming one with humanity. Indeed, in Qur'anic terms, God would be denying Himself if He did. The incarnation of God and the invitation to human beings to a participation in the life of God by divine grace are, for the Qur'an, simply inconceivable. This is because the constant confessional affirmation of the Muslim, *Allahu Akbar*, 'God is greater', implicitly denies to God the greatness of love that consists in binding Himself in solidarity with his creation to the extent of being willing to suffer and die on a cross, without thereby ceasing to be God. The Qur'an is thus being entirely consistent with itself when it strictly rejects any statement about Jesus that goes beyond what it says about him: that he was neither more nor less than a servant of God and a prophet in the line of the other prophets. The special titles that the Qur'an applies to Jesus, such as 'word of God', are thus ultimately emptied of their genuine, biblical significance. They are given an entirely new meaning in the Qur'an.

The denial of the death of Jesus on the cross implies also the denial of the mystery of redemption, a central theme of the Christian faith. Jesus Christ, who in Christian perspective is the incarnate Word of God to humankind, in the Islamic vision of faith becomes one with the prophets and leaves for Muhammad, the last in the line of prophets, the title 'seal of the prophets'. For Islam, the Qur'an contains the truth of all the earlier scriptures, which no longer exist in the authentic form in which they were originally revealed. For the Qur'an, it is thus the Muslims who are the true disciples of Jesus.

Two types of texts of the Qur'an can be identified as belonging to the category of *areas of ambiguity in Islamic teaching*. *First*, there are texts concerned with core features of beliefs and ethics that are open to fundamentally different interpretations. For example, alongside Qur'anic verses that are very open towards the 'People of the Book', especially the Christians (see Q. 2.62; 5.82), we find other verses that put such relationships in a much more negative light. In Q. 9.29 the Muslims are called upon to fight not only the pagans but also the 'People of the Book' until they accept the subordinate role of the protected position as *dhimmis* which is appropriate to them in the framework of Islamic rule. Everything depends on the particular emphasis of different individuals and groups and on their interpretation of the Qur'an. These interpretations are extremely varied and not infrequently at odds with each other. Since there is no central authority in Islam, legitimate plurality is accepted, although some groups claim to have greater authority in the area of interpretation.

Another type of ambiguous text can arise when the Qur'an confronts the conscience of the believer with two ultimately incompatible moral options. For example, when someone has innocently suffered injustice, what kind of response would be in keeping with God's will? Q. 5.45 mentions the law of retribution but the same verse adds that to forgo one's right to retribution brings atonement for one's sins. Ambiguities of this kind are interpreted in a great variety of ways by Muslims, and Muslims practice a wide range of approaches to Qur'anic interpretation, even including the interpretation of those verses that have a significant relation with doctrine. To the extent that the interpretation of a given Qur'anic doctrine or ruling opens the heart of the Muslim believer to the self-giving love of God, such an interpretation would dispose him or her to the effect of God's grace and could thus lead him or her to God. From the perspective of the Christian faith, the Muslim who is seeking God with an open heart is, without knowing it, oriented towards the person of Jesus Christ, who has conquered death and in his unlimited love enables all people in ways known only to him, to participate in the paschal mystery.

Conclusion

The history of religions has come under the influence, not only of the Holy Spirit, but also of human sinfulness. The history of religions has been characterized by moral blindness, corruption and compromise, hypocrisy, injustice and crime. In other words, the history of religions has suffered from a partial or even sometimes a total rejection by the adherents of religion, of the call to wholeness and holiness. Error and evil in the lives of religious believers have influenced the normative dimension of the religions, that is, their doctrines and laws. Catholic believers, too, have been susceptible to these negative influences. The Catholic Church, however, believes that she has received the gift of indefectibility from the fullness of truth received in Christ through the Holy Spirit.[16] Hence, it is part of the missionary task of the Church, guided by its teaching office (*magisterium*), to engage with Muslims (and so also with Islam in its manifold forms and expressions, past and present) in a spirit of attentiveness and openness to learning but also in a spirit of critical discrimination. It is also the Church's task at every God-given opportunity (*kairos*) to proclaim the fullness of the truth entrusted to it by Christ. This includes the prophetic responsibility to ask critical questions regarding certain ways in which Islam is taught and practiced.

Although 'the Church of the living God' consists of sinners, it is also, rightly understood, 'the pillar and bulwark of the truth' (1 Tim. 3.15), as it is founded on Jesus Christ and guided by the Holy Spirit. Through being always ready to discern and to learn anew in every historical situation, the members of the Church are called to follow their vocation ever more effectively by being guided by the Holy Spirit according to the teaching of Jesus Christ, who is the salt, the light and the yeast of human society. In faith, hope and love, the Church in the power of the Holy Spirit witnesses to Jesus Christ, the Son of God, invites men and women to become her members and looks forward to the fullness of the Kingdom of God, the Three-in-One.

Notes

1 Hadiths or Traditions relate the deeds and utterances of the Prophet Muhammad as recounted by his Companions. The most authoritative Sunni collections of

Hadith are those of Bukhari and Muslim. Hadiths are the basis, second only to the Qur'an, for Islamic Law.

2   In this essay we present central elements of the creedal dimension of Islam and discuss it from the perspective of Christian faith and practice. Our approach, here, is normative and theological rather than empirical.
3   All renderings of Qur'anic texts in this chapter are taken from the translation by M. A. S. Abdel Haleem (Oxford: Oxford University Press, 2004).
4   The Hanbalites are followers of the School of Law established by the disciples of Ibn Hanbal (780–855). Ibn Hanbal also is the compiler of a large collection of Hadith, the *Musnad*.
5   Some Shiites hold in faith that the community of believers is redeemed by participating in the sufferings of the *Ahl al-Bayt*, the Holy Family (i.e. Muhammad, Ali, Fatima, Hasan, Husayn). See Mahmoud Ayoub, *Redemptive Suffering in Islam* (The Hague/Paris/New York: Mouton, 1978), 168–205.
6   Die Qur'an commentators are divided on the question whether Iblis and his followers are fallen angels or belong to the Jinn (see Q. 18.50).
7   For a thorough study of jihad see David Cook, *Understanding Jihad* (Berkeley/Los Angeles/London: University of California Press, 2005).
8   With this term we designate Muslims who interpret the Qur'an as demanding the establishment of Islam as a comprehensive political system, not only by political but also by military means.
9   See also the entries 'Taqiyyah' (dissimulation of religious beliefs) and 'Mut'ah' (temporal marriage) in Cyril Glassé, *The Concise Encyclopedia of Islam*, 2nd ed., (London: Stacey International, 1991).
10 The Council does not of course intend any kind of irresponsible disregard for Christian-Muslim history or for the lessons to be learned from it. On the contrary, as the renowned scholar of Islam, George Anawati OP (1905–1994), one of the Council's experts, who was involved in formulating *NA*, commented shortly after the Council, 'it will be necessary that many concrete situations [. . .] be resolved before the clashes of the past can be wiped with a sponge.' ('Exkurs zum Konzilstext über die Muslime' in *Lexikon für Theologie und Kirche. Das Zweite Vatikanische Konzil, Kommentare*, Teil II (Freiburg: Herder, 1967), 487.
11 For a masterly discussion of the qualities of the Muslim faith see R. Caspar, *Théologie musulmane*, Tome II, *Le Credo* (Roma: PISAI, 1999), 1–40, esp. 3. 'Réflexions sur la foi musulmane', ibid., 23–29.
12 Were it not out of context, we should say: 'between the three religions' since what we have said here about Christian and Muslim faith applies also to the Jewish faith tradition.
13 See R. Caspar, *Théologie Musulmane, II* (Roma: PISAI, 1999), 29.
14 'In relation to Muhammad's understanding of his mission, the basic problem for Christians is the use of force, understanding this to be a divinely sanctioned response to rejection of the authority of God and his messenger. For, from the perspective of a genuinely Christian understanding of prophethood, to the extent that a prophetic mission is carried out with the use of political and military force, it thereby loses the qualities of truth and righteousness that it seeks to uphold.' Troll, *Dialogue and Difference*, 123–124.
15 Edmond Farahian and Christiaan van Nispen, 'Approches biblico-théologiques de l'Islam', in Peter-Hans Kolvenbach et al. (eds), *Understanding and*

Discussion: Approaches to Muslim-Christian Dialogue (Rome: Pontificia Università Gregoriana, 1998), 31–57, esp. 44.

16 The Vatican II 'Dogmatic Constitution on the Church' teaches: 'The holy People of God shares also in Christ's prophetic office: it spreads abroad a living witness to him, especially by a life of faith and love and by offering to God a sacrifice of praise, the fruit of lips praising his name (cf. Heb. 13.15). The whole body of the faithful who have an anointing that comes from the holy one (cf. 1 Jn 2.20 and 27) cannot err in matters of belief. [. . .] The People unfailingly adheres to this faith, penetrates it more deeply with right judgment, and applies it more fully in daily life' (*LG* 12; cf. also *LG* 25).

Further Reading on Islam and on Catholic Thinking on Islam

Islam

Cook, David (2005), *Understanding Jihad*, Berkeley/Los Angeles/London: University of California Press.
al-Faruqi, Ismail Raji (1998), *Islam and Other Faiths* (ed. Ataullah Siddiqui), Leicester: Islamic Foundation.
Haleem, M. A. S. (2004), *The Qur'an*, Oxford: Oxford University Press.
Hewer, C. T. R. (2006), *Understanding Islam. The First Ten Steps*, London: SCM Press.
Momen, Moojan (1985), *An Introduction to Shi'i Islam*, New Haven: Yale University Press.
Nasr, Seyyed Hossein (2002), *The Heart of Islam*, San Francisco: Harper Collins.
Omar, Irfan A. (ed.) (2007), *A Muslim View of Christianity. Essays on Dialogue by Mahmoud Ayoub*, Maryknoll, NY: Orbis.
Rahman, Fazlur (1979), *Islam*, Chicago: Chicago University Press.
Schimmel, Annemarie (1975), *Mystical Dimensions of Islam*, Chapel Hill: University of North Carolina Press.
Taji-Farouki, Suha and Basheer Nafi (2004), *Islamic Thought in the Twentieth Century*, London: I. B. Tauris.

Catholic approaches to Islam

Borrmans, Maurice; for the Pontifical Council for Interreligious Dialogue (1990), *Guidelines for Dialogue between Christians and Muslims*, New York/Mahwah, NJ: Paulist Press.
Catechism of the Catholic Church (1994), London: Geoffrey Chapman.
Flannery, OP, Austin (ed.) (1987), *Vatican II. The Conciliar and Post Conciliar Documents*, Study Edition. Northport, NY: Costello Publishing Company/Grand Rapids, MI: William Eerdmans Publishing Co.
Gioia, Francesco (ed.) (2006), *Interreligious Dialogue. The Official Teaching of the Catholic Church from the Second Vatican Council to John Paul II (1963–2005)*, Boston: Pauline Books & Media.

Islamochristiana (1975–), Annual publication of the Pontificio Istituto di Studi Arabi e d'Islamistica, Roma.

Kolvenbach, Peter-Hans, Edmond Farahian, Christiaan van Nispen and Ary Roest Crollius (1998), *Understanding and Discussion: Approaches to Muslim-Christian Dialogue*, Rome: Pontificia Università Gregoriana.

Troll, Christian W. (2007), *Muslims Ask, Christians Answer*, Anand, India: Gujarat Sahitya Prakash. See also http://www.answers-to-muslims.com

Troll, Christian W. (2009), *Dialogue and Difference: Clarity in Christian-Muslim Relations*, Maryknoll, NY: Orbis.

Wansbrough, Henry (1985), *The New Jerusalem Bible*, London: Darton, Longman & Todd and Doubleday & Company, Inc.

CHAPTER 4

CATHOLICISM AND HINDUISM

Martin Ganeri OP

Section 1: What is Hinduism?

There are estimated to be between 850,000 million and 1 billion Hindus living in the world today, or around 15 per cent of the world's total population. The vast majority of Hindus live in India and the other countries of South Asia, especially Nepal, where, as in India, they form the vast majority, but Hindus are also to be found all around the world as sizeable minorities. Hindus thereby form the third largest religious grouping in the world after Christianity and Islam (www.adherents.com).

Both the terms, 'Hindu' and 'Hinduism' can be misleading. The term, 'Hindu', has long been used to refer very generally to those inhabitants of India (*al-Hind* in Arabic), who were not easily identifiable as Muslims or members of another religious tradition. The term 'Hinduism' itself was coined in the nineteenth century by Europeans to refer to the religious culture of the Hindus. Because any '-ism' suggests a single system with a definable set of beliefs and practises, it has often been assumed that there is a single religion that all Hindus ascribe to or at least that there is some system within Hinduism that might be taken to represent the 'essence' of Hinduism and might serve as a parallel for the kind of religion represented by Christianity or Islam. In reality, there is no single system of this sort to be found in Hinduism. There is no single founder, or commonly accepted sacred book or creed. As the German Indologist, Heinrich von Stietenchron has put it, Hinduism is best understood to denote a 'civilisation that contains a plurality of distinct religions' ('Hinduism: On the Proper Use of a Deceptive Term', in G-D. Sontheimer and H. Kulke (eds), *Hinduism Reconsidered*, Delhi, Manohar, 2001, 33). 'Hinduism' thus simply refers to everything that is present in Hindu culture, including its religions.

In fact, Hinduism includes a vast array of divergent religious traditions and ways of living. As we shall see, what some Hindus believe is in marked opposition to what others believe, and what counts as good practice by some Hindus is rejected by others. This does not mean, as has again often been supposed, that Hindus are relativistic when it comes to claims about truth or ethics, but it does means that there is *no single system* of beliefs or practices in Hinduism. Thus, the best approach to Hinduism, either in order to describe what is found in it or to consider a Catholic Christian engagement with it, is one that keeps the focus on the beliefs and practices of particular Hindu traditions or individuals, paying careful attention to the way any tradition or individual modifies, or even rejects, the terms, concepts and ethical norms used by others.

Hinduism as a 'civilisation that contains a plurality of distinct religions' has developed over many millennia. The varied traditional types of Hinduism continue and flourish in the modern world, adapting themselves to such new developments as the modern mass media. But there have also arisen forms of Hinduism that have been radically shaped through the encounter with the ideas and realities of Western modernity and of Christianity. Thus, from the late eighteenth century there developed what is known as the 'Hindu Renaissance' or 'Reformed Hinduism', promoted by such figures as Swami ('Lord', a term of respect used for a Hindu monk) Vivekananda (1963–1902) and Mahatma ('Great Soul', an honorific title) Gandhi (1869–1948), who rejected many of features of traditional Hinduism and who revisioned Hinduism as an ethical spirituality and world religion tolerant of other religions and open to all. Likewise, the twentieth century has also seen the emergence of what is known as 'Political Hinduism' or 'Hindu Nationalism', in which Hinduism is depicted as the national and ethnic identity of Hindus exclusive of Muslims and Christians in India, and whose groups have campaigned for India to become a Hindu state or at least for Hindu culture to be publicly privileged. These distinctly modern forms of Hinduism have also had an immense, if very different, impact on India in the modern period and on Hindu-Christian relations in India and abroad.

In what follows no attempt is made to describe or engage with Hinduism as a whole. Most emphatically, no claim is being made to define Hinduism or set out the 'essence' of Hinduism. Instead, three important concepts and associated features of Hinduism are picked out, which are very significant for a very large number of Hindus and which continue to be very important for Christian approaches to Hindus and Hinduism: *dharma* (proper nature or order) and Hindu approaches to right social living and social religion; *mokṣa* (spiritual liberation or release) and the pursuit of world transcendence, together with the traditions of philosophy and theology that have developed around this; and *bhakti* (attachment or devotion) and the Hindu traditions of devotional theism that have emerged centred on different Hindu gods and goddesses. For most Hindus *dharma*, *mokṣa* and *bhakti* are interrelated aspects of what they believe and do as Hindus, rather than wholly separate alternative ways of being a Hindu.

Unless indicated otherwise, these and other Hindu terms are given in the form used in Sanskrit, the Indo-European language that has from ancient times served as the medium for much of Hindu religious and cultural expression. In order to indicate the particular sounds of Sanskrit and other Indian languages a standard system of diacritics is used throughout (for an explanation of which see, for instance, Gavin Flood, *An Introduction to Hinduism*, Cambridge, Cambridge University Press, 1996, xiii–iv).

Dharma: *Right Social Living and Religion*

The concept of *dharma* has many meanings. It comes from a verbal root, *dhṛ*, which means 'to uphold' or 'to support'. It may perhaps be characterized in general as referring to the proper nature or order things have, either which they actually do have or which they should have. *Dharma* both describes and prescribes the proper order that upholds the natural world and human society. In part, it means the natural properties that things have in virtue of what they are. It is, for example, the *dharma* of fire to heat other things up. *Dharma* also refers to the right way that human society should be, and the right social norms, ethical practices and ritual activities that human beings should follow. It also refers to the right way of the world as a whole, the natural laws and order that should be manifest in the world. Living according to *dharma* is of immense importance for Hindus as being the way to have success in the current life and a good state after death, and serves to preserve the well-being of the world as a whole. In the modern period Hindus have started to use the term *dharma* as a word to correspond to the English term 'religion'. Many Hindus today prefer the term *Sanātana Dharma* (Eternal *dharma*) as a Hindu term for 'Hinduism'. For some Hindus *dharma* is fixed and unalterable, while for others it has a more dynamic quality, open to revision and reapplication as times and situations change.

Dharma is about right living and the primary context for Hindus where this takes place is the family. It is as a member of a family that a Hindu learns his or her own identity within the set of relationships he or she has within the family and the wider community of which the family is a part. It is as a member of a family that he or she develops an understanding of how to act well and what to believe. The family or household is, then, the fundamental reality for most Hindus, the primary context in which the joys and the sorrows of life are experienced.

Most of what follows in this section relates closely to the form of Hinduism otherwise known as 'Vedic' or 'Brahmanical Hinduism', which developed in the second millenium BC and gradually became a dominant strand within Hinduism as a whole. It refers to the Hindu traditions developed and promoted by the Brahmins and other high caste Hindus. Such Hindus accept the authority of a body of sacred literature called the Vedas, composed in Sanskrit, revered as revelation and held to be the principal source of *dharma*. Brahmanical Hinduism refers more widely to the whole religious and non-religious culture described and promoted in the vast and diverse body of Sanskrit literature that has developed over the centuries, including the *Dharma Sūtras* (the extant ones mostly dating from about the sixth to the third century BC) and *Dharma Śāstras* (from about the end of the third century BC onwards), texts that set out ritual and social *dharma* in great detail.

Hinduism, however, also contains many non-Vedic and non-Brahmanical traditions. In the long history and complex reality of Hinduism many alternatives to the *dharma* found in Brahmanical Hinduism have arisen. Alongside the Vedic tradition there is, for instance, that of Tantra, which is of great importance within Hinduism as a whole. Tantra (meaning 'loom'), refers to a range of texts and traditions that have origins outside of Vedic Hinduism, but now permeates Hindu thinking and practice as a whole, having come to prominence around the eighth century AD. There are also the traditions of world renunciation, emerging from the middle of the first millennium BC as well as the many popular and regional movements arising down the centuries, often explicitly rejecting Brahmanical teaching and values. Many of these other traditions remain as alternatives to Brahmanical Hinduism, or in marked tension with it, while there has also been a continuous process of assimilation of non-Vedic traditions into Brahmanical Hinduism itself.

Caste

For centuries, Hindu society has been divided up into different high and low castes. The word 'caste' is derived from a Portuguese term (*casta*) meaning 'breed' or 'race'. In reality it refers to two schemes by which Hindus have structured and classified society: the scheme of *varṇa* (colour or class) and the scheme of *jāti* (birth or kind).

Varṇa

Within Brahmanical Hinduism, the *varṇa* scheme depicts Hindu society as made up of four broad classes of people having different natural characteristics and functions in society: the Brahmins, who study the Vedas and perform Vedic rituals of different sorts; the Kṣatriyas, who are the warriors and kings; the Vaiśyas, who are the merchants and agriculturalists; and the Śūdras, who are the servants. Outside of this scheme are those on the edges of settled Vedic Hindu society, historically the tribal people and forest-dwellers, who are said to be *avarṇa* or classless. The *varṇa* scheme is a ritual and social hierarchy with the Brahmins at the top and the Śūdras at the bottom. The top three *varṇas* are also said to be 'twice-born' (*dvija*), meaning that they are reborn through certain life-rituals. The top three *varṇas* and they alone are entitled to know the Vedas and to have Vedic rituals performed for them. Within this scheme, Śūdras and others are excluded from Vedic religion and so tend to have other forms of religion and ritual and to have non-Brahmin ritualists serving their needs. Within traditional Vedic Hinduism, then, there has never been the expectation that there should, or could be, one religion for all people, be it in India or elsewhere.

The *varṇa* system is held to be part of the natural order of the world, part of the original structure of the world from its creation. One very important hymn of the Veda (Ṛg Veda X.90) describes the production of the world in terms of the sacrifice of the Cosmic Man and depicts the *varṇas* as made from different parts of his dismembered body: the Brahmins from the head, the Kṣatriyas from the arms, the Vaiśyas from the thighs and the Śūdras from the feet.

Jāti

The other scheme of *jāti* corresponds more closely to the original Portuguese meaning of caste. Although the origins of *jāti* are not easy to identify, this way of viewing human society has been of great importance for very many Hindus. *Jāti* means 'birth' or 'kind' and refers to the thousands of different kinship groups that exist across India. A person is born into a particular *jāti* and is thought of as being a particular kind of person as a member of it, different from members of other *jātis*. The *jāti* scheme is also a hierarchy, based on the idea of purity, with some *jātis* being more or less pure than others. Members of *jātis* avoid the defilement that comes through contact with less pure ones. Thus, while *jātis* are often distinguished by occupation, the principal markers of difference centre on restrictions on intermarriage and eating together. At the bottom of the *jāti* scheme are those who are known as 'untouchable', whose occupations such as leather working or removal of human waste products render them so unclean that the other *jātis* avoid any form of contact with them. Traditionally, untouchables have tended to live in separate areas.

These two schemes of *varṇa* and *jāti* have tended to merge in the historical reality of Hindu society. However they remain different schemes, this distinction has been important for modern Hindu reformist movements.

Social and ritual life

Upholding the *dharma* of society is an integral part of upholding the right order of the world as a whole and the *dharma* of society is upheld when the members of each *varṇa* or *jāti* do the work appropriate to them. Certain types of behaviour are considered generally right for all people to do (*sādhāraṇa dharma*, 'common *dharma*'), such as truthfulness, non-violence, abstinence from theft and giving. However, great emphasis is put on the actions that are right for an individual within the particular stage of life and group to which he or she belongs, his or her *svadharma*, or own-*dharma*. The Hindu idea of *dharma* is thus said to be 'context-specific'. Thus, the *dharma* of a Brahmin is to study the Vedas and perform ritual duties, the *dharma* of a Kṣatriya is to fight and to rule, and so on. One widely revered sacred text, the *Bhagavad Gītā*, affirms the idea of *svadharma* in these much repeated words, 'Better the doing of one's own duty (*svadharma*), badly done, than that of another, done well. Better death in one's own duty, the duty of another causes fear' (BG 3.35).

Within Brahmanical Hinduism this idea of *svadharma* has also been expressed within the scheme of *varṇāśramadharma* (the *dharma* of class and stage of life). We have already considered what is meant by *varṇa*. There are also said to be four *āśramas*: that of the celibate student in Vedic study (*brahmacarya*), that of the married householder (*gṛhasta*), that of the forest dweller (*vānaprastha*), and that of the renouncer (*saṃnyāsa*). The last two stages represent increasing degrees of withdrawal from ordinary social and ritual life. This is an idealized scheme of the life of a high caste Hindu and most Hindus ordinarily only move from being a child and student to being a married householder, while the option of world renunciation is open for anyone at any time of life. At the heart of this vision of Hindu society is the figure of the married householder, who maintains the *dharma* of the world and human society, through the performance of proper rituals, the production of offspring and the carrying out of the occupations proper to the different sections of society.

This Brahmanical Hindu understanding of right human living is manifest in another important scheme: that of the four legitimate goals to be pursued by human beings (*puruṣārtha*). These are honestly gained wealth (*artha*), pleasure within the bounds of social norms (*kāma*), ritual and social obligations (*dharma*) and liberation from the world (*mokṣa*). The final goal of liberation links to the fourth stage of life and liberation from the world cycle is indeed held by very many Hindus to be the ultimate goal to be aspired for. However, the other three goals are also thought to be legitimate and worthwhile and this scheme of the four goals should serve to dispel a popular misconception that Hindus are solely concerned with liberation from the world. Most Hindus have valued the enjoyment of mundane goods and a successful life and concentrated their energies on their pursuit, just as they have valued the family life of the householder as the normative mode of human living.

Vedic and non-Vedic Hindu ritual

Ritual plays a major role in the lives of almost all Hindus. Common rituals often serve as a unifying force for Hindus, who otherwise hold very different beliefs and ethical values, the function and meaning of any ritual being open to a number of different interpretations. Such ritual draws upon a number of authoritative sources in addition to the Vedic, especially those of Tantra. Indeed, central to Tantric Hinduism is an emphasis on rituals in the worship of deities, as a means to get powers and goods in the present life as well as final release from mundane existence.

For its part, Vedic ritual comprises a complex and comprehensive scheme for the public and domestic lives of the three upper castes. Vedic ritual is sacrifice (*yajña*) in the wider sense of 'that which is made sacred', a central part of which is making oblations (*homa*) of different sorts into a sacred fire. Such ritual serves to uphold the *dharma* of human society and of the world as a whole. A member of the higher castes, especially a Brahman, should also ideally carry out rituals throughout the day, although many contemporary Hindus often perform only some of these or replace them with other non-Vedic ritual or devotional practices.

An important type of ritual is *saṃskāra*. These are rituals performed at different stages of a high caste Hindu's life, from conception to death, and which enable a Hindu to progress from one stage to another and to the duties and entitlements that go with them. These include *upanayana*, when a male member of the three higher classes (*varṇa*) receives the sacred thread and becomes ritually one of the 'twice-born', moving from childhood to being a student. Central to Hindu life is marriage (*vivāha*), whereby a Hindu becomes a householder, having the right and obligation to have rituals performed and to pursue the three goals of ordinary life, *dharma*, wealth and pleasure. The final *saṃskāra* is *antyeṣṭi* (the final sacrifice), the death rites. For most Hindus this means cremation and a set of rituals known as *śrāddha*, performed for ten days after the death, whereby the spirit of the dead person is enabled to move to the realm of the ancestors and the living are cleansed from the pollution that death brings.

One important type of ritual is that of *mantra*. Hindu ritual is suffused by the use of *mantra*s drawn from Vedic, Tantric and other traditions. The importance and ubiquity of use of *mantra*s in Hinduism testifies to the centrality of the spoken word in Hinduism as a creative and powerful force. A *mantra* is a verbal utterance, which may be a short phrase from a sacred text, or an invocation of a deity, or one or a set of syllables that may or may not have any recognizable meaning. *Mantra*s are held to have great effectiveness when used properly by those entitled to do so. They are 'verbal instruments' containing the power of the transcendent reality that they express or address. In Vedic sacrificial ritual *mantra*s drawn from the Vedic texts are essential components of what makes the ritual effective. Among Vedic *mantra*s is the *gāyatrī mantra*, addressed to Savitar, the Sun, which while strictly something only a 'twice-born' male is supposed to recite each day, is now also far more widely used as a form of ritual activity, often in a recorded form. An even more important *mantra* is the sacred syllable, Oṃ, which is held to express the ultimate reality, the fundamental structure of the world and the essence of the Veda. Other non-Vedic *mantra*s may invoke and serve as a way to experience the reality and grace of particular deities, such as Oṃ namo Nārāyaṇāya or Oṃ namaḥ Śivāya addressed to the male deities, Viṣṇu and Śiva. A Tantric *mantra* held to express the reality and power of the Goddess, Tripurasundarī, *ha sa ka la hrīṃ, ha sa ka ha la hrīṃ, sa ka la hrīṃ*, exemplifies the use of *mantra*s made up of syllables without any ordinary meaning.

Festivals (*utsava*), pilgrimages (*yātrā*) and religious fairs (*melā*) are also important parts of Hindu ritual and have a wide appeal, open to a wide number of Hindus from different sections of society, and invested with a wide variety of meanings by different groups. They are immensely popular, with thousands, often millions taking part. Festivals, such as Dīvalī, the festival of lights, celebrated throughout the Hindu world, punctuate the year, while pilgrimage sites, such as Vārāṇasī (Benares), are held to be 'fords' (*tīrtha*), crossing places where the transcendent realm is open to the mundane. The *Pūrṇa Kumbha Melā*, held at Prayaga (modern Allahabad), every 12 years, has in modern times been attended by crowds of up to 20 million.

Hindu ritual in general is informed by a number of important distinctions. One is between what is auspicious (*śubha, mangala*) and what is inauspicious, the idea being that certain times and certain things are auspicious and others not. Hindus will routinely aim to discern the auspicious time to hold a ritual such as marriage or undertake some activity, such as a business venture. Likewise, there is the distinction between purity (*śauca, śuddhi*) and impurity. Activities such as bathing or some types of food or substances, such as the products of the cow, promote purity, while other types of food or substances or people bring impurity. The idea of purity becomes a way of characterizing life as a whole, covering attitudes of mind and morals as well as ritual activities. A further important distinction is between merit (*puṇya*) and sin (*pāpa*). Merit is that which conduces to a good state of life or to a good state after life, for oneself or others, and can be gained from acting according to *dharma*, as well as by particular activities that are meritorious in character, such as properly performed ritual, or devotion to a deity, or giving, while sin accrues through acting against *dharma*. Sin can be of greater or lesser degree, but most sins can be expiated through the performance of penances, often determined by the community to which the individual belongs. Such penances include washing, fasting, pilgrimage or taking purifying substances from the cow.

Dharma and Sādhanā
The emphasis on *dharma* or right behaviour (orthopraxy) has also gone along with considerable tolerance of diverse beliefs (orthodoxy). Hindu individual and groups certainly regard some beliefs as more true than others and have engaged in vigorous intellectual debate with each other over this. Hinduism is not relativistic as such. However, since the upholding of *dharma* is primarily about right behaviour, there has been less emphasis that all publicly conform to one set of beliefs. Hindu society has thus accommodated many different world-views (*darśana*), theistic traditions and paths of spiritual practice (*sādhanā*) and allowed a considerable freedom of choice in what to believe and follow, even for those who belong to the same caste, community or family.

Social conflict and reform

The historical reality of the caste system has very often been experienced as exclusive and oppressive by those who are not 'twice-born' within the *varṇa* scheme, or those who are less pure within the *jāti* scheme, above all by those who are 'untouchable'. Lower castes have often been regarded as naturally inferior, enjoyed the least power, tended to have the worst occupations and the least wealth. Insofar as the caste system means the affirmation of a social and ritual hierarchy fixed by birth and justifies oppressive attitudes and conditions, it has received a number of challenges over the centuries within Hinduism. Within traditional Brahmanical Hinduism itself there has long been a counter suggestion that the behaviour rather than the birth of an individual determines where in the caste system that individual should be classified. Moreover, in the course of Hindu history there have been ways in which the lower castes have tried to improve their status, either through simply claiming a higher caste status, or changing to a more pure lifestyle in order to get a higher status, or through adopting forms of religion that offer escape from the caste system. Thus, many theistic and devotional (*bhakti*) movements have developed in Hinduism that reject the caste hierarchy and exclusiveness, insisting that all people have equal and direct access to the divine. Moreover, mass conversion to other religions such as Islam, Christianity or Buddhism has always been a favoured option for lower castes in India.

In the modern period the inequalities manifested in the practice of the caste system was an important factor of the reforms promoted by the leaders of the Hindu Renaissance or Reform. Hindu reformers often called for a retrieval of an idealized form of the *varṇa* scheme, as a system that simply distinguishes occupations within a harmonious society, based on individual talents and merits rather than birth. Moreover, they campaigned for the social emancipation of the poor, seeing it as an integral part of human duty and of the spiritual life. Central to Swami Vivekananda's teaching is the idea of the common divinity of all people, meaning that all have one and the same divine spirit within them. He thus argued that service to the poor is both service to God and service to oneself. Mahatma Gandhi insisted that all people have an equal dignity and campaigned relentlessly against untouchability, renaming them Harijans (children of God) and insisting that they be accepted as equal members of the Āśrama communities he set up. At the heart of Gandhi's vision of religion is that it is a spiritual quest for God as Truth, realized through promoting a common ethic of non-violence (*ahiṃsā*) and service of all (*sarvodaya*).

The call and work for such reform has now become part of the modern political life of India. The Indian constitution that came into effect after Indian Independence in 1947 also made untouchability illegal and made provision for positive discrimination for disadvantaged castes, who may form as much as 50 per cent of the present Hindu population. Moreover, in the twentieth-century lower caste groups, especially the 'untouchables' have often renamed themselves as Dalits (derived from Sanskrit, meaning the 'broken' or 'oppressed') and actively asserted their voice and rights in the modern Indian state, even rejecting all association with the Hinduism of the upper castes, and insisting that they have a distinct culture and religion of their own.

Mokṣa: *World Renunciation and the Pursuit of Liberation*

An abiding image of Hinduism for many people is the figure of the holy man (*saṃnyāsin* or *sādhu*), who has renounced the world (i.e. the ritual and social world of *dharma* we have just considered), and who wanders as a mendicant, practising feats of great asceticism and meditation. The ultimate goal of these efforts is *mokṣa* (liberation from the world). Here we encounter an understanding of reality and of human life that permeates wider Hindu life and thought: the idea that a human being is composed of a spiritual core (*ātman*, the self or soul), which is immortal and an integral substance, but which comes to have a material body; that all embodied human beings are enmeshed in a cycle of countless rebirths (*saṃsāra*) generated by earlier good or bad actions (*karma*); and the idea that the life we experience in the world is fundamentally unsatisfactory and the source of suffering (*duḥkha*), but that it is possible to be liberated from the cycle of rebirth and come to experience a transcendent and blissful type of existence (*mokṣa*).

Over the course of the centuries many very different views have developed in Hinduism about what the precise nature of reality is, what the transcendent state of liberation is like, what relationship there is between ultimate reality and the finite things that make up the world, especially the finite self (*ātman*), and what the way to get to liberation is. There is a dualist view, which divides reality into material and spiritual causal principles. There is a monist view that views reality as ultimately just spirit. There is the realistic theist view that posits a divine Lord (*Īśvara*), who produces, sustains and destroys the world of spiritual and material entities. Over the centuries these views have been developed into highly sophisticated and intellectually rigorous traditions of theology and philosophy (*darśana*), engaged in active debate with each other, and producing textual accounts quite similar to Western Scholastic theology.

Vedānta

One of the most influential such tradition is that of Vedānta. Vedānta means the 'end of the Veda', referring both the final section of the Vedic revelation, the sacred texts known otherwise as the *Upaniṣads*, and the traditions of theology that are based on them, the Vedāntic schools. Following the *Upaniṣads*, the Vedāntic traditions commonly call ultimate reality, *Brahman*, but they differ on whether they take a monist or a theistic view of how *Brahman* relates to the world, that is to say, whether they conceive of *Brahman* as the sole impersonal spiritual reality with which the finite self is identical, or whether they conceive of *Brahman* as a personal divine Lord with whom the finite self is in communion. The *Upaniṣads* teach that there is a close relationship between *Brahman* and the finite self, saying for instance, 'this self is *Brahman*' (*ayam ātmā brahma*), or 'you are that' (*tattvamasi*), 'I am *Brahman*' (*aham brahmāsmi*). The Vedānta schools differ on how precisely to interpret these and other texts. The monist tradition is known as Advaita (Non-dualism) and its most important teacher is Śaṃkara (788–820 AD). The theist traditions are many, but among them two of the most important are Viśiṣṭādvaita (Non-dualism of the Differentiated), whose great teacher is Rāmānuja (1017–1137 AD) and Dvaita (Dualism), whose great teacher is Madhva (*c*. 1238–1317 AD). For monists, liberation from the world consists in the blissful realization of identity with *Brahman*, whereas for theists it is the realization of a communion of knowledge and love with God.

The later tradition of Advaita Vedānta that developed after Śaṃkara and which has become accepted as the standard form of Advaita asserts that *Brahman* is ultimately the only reality that there is, being spiritual and pure blissful consciousness, and that the conscious core or self within each of us is identical with Brahman. The world as we experience it in all its diversity, including the experience that each of us has a finite self distinct from others and from *Brahman*, seems real enough to us as we live ordinary lives. It is thus said to be practically real (*vyāvahārika-sat*), in contrast to Brahman, which is ultimately real (*pāramārthika-sat*). But this is actually the product of ignorance (*avidyā*). It is said to be indescribable either as existent or non-existent. As long as we remain in ignorance we go about our business, doing good and bad deeds, gaining their fruits, meritorious or sinful as the case may be, and so end up undergoing rebirths again and again. We also experience the shortcomings of such life; the fact that all good things come to an end and that often life is full of trials and suffering. It is only when we are liberated from this worldly existence that we see clearly that it is a product of ignorance and illusory. Liberation comes through renouncing the ordinary life of *dharma*, through ascetical practice and above all through meditation on the teaching of the *Upaniṣads*, guided by a guru, a teacher who is already liberated. The central teaching of Advaita has often been summed up as '*Brahman* is real, the world is false, the self is *Brahman* not other.'

In Viśiṣṭādvaita Vedānta, on the other hand, Brahman is identified with the personal divine Lord of theism. The permanent reality and distinction of God, spiritual finite selves and material things are affirmed. At the same time, the relation between them is described as *advaita* (non-dualism), because the finite selves and material things are contingent on the Lord for their existence at all times. In the teaching of the great teacher of this tradition, Rāmānuja, the central conception of this relationship is that the entities of the world form the body of *Brahman*. Liberation consists in the blissful realization of this relationship and of the direct knowledge or vision of *Brahman*. In this state the self regains its proper nature as a non-material being, characterized by consciousness and bliss, enjoying an integral existence free from any material body. This comes about through *bhakti* (devotion), which Rāmānuja depicts in Vedāntic terms as a form of devotional mediation on the Vedāntic texts, a steady calling to mind of God that leads into vision of God. This process and the attainment of the final goal are, however, dependent on the God's own choice for the devotee and the gift of his grace (*anugraha*).

Yoga

The term 'yoga' comes from a verbal root (*yuj*) meaning 'to yoke together' or 'to unite'. Yoga refers to a wide range of ethical, physical and meditational disciplines, which serve to control human behaviour, the body and the consciousness. Yoga is used as a general term in many different traditions for such disciplines, but also more specifically for the Yoga traditions, where there is systematic exposition of yoga as a discipline and path to liberation from the confines of material embodiment.

One of the most important systematic traditions of yoga is the *Rāja Yoga* found in Patañjali's *Yogasūtra* (around third century AD). Here yoga is said to be an 'eight-limbed' (*aṣṭāṅga*) process, whose aim is 'the suppression of the fluctuations of the consciousness (*citta*)' (*Yogasūtra* 2). Yoga accepts a dualist view of reality, in which there are two separate principles: a plurality of non-material conscious selves (*puruṣa*) and matter itself in its different forms (*prakṛti*). The self mistakenly thinks that it has a connection with matter and thus becomes bound up with bodily rebirths and experiences the suffering that this entails. The consciousness fluctuates because it has lost control of itself, influenced by the sense impressions and memories generated in the embodied state. One much favoured simile for yoga is that of a horse-drawn chariot. The fluctuating consciousness is like a man in a chariot when the horses are out of control, whereas yoga is like learning to control the horses. Yoga enables the consciousness to be controlled and to become 'one-pointed' (*ekāgra*), restraining human behaviour and the body.

The 'eight limbs' of *Rāja Yoga* are restraint, observance, posture, breath-control, sense-withdrawal, concentration, meditation and absorbed concentration. By 'restraint' is meant general ethical practices of refraining from injuring other beings, lying, stealing, unchaste behaviour and greed. By 'observance' is meant the promotion of purity, contentment, austerity, study of sacred texts and devotion to the Lord. The stages of ethical, physical and mental control lead onto each other and allow the practitioner to control his or her consciousness. In the final stage of absorbed concentration (*samādhi*), the practitioner becomes no longer conscious of his or her body and environment. This leads eventually to final liberation (*mokṣa*), which in yoga is thought of as a state of 'isolation' (*kaivalya*). Liberation is, thus, a freedom from any involvement with matter, the self becoming isolated in blissful absorption in its own consciousness.

Bhakti: *Hindu Theism and Devotional Religion*

Within Hinduism as a whole there are a vast number and huge variety of theistic cults and gods and goddesses. Theistic religion is the primary religious expression of the majority of Hindus. These theist religious traditions (*sampradāya*) have also developed sophisticated systems of theology and demanding paths of ethical and spiritual practice, centred on the particular deity worshipped in them, with their own understanding of what constitutes *dharma* and *mokṣa*.

Theistic traditions

While the many different local and regional cults and traditions have diverse historical origins, they are often depicted as all being forms of three great pan-Indian theistic traditions: Vaiṣṇavism centred on the god Viṣṇu; Śaivism centred on the god Śiva; and Śākta religion centred on the goddess often simply known as Śakti. Vaiṣṇavism includes a variety of cults and traditions either centred on a form of Viṣṇu or on his *avatāras* (descents). Images of Viṣṇu may be either anthropomorphic or theriomorphic, depending on which form of his manifestation or descent they represent. Śaiva cults and traditions likewise show a considerable variety of forms, some highly devotional in character, others centred on initiation and ritual practice, some of which are on the edges of or reject the norms of society. Śiva is depicted in a variety of forms, both benign and terrifying, represented as a great ascetic and world renouncer, or as a great lover and perfect householder. His images are either anthropomorphic or in the aniconic form of the *linga*. Śakti or the goddess is worshipped either as a local deity, the consort of a male deity or as the 'Great Goddess', the one who produces, sustains and destroys the world. She too has benign and terrifying forms, and is the focus either of devotional worship or ritual practice. Often she is a force to be placated and animal sacrifice is a common feature within the Śākta traditions. Yet she is also the divine mother, whose ferocity liberates her devotees from the forces of ignorance and bondage.

The different theistic traditions in various ways draw on the many sources of Hinduism, such as the Vedic, Tantric, Purāṇic (of the sacred literature known as Purāṇas and hence the religion expressed by them) and more local traditions. The South Indian Śrī Vaiṣṇava tradition, for example, is centred on Viṣṇu in the form of Nārāyaṇa together with his consort or Śakti, Śrī. This tradition bases its theology and practice on the theistic Vedānta of Rāmānuja, the Viṣṇu Purāṇa, the Tantric Pāñcarātra texts, as well as the devotional hymns of the Tamil saints, the Ālvārs. Within this tradition Viṣṇu is depicted as having five forms or modes of manifestation: his supreme form; his creative manifestations; his descents in human or animal form (the *avatāras*); his descents into consecrated images (*arcāvatāra*) and as the inner controller immanent in all things. Śrī Vaiṣṇava practice affirms variously the Vedāntic path of meditation on Upaniṣadic texts, yogic discipline similar to that found in the *Yoga Sūtras*, the performance of the ritual and social *dharma* we have considered, and the devotional worship of the deity, focused especially on the images found in the South Indian temples of the tradition. Another South Indian tradition, Śaiva Siddhānta, is centred on Śiva, as the one who, along with his Śakti, has the fivefold action of producing, maintaining and destroying the world, and of concealing and revealing himself. Within this tradition reality is divided into a characteristically Śaiva scheme reflecting the depiction of Śiva as 'Lord of beasts' (*Paśupati*). Accordingly, there is said to be: *pati* (the Lord, Śiva); *paśu* (the 'beast', the finite conscious self); and *pāśa* (the 'bond', the material substrate, which binds the selves through impurity, karma and the obscuring power of the Lord). Through ritual action and the grace of Śiva, the *paśu* becomes freed of pāsa and comes to be like Śiva. Śaiva Siddhānta has its own Tantric Āgama texts as well as the devotional hymns of the Tamil Śaiva poet-mystics, the Nāyaṉmārs.

Forms of worship

Images or symbols of these deities are housed in temples, found in domestic or wayside shrines. The actions of the deities are recounted in the vast traditions of Hindu mythology as recorded in sacred literature, portrayed on temples, or enacted in dramatic performances. The gods are worshipped in their shrines with offerings, lamps and chants (*pūja*). They are celebrated in the many festivals that punctuate the year. In the modern period, traditional forms of Hinduism have found fresh expression through the media, so that there have been television serializations, such as of the epic Rāmāyaṇa centred on the Vaiṣṇava deity, Rāma. Broadcast in 1987–1988 every Sunday morning it captivated the Indian nation, with many millions watching every week.

Hindu theistic religion is also called *bhakti* religion. *Bhakti* means 'attachment' or 'devotion' and this encompasses all the different ways in which the deities are worshipped and human beings are attached to them, be it in the performance of rituals, recitation of sacred texts, singing of devotional hymns or meditating on the deity. Theist traditions often distinguish between lower and higher forms of *bhakti*. Lower *bhakti* is shown to deities for protection and success in this life. A higher *bhakti* is when men and women cultivate intense devotional relationships of love and service for the deities, patterned on human relationships, such as that of parent and child, servant and master, or two lovers. Such devotion is focused on the deity as himself or herself the supreme object to be obtained, rather than the lesser motivation of protection or mundane goods. This is a source of delight in this life, as well as the means to get release from rebirth and realize blissful communion with the deity. Such release (*mokṣa*) is experienced as the fullest manifestation and eternal enjoyment of the relationship cultivated in this life. A central emphasis in different Hindu theistic traditions is the human need for divine grace (*anugraha*) and God's willingness to give it to those who wish it either for success in this life or liberation from the world.

Conception of deity

Are Hindus polytheists or monotheists? We have noted that Hinduism embraces all the different religions present in Hindu culture. Thus, Hindus cannot just be labelled as polytheist simply because of there being many theistic traditions. It is true that many Hindus treat the deities as distinct and localized forms of divine presence. However, within the sacred texts and practice of the developed theistic traditions there is the assertion that there is only one God and they relate the vast number of gods and goddess to that God in some way, as manifestations of it or as inferior beings. We have already seen that in Vedānta the concept of *Brahman* is that there is one ultimate reality, which is the source, or the reality, of everything else.

Within the sacred literature of Hindu theism there is also found the concept of *Bhagavān* (the Lord) or *Bhagavatī* (the female form), which asserts that is one God or goddess who is the creator, sustainer and destroyer of all the world, who is concerned for the welfare of human beings and who reaches out to them out of love for them. The members of the different theistic traditions, be they Vaiṣṇava, Śaiva, or Śākta, simply identify the deity they worship as *Bhagavān/Bhagavatī* with all that that entails in terms of attitudes towards other religious traditions. In theistic forms of Vedānta, moreover, the two concepts of *Brahman* and *Bhagavān* are naturally identified. Thus, it is fairer to say that Hinduism as a whole contains many different monotheist religions within it, as well as some polytheistic elements. As we have seen in the examples of Śrī Vaiṣṇavism and Śaiva Siddhānta, the male deity is conceived along with his Śakti, who is regarded as an eternal and integral aspect of that deity's reality and activity. Since the unicity of the divine is also affirmed in such traditions such a conception of deity should not be regarded as polytheistic, since neither male nor female aspect has a separate existence. Rather the Hindu concept of deity here is perhaps better characterized as 'binitarian' in nature.

Most Hindu theistic traditions make much of the worship of images. Emphasis is placed on the proper ritual consecration of an image, especially the rite of *prāṇa pratiṣṭhā*, whereby the power and presence of the deity is installed into and enlivens the image. The consecrated image is thus regarded as the deity present in the image and treated as the deity. In the Pāñcarātra system, as we have noted, the consecrated image is said to be the 'image-descent' of God. For members of the South Indian Śrī Vaiṣṇava tradition the consecrated image is considered to be the most important way in which God makes himself easily accessible to human beings everywhere in the vulnerability of the materials used and is therefore the focus of intense devotion and reverence. As the Śrī Vaiṣṇava scholar, S. M. Srinivasa Chari, puts it, 'The *arcāvatāras* (image-descents) are similar to the water present in the pools of the river bed and available at all times for a thirsty person' (*Vaiṣṇavism*, Delhi, Motilal Banarsidass, 1994, 225).

Section 2: A Catholic Approach to Hinduism

Official Church Teaching

The Second Vatican Council gives a basis on which any Catholic approach to Hinduism should be formed. *NA* (the Declaration of the Relation of the Church to Non-Christian Religions), says of Hinduism:

> Thus in Hinduism men explore the divine mystery and express it in the limitless riches of myth and the accurately defined insights of philosophy. They seek release from the trials of this present life by ascetical practices, profound meditation and recourse to God in confidence and love. (*NA* 2)

This statement clearly points to some of the important aspects of Hinduism we considered in Section 1, in particular to the pursuit of *mokṣa* ('release from the trials of this present life') and to the intellectual traditions that have developed around this, such as Vedānta and Yoga ('the accurately defined insights of philosophy') and to *bhakti* devotional theism ('recourse to God in confidence and love') and the rich and diverse narrative traditions with which Hindus celebrate and explore this ('the limitless riches of myth').

This short passage should be read in the wider context of what the rest of *NA* and other Conciliar documents teach about the Church's relationship with other religions. *NA* affirms the unity of humanity, which is rooted in the fact that all human beings have a common origin and destiny in God. Human beings look to their different religions for answers to the fundamental questions facing human life:

> What is man? What is the meaning and purpose of life? What is upright behaviour, and what is sinful? Where does suffering originate and what end does it serve? How can genuine happiness be found? What happens at death? What is judgement? What reward follows death? And finally, what is the ultimate mystery, beyond human explanation, which embraces our entire existence, from which we take our origin and toward which we tend? (*NA* 1)

Thus, the features of Hinduism pointed out represent the answers Hinduism gives to these universal human questions. They also point to possible common ground between Hinduism and Christianity. *NA* goes on to establish the principles that govern the Church's attitude and relation to other religions in general. The Church:

> rejects nothing that is true and holy in these religions. She has a high regard for the manner of life and conduct, the precepts and doctrines which, although differing in many ways from her own teaching, nevertheless often reflect a ray of that truth which enlightens all men. Yet she proclaims and is in duty bound to proclaim without fail, Christ who the 'the way, the truth and the life'. (Jn 1.6) (*NA* 2)

The Church's approach, then, is one of openness to common ground, the 'true and holy', as it may be found in Hinduism, as being a reflection of the truth and holiness, the saving revelation, that she proclaims to be fully present in Jesus Christ and which the Church manifests in her life and teaching.

In *AG* (the Decree on the Church's Missionary Activity), Christians are encouraged to 'be familiar with their national and religious traditions and uncover with gladness and respect those seeds of the Word which lie hidden among them' (*AG* 11). Whatever truth or holiness is to be found in other religions serves as a 'preparation for the Gospel' (*AG* 3). The 'true and holy', wherever it is to be found, is a participation in, and points towards, the truth and holiness of Christ, just as the 'seeds of the Word' are a sharing in the Word that is incarnate as Christ. In like manner, *LG* (the Dogmatic Constitution on the Church) talks of ways in which other religious traditions are 'ordered' or 'related' (*ordinatur*) to the Church (*LG* 16). Again, *GS* (the Pastoral Constitution on the Church in the Modern World) affirms that the 'Holy Spirit offers to all the possibility of being made partners, in a way known to God, in the paschal mystery' (*GS* 22).

In continuity with this, Papal teaching has affirmed that there are areas where Christians encounter common ground in Hinduism. Pope Paul VI characterizes India as:

> the home of a nation that has sought God with relentless desire, in deep meditation and silence, and in hymns of fervent prayer. Rarely has this longing for God been expressed with words so full of the spirit of Advent as in the words written in your sacred books many centuries before Christ, 'from the unreal lead me to the real; from darkness lead me to light; from death lead me to immortality' (*Bṛhadāraṇyaka Upaniṣad* 1.3.28). (To the Representatives of Various Religions of India, Bombay, 3 December 1964, in Francesco Gioia (ed.), *Interreligious Dialogue: The Official Teaching of the Catholic Church (1963–1995)*, Boston, Pauline Books and Media, 1994, 125)

He also points to the 'religious disposition and a deep attachment to family life' that 'characterises India, and in general all the peoples of Asia' (To the People of India, Bombay, 4 December 1964, Gioia, 127).

In *RM*, Pope John Paul II states that relations with members of other religions are governed by 'Respect for man in his quest for answers to the deepest questions of his life, and respect for the action of the Spirit in man' (*RM* 29). This refers both to the natural dignity of all human beings and for what safeguards and promotes this, and to the spiritual calling of man, which finds its fulfilment in God, urged on by the universal presence and activity of the Holy Spirit drawing men and women to God. In keeping with this, the Pope praises the 'spiritual vision of man' found in the religious traditions of India:

India has so much to offer to the world in the task of understanding man and the truth of his existence. What she offers specifically is the noble and spiritual vision of man – man, a pilgrim of the Absolute, travelling toward a goal, seeking the face of God. (To Followers of the Various religions of India, New Delhi, 2 February 1986, Gioia, 314)

In *FR*, Pope John Paul II also promotes a Christian theological engagement with the intellectual traditions of India:

In preaching the Gospel, Christianity first encountered Greek philosophy; but this does not mean at all that other approaches are precluded . . . My thoughts turn immediately to the lands of the East, so rich in religious and philosophical traditions of great antiquity. And among these lands, India has a special place. A great spiritual impulse leads Indian thought to seek an experience which would liberate the spirit from the shackles of time and space and would therefore acquire absolute value. The dynamic of this quest for liberation provides the context for great metaphysical systems. (*FR* 72)

Earlier in the encyclical the Pope points to the continuing importance of the work of the St Thomas Aquinas as a model for how Christian theology can engage with non-Christian thought:

A quite special place in this long development belongs to Saint Thomas, not only because of what he taught but also because of the dialogue he undertook with the Arab and Jewish thought of his time. In an age when Christian thinkers were rediscovering the treasures of ancient philosophy, and more particularly of Aristotle, Thomas has the great merit of giving pride of place to the harmony which exists between faith and reason. (*FR* 43)

The Pope's words suggest, then, that there can also be a dialogue between Christianity and Hindu thought, rooted in the same concern that Aquinas had for the harmony between faith and reason.

Pope Benedict XVI's approach to interreligious relations, for its part, represents a continuation and reaffirmation of this tradition. In his teaching as Cardinal and Prefect of the Congregation of the Doctrine of the Faith, as well as Pope, a number of abiding themes emerge: a commitment to the objectivity of truth against relativism and the call for all to engage in a mutual search for truth; the affirmation of the importance of the use of reason in the exploration of faith; and the need for Christian theologians to consider the relationship that other religions actually have to Christianity, with a careful discernment of the difference between those traditions within a religion that have something in common with Christianity from those that are opposed to it (as, for instance, in Joseph Cardinal Ratzinger, *Many religions – One Covenant: Israel, the Church and the*

World, San Francisco, Ignatius Press, 1998; *Truth and Tolerance: Christian Belief and World Religions*, San Francisco, Ignatius Press, 2004).

Such Conciliar and Papal teaching provides a set of principles and models that govern any Catholic account of Hinduism as a religion and any Christian theological engagement with Hindu religious traditions, as well as gives some concrete points of common ground with Hinduism. The Indian Christian community has itself sought in different ways to engage with the religious traditions of Hinduism in order to embed Christianity more fully in the religious cultures of India and to develop an authentically Indian Christian theology and spirituality. Catholics outside of India, for their part, encounter Hinduism both through the work of Christians in India, through Hindu communities in the West, and through academic and popular theological and spiritual writing promoting different forms of engagement.

In what follows we shall consider what a Catholic approach to those particular aspects of Hinduism we outlined in Section 1 might be, giving some examples of existing Catholic engagements.

Dharma *and Caste*

Christian attitudes to Hindu *dharma* and to the caste system in particular are matters of great sensitivity in the modern encounter between Christians and Hindus, both in India and the rest of the world. What is required is a careful and balanced approach. There is a need to avoid generalizations. Hindus have had many different views on and ways of realizing the *dharma* of society, some of which have greater common ground with Christian teaching, some less.

For instance, Catholic teaching about the structure of Church life and social teaching would seem to be comfortable with the principle of *svadharma* in itself. Catholic Christianity teaches that the Church has a hierarchical structure instituted by Christ, in which there is a variety of offices as well as charisms (*Catechism of the Catholic Church* (CCC), Revised English edition, London, Geoffrey Chapman, 1999, paras 874–945). Moreover, as articulated especially in canon law and social doctrine, the Church depicts Christian life as a matter of different duties and rights that pertain to the states of life and the offices that particular members of the Church may have (*Compendium of the Social Doctrine of the Church* (*Compendium*), Pontifical Council for Social Justice, English translation, London and New York, Continuum, 2005, para. 156). Catholic social teaching also recognizes the diversity of human beings, with different characters and talents, as part of the divine will that people find their fulfilment through sharing their abilities and resources with each other (CCC 1936–1937).

At the same time, the Church teaches that all people have a common and equal natural dignity and set of rights that follow from this, as created in the image and likeness of God (CCC 1934; NA 5; *Compendium* 144–148) and that within the redemptive order brought about by Christ there is a fundamental unity and inclusiveness that means that there is 'neither Jew nor Greek, male or female, slave nor free' (Gal. 3.28). Christianity does not restrict access to the Bible or to the sacraments to any particular group. As a religion, Christianity has also moved away from laws of ritual impurity or restrictions on contact or eating. The fundamental unity and equality of all members of the Church is expressed above all in the central Christian act of religion, the Eucharistic meal. The Church teaches also that all people have the duty to work in solidarity with other members of society against unjust inequalities and for the just distribution of goods, out of respect for the human dignity of all (CCC 1938–1942; *Compendium* 192–196).

Catholic teaching, then, balances a recognition of the good of diversity in occupations and gifts with an insistence on the common dignity of all people. Inevitably it approaches Hindu accounts of caste from this perspective and welcomes Hindu accounts of *dharma* that also affirm this. We have already noted that there have been many traditions or individuals within Hinduism, such as the devotional or *bhakti* movements, or modern reformist Hindus like Swami Vivekananda and Mahatma Gandhi, that have sought to counter inequalities and oppressive attitudes and practices present in Hindu society and to affirm the equal dignity of all people. The teaching of these Hindu reformers represents, for its part, an important manifestation of the influence of Christian social ethics has had on Hindus in the modern period, since the leaders of Reformed Hinduism had great admiration for the ideas they found in the New Testament, allowing them to inform their own understanding of what Hindus should think and behave.

On his first visit to India, Pope John Paul II made a point of praising Gandhi and promoted Gandhi's teaching as a model for India and the world:

> Mahatma Gandhi taught that if all men and women, whatever the differences between them, cling to the truth, with respect for the unique dignity of every human being, a new world order – a civilisation of love – can be achieved. Today we hear him still pleading with the world: 'Conquer hate by love, untruth by truth, violence by self-suffering.' (Tribute to the Monument of Gandhi, New Delhi, 1 February 1986, Gioia, 309)

Likewise, in calling on all the people of India to affirm that working for the social emancipation of those who are suffering or in want is part of genuine spirituality, he drew attention to the words of one of the many leaders of the devotional movements, the Śaiva Siddhānta Nāya<u>n</u>mār, Pattinattar:

> Because we believe in man, in his value and in his innate excellence, we love him and serve him and seek to relieve his sufferings. As the sage of Tamilnadu, Pattinattar, puts it: 'Believe the One above. Believe that God is. Know that all other wealth is naught. Feed the hungry, know that righteousness and good company are beneficial; be content that God's will be done. A sermon unto you, O heart!' (To Representatives of the Various Religions of India, Madras, 5 February 1986, Gioia, 325)

The Catholic community in India has had to evolve its own approach to the teaching and realities of *dharma* and caste. Low caste Hindus have, in the course of the centuries, been attracted to Christianity in large numbers, but Catholic missionaries have also tried to accommodate higher castes' concerns as well. This has meant that attempts were often made to accommodate some caste distinctions, though always in a much reduced form. Thus, the early Jesuit missionary, Roberto de Nobili (1577–1656) argued that certain aspects of caste were social rather than religious and could therefore be accepted by Christianity. He adopted the lifestyle of a high caste Hindu and make provision for separate space for Brahmins within Christian churches. And as late as the early twentieth century, there were attempts to set up separate establishments for Brahmins. However, to what extent caste traditions could and should be accommodated within the Indian Christian community always remained a matter of contention.

In the second half of the twentieth century the Indian Catholic community has come to be much more sensitive to the particular difficulties and perspectives of Dalit Christians (those Christians belonging to the lower caste groups, especially the 'untouchables'), who now make up the overwhelming majority of the Church community. Dalit Christians argue that the Church should reject any association with Hindu caste hierarchy, be it with its social customs and the distinctions made within it, or with those elements of Hindu theology and spirituality that have supported caste hierarchy. Some Indian Catholic theologians have accordingly developed forms of liberation theology that critiques Hinduism from a liberational perspective, accepting only those elements that affirm equality and social emancipation in this life as well as spiritual liberation.

Dalit Christians also complain of the continuing presence of the exclusivity of the caste system within the Church community itself, because the Church hierarchy tends to be dominated by a high caste minority, with very few Dalit clergy. It also remains the case that in some places high caste and Dalit Christians worship separately and are buried in different cemeteries. Dalit Christians feel that they are subject to a double discrimination with modern Indian society. As Christians they do not enjoy the same rights as Hindu Dalits under the Indian Constitution, because, whereas Dalit Hindus receive forms of positive discrimination, Christians get none on the grounds that there is no caste in Christianity.

The perspective and concerns of Dalit Christians thus represent an important challenge to the long-standing tendency on the part of Western missionaries working in India to privilege Brahmanical Hinduism when they seek to develop Indian Christianity by adopting forms of Hindu culture or engage in Christian-Hindu dialogue. For Dalit Christians this represents a form of collusion with the ideologies of oppression found within Hinduism. Moreover, they argue that in any case they have a different culture and that this is the one with which Christianity should engage and find an authentically Indian expression. At the very least, we can see here something of the difficulties in the inculturation of the Gospel when it comes to something as complex and contested as Hinduism.

Vedānta

Vedānta is a tradition where Hindus 'seek release from the trials of this present life by ascetical practices and profound meditation' (*NA* 2). Vedānta is also a system of exegesis and reasoning, which manifests the 'the accurately defined insights of philosophy' (*NA* 2) to be found in Hinduism. Theological and spiritual engagement with Vedānta has, in fact, proved very significant in Catholic engagement with Hinduism, especially in the modern period. Because of the particular importance of Thomism (the theology based on the thought of Thomas Aquinas) for Catholic theologians, there has been a particular emphasis on exploring what relationship Thomism might have with Vedānta both in the general assessment of how Christianity and Hinduism relate as religious traditions, as well as within a particular interest in how Vedāntic ideas might help develop an Indian Christian Thomist theology. Thus, in the modern period, a considerable number of theologians working in India, such as Fr Pierre Johanns SJ (1885–1955), Fr Richard de Smet SJ (1916–1998) and Sr Sara Grant RSCJ (1922–2000) all studied the Vedānta and sought to relate it to the Thomist account. This particular encounter, then, serves as a good example of what Pope John Paul II promotes in *FR*. Just as Christian theology in the mediaeval period could engage with different forms of non-Christian thought, so Christian theology might also engage in a similar manner with Hindu traditions, such as the Vedānta.

Likewise, there has been an interest in a deep experiential encounter with Vedāntic spirituality in a monastic context, bearing fruit in the development of Christian Ashrams, modelled on Hindu religious communities. Thus, the French Benedictine monk, Fr Henri Le Saux (otherwise known as Swami Abhishiktananda) (1910–1973), founder of the best-known Christian Ashram, Shantivanam, immersed himself totally into the lifestyle of a Hindu saṃnyāsin and into Vedāntic spirituality as he found it in the *Upaniṣads* and in the teaching of the contemporary Hindu guru, Ramana Mahārshi (1879–1950).

Thus, the possibilities, as well as the problems, associated with Catholic engagement with Vedānta can serve as a representative model for engagement with the many other intellectual and spiritual traditions of Hinduism. Clearly, the general problem is that Vedānta has developed in such a very different context, drawing on sacred texts and paradigms ideas that have no historical connection with those of Christianity. Much of Vedānta would seem simply incompatible in its present form with Christian faith and practice. The model of the medieval period is, however, instructive for what might be involved in a Christian appropriation of Vedānta, since when a theologian like Aquinas engaged with Greek, Jewish or Muslim thought, there was a process of transformation as well as adoption of ideas and we should expect the same to take place when it comes to engagement with Hindu traditions. Yet, there is also the problem of how to find the right balance between what any Christian theologian or spiritual practitioner might want to conclude or do as an individual and what accords with the ecclesial responsibility that person has to the wider Christian community not to promote ideas or to engage in activities that contradict or undermine what that community in India or in the Church as a whole can make sense of or accept at any given point. Unfortunately, that balance has often not been maintained, when it comes to Christian engagement with Vedānta in the modern period.

Much of the encounter with Vedānta in this period has been an engagement with the particular tradition of Advaita Vedānta, for the historical reason that at the end of the nineteenth century and into the first half of the twentieth century, Advaita Vedānta was given huge prestige by Western and modern Hindu scholars, so that it seemed that this was *the* Hindu tradition that Christians should engage with, often to the relative neglect of other traditions, Vedāntic or otherwise. In its standard form outlined in Section 1, Advaita is, however, clearly incompatible with the articles of Christian faith. Christianity is theistic and Trinitarian, whereas the

Brahman in Advaita Vedānta is not the personal Lord of theism, nor is there any real parallel for the Trinitarian distinction within Brahman. Christianity holds to the reality and goodness of a created world, whereas Advaita takes the world to be the product of ignorance and the arena of rebirth and suffering. Christianity maintains that the human being is an integral composite of body and soul, created in the image of God and an entity distinct from God, whereas Advaita maintains a dualist understanding of the human person, in which the spiritual core, the self, is identical with Brahman. Christianity is concerned with the redemption of the world, whereas in Advaita the goal is the transcendence of the world.

Some theologians engaging with Advaita, such as Richard de Smet SJ and Sara Grant RSCJ, however, have suggested that Thomism and Advaita are in fact compatible (for de Smet see Malkovsky, B. J., ed., *New Perspectives on Advaita Vedanta; Essays in Commemoration of Professor Richard de Smet S.J.*, Leiden, Brill, 2000 and for Grant see Grant, S., *Towards an Alternative Theology: Confessions of a Non-Dual Christian*, Indiana, University of Notre Dame, 2002). Śaṃkara, the greater teacher of Advaita, they argue, has a theist and a realist account very different from the later form Advaita takes. De Smet and Grant argue that in Śaṃkara's account the Advaitic distinction between the ultimately real and practically real should be taken as one between self-subsistent being and contingent being, rather than between what is real and what is the product of ignorance. Likewise, Śaṃkara's affirmation of the identity of the soul with Brahman is to be understood as teaching only that the soul has no independent existence apart from Brahman. Statements that seem to deny the real production of the world, likewise, only deny that Brahman undergoes change in the production of the world. Śaṃkara's account can, thus, be said to be compatible with the Thomist account of God and creation, concerned to express the same non-reciprocal relation of dependence that Aquinas does through his account of mixed relations. The central concept of non-dualism (*advaita*) in Śaṃkara is thus not the same as monism, for it affirms dependence not identity of being.

For de Smet the difference between Śaṃkara and Aquinas is one of expression, not of content. Śaṃkara affirms contingency by a more negative approach, whereby the reality of finite pales into insignificance when set against that of absolute being, whereas Aquinas has a more positive approach, using the language of participation. De Smet and Grant have also come to talk of the Advaitic account as a complementary expression that might enrich the Thomist account and Christian experience. Grant argues that non-dual language and experience, as well as the Vedantic emphasis on the immanence of Brahman, challenges tendencies in Western theological discourse towards a dualism between God and the world, in which God is depicted as outside and remote from the world.

This attempt to argue for an alternative reading of Advaita remains problematic, since it has won little wider acceptance, despite the painstaking efforts of de Smet and Grant to argue that this is the meaning of Śaṃkara's own account. Nonetheless, we could say that it is at the least a possible Christian re-reading of Śaṃkara's Advaita in the light of Thomas Aquinas and very much in the tradition of what Aquinas himself did with non-Christian accounts. Likewise, spiritual or contemplative encounter with Advaita has often worked well as a form of a Christian transformation of the Advaitic experience. This is the case with the early work of Henri Le Saux. In his earlier encounter with Advaitic spirituality, Le Saux sought to find ways in which Advaita might be transformed by and fulfilled in Christian Trinitarian faith. Contemplating the Vedāntic description of Brahman as 'being, consciousness and bliss' (*sat-cit-ānanda*), he found there a Vedāntic understanding of Brahman that could be transformed into a Trinitarian concept, of Father (*sat*), Son (*cit*) and Spirit (*ānanda*). In this he picked up a long-standing Christian Trinitarian reading of this Vedāntic formula that still remains popular in India.

Unfortunately, later in life, Le Saux failed to maintain the balance needed in such encounter. Instead, he allowed his Christian faith in the Trinity to be sublimated by the Advaitic experience of the unity of all in Brahman. For Le Saux Christian faith about the incarnation of Christ had to be transformed into Advaitic categories, so that Christ is no longer the unique union of God and man, but an exemplar of the relationship that all human beings have with Brahman. (For an insight into the evolution of Le Saux's thought, see James Stuart, ed., *Swami Abhishiktananda: His Life Told through His Letters*, India, ISPCK, 1995. His final assimilation to the Advaitic perspective is evident in the letters written in his last year of 1973).

Catholic theological and spiritual encounter with Advaita Vedānta, then, works best when it results in a Christian transformation of Advaita, similar to the transformation of Greek, Jewish and Islamic thought by Aquinas. The fact that in the case of some thinkers it appears to have done the reverse makes clear the need for careful discernment on the part of the Church community as a whole before adopting any such account.

Apart from Advaita, there are the many theistic traditions of Vedānta with which Christianity might seem to have more immediate common ground. Such forms of Vedanta, such as that developed by Rāmānuja, are monotheistic and realist and so already lack some of the marked incompatibility that Advaita has with the Christian account of God and creation. Theistic Vedānta, moreover, serves as the intellectual system supporting many of the devotional (*bhakti*) traditions in Hinduism, which would also seem to have much in common with Christian theism.

Theistic Vedānta would, in fact, seem to have much that is compatible with the particular account of God and of the creation and governance of world found in the *Prima Pars* of Aquinas' *Summa Theologia*, although also manifestly different in certain respects. The concept of God found in theistic Vedānta is in many ways fundamentally similar to Aquinas' account of God considered in the unity of the divine essence. Both traditions affirm that God is one, omniscient, omnipotent, wholly perfect and immutable, intimately present in all things. On the other hand, theistic Vedānta affirms the real distinction of attributes in God in a way that contrasts with the absolute simplicity emphasized by Aquinas. Moreover, the God of theistic Vedānta remains Unitarian rather than Trinitarian in character, although when this is combined with the other theistic traditions, such as that of Śrī Vaiṣṇavism, which affirm the existence of the divine consort, Śakti, as an eternally existing and integral part of the divine being, then the concept of God does acquire a binitarian character.

Theistic Vedānta can also be said to teach a creational relationship between God and the world, insofar as it maintains both that the world depends on Brahman at all times for its existence and that God governs the world in general and exercises a particular moral rule over human affairs, without undermining the freedom of human beings. On the other hand, theistic Vedānta also affirms the eternity of the world. The world as we experience it is produced from a more subtle state at each beginning of a new cycle of time, rather than created *ex nihilo* in the sense of created in or with time. Like Advaita, much of theistic Vedānta uses language and imagery that affirm a unity between God and the world in a way unfamiliar to Christian imagery, as in Rāmānuja's depiction of the world as the body of God. However, it is a mistake to think that theistic Vedānta is pantheistic as a result, since the language and images are interpreted in such a way as to affirm the transcendence of God, as well as the world's difference from God.

At the same time, when it comes to the understanding of human nature and hence human destiny, theistic Vedānta remains the product of a very different tradition from the Thomist account. As with other Hindu traditions it affirms a fundamentally dualist anthropology that contrasts with the Christian understanding of the human person as a body and soul composite. (For a fuller account of the relationship between theistic Vedānta and the Thomist account, see Ganeri, M., *Indian Philosophy and Western Theism*, Abingdon, Oxon, Routledge, forthcoming.)

Yoga

Many Christians have been on courses in Yoga and found it to be of considerable value as a method of control over the body and mind, whether for therapeutic purposes or better concentration. However, it is important to bear in mind that Hindu traditions of yoga and meditation are also embedded in spiritual paths with goals somewhat different from those found in Christianity. There is a need for a certain caution, then, in taking up these forms of practice.

A considered official guide on these matters is to be found in *Some Aspects of Christian Meditation*, a document issued by the Congregation for the Doctrine of the Faith in 1989. The document notes the interest many Christians have in Eastern methods, be they derived from Hindu or Buddhist traditions. As the document asserts, however, the value of engagement with such traditions is determined by the degree to which it accords with authentic Christian spirituality, which is determined by the principles and goals of Christian faith. Christian spirituality is Trinitarian and incarnational in character and aims at a personal encounter with God and a communion of knowledge and love with God's triune life. Thus, while the Church rejects nothing that is true and holy in Eastern traditions, 'one can take from them what is useful so long as the Christian concept of prayer, its logic and requirements, are never obscured' (*Some Aspects of Christian Meditation*, para. 4, Gioia, 600).

In terms of the systematic yoga of the *Yoga Sūtra*s the difference in goals and the means to them is quite marked. The dualist metaphysics of Yoga and the goal of separation from any materiality contrast with the Christian view of creation, human nature and the goal of bodily resurrection. Although, in Yoga the concept of a Lord is affirmed, this is simply an object for meditation. The goal is not union with the Lord, nor is the Lord the creator of the world. Moreover, the path of Yoga remains something the practitioner has to achieve for him- or herself, in contrast to the fundamental Christocentric and grace-dependent path of Christian soteriology.

Bhakti

In Section 1 we also considered Hindu devotional theism (*bhakti*). Here too Hindus 'seek release from the trials of this present life by ascetical practices, profound meditation and recourse to God in confidence and love' and express it through 'the limitless riches of myth and the accurately defined insights of philosophy' (*NA* 2). What should a Catholic attitude to

Hindu theism be? What sense should Catholics make of the Council's words that Hindus have 'recourse to God in confidence and love?' This is also a difficult area and what follows is meant simply as a possible pointer to a Catholic approach that upholds the two principles of Church teaching: that the Church 'rejects nothing that is true and holy' and that the Church 'proclaims and is in duty bound to proclaim without fail, Christ who is the way, the truth and the life' (Jn 1.6) (*NA* 2).

Hindu theism abounds in a rich mythology, which includes many vivid accounts of the exploits of the gods and goddesses depicted within them. Christians have often found the events and the imagery contained in these myths to be surprising and even shocking. A particularly difficult case for Christians has been the rich and very important body of erotic mythology, which comes to play a central part in the formation of Hindu devotional attitudes towards the divine. A good example of this is the account of the male deity, Kṛṣṇa, who descended as a human being to live with the cow-herding people of the North Indian region of Vraja. Here he grew up and as a young man engaged in various love-games with the cowherd women (*gopīs*), even though many of them were already married, and hence such a relationship flaunted the established *dharma*. Enchanted by the sound of his flute and driven by intense desire for him, they abandoned homes and husbands to dance with their divine lover in the autumnal moonlight. The pain of separation, and the bliss of erotic union, especially the love-affair between Kṛṣṇa and his favourite cowherd woman, Rādhā, has been retold time and again in the devotional literature, often in quite graphic detail.

Here, however, it is important to have an informed understanding of what myths and imagery do within Hinduism. For Hindus, these serve as vehicles for expressing the nature of the divine and to promote human relationships with the divine. They serve to explore and evoke devotional and ethical attitudes. The mythology and imagery are also interpreted according to the norms of *dharma* and the sophisticated theologies that have developed in Hinduism, such as the Vedānta. It is, then, these, truths and models for behaviour that Hindus derive from the myths and imagery that need to be considered in any Christian approach to Hindu mythology. In the mythology of Kṛṣṇa, for example, the erotic exploits of the deity with the cowherd women of Vraja serve as a vehicle for promoting intense devotion to God, both with the blissful delight of mystical union with God and the unbearable pain of separation from God. The mythology itself is not understood to encourage sexual licence between human beings. The problematic nature of such mythology is acknowledged and addressed in the devotional literature and their commentaries. In the case of Kṛṣṇa and the women of Vraja, one explanation is that Kṛṣṇa remains untouched by such acts and engages in them only in order to arouse devotion in human beings (*Bhāgavata Purāṇa* X.33).

The imagery and modes of Hindu *bhakti* find their counterpart in the rich devotional traditions of medieval Christian spirituality. As we have seen, Hindu devotional theism emphasizes and explores the cultivation of a range of devotional relationships found expressed in the mythology and which mirror the different relationships human beings have with each other, such as that of master and servant, parent and child, as well as that of two lovers. Christian spirituality has likewise explored and cultivated these relationships in developing the devout and mystical life. We might call to mind here the long tradition of Christian commentary on the *Song of Songs*, such as that by Bernard of Clairvaux, and the 'bridal mysticism' of the medieval period, or the exploration of the motherhood of God in the writings of Julian of Norwich.

Christianity would, then, find some common ground in those traditions of Hindu theism that are centred on *bhakti*, when this cultivates a loving relationship with God, and when the need for divine grace is emphasized. Here we might identify 'recourse to God in confidence and love' (*NA* 2). In one sense Christians and Hindus still do not worship the same God, since the particular accounts of God found in these traditions and the modes of worship are different. To say that Hindus have 'recourse to God' is not then to say that Hindus have recourse to the same concept of God, but to the same reality behind the conception of God. At the same time, however, there are also common elements in the conception of God and common modes of approaching God. So, a Hindu might be also said to participate in the 'true' (*NA* 2) of the Christian understanding of God. We have already noted the theistic Vedānta traditions as a case of this.

Above all, it is with Hindu *bhakti* traditions that Christianity finds a common experience of divine love as being at the heart of the human encounter with God and as the dynamic within a God-centred life. Reflecting his own deep knowledge of the South Indian devotional tradition of Śaiva Siddhānta and affirming his sense of the common ground between this tradition and Christianity, the Indian theologian M. Dhavamony, for instance, describes the Hindu *bhakti* religions as India's 'Religions of Love'. He sees this as the proper meeting point of Christianity and Hinduism. As he puts it:

> Of all Hindu religious experience, *bhakti* experience comes close to Christian experience, for in this experience we come across the necessity of repentance and of a purified heart before God's grace can become effective, the need of realizing fellowship with God in union with Him, and the profound sense of dependence on Him alone and of loyal service and surrender to Him

(*Hindu-Christian Dialogue: Theological Soundings and Perspectives*, Amsterdam-New York, Rodopi, 2002, 47)

Such *bhakti* experience might be a point where a Christian can also identify the presence of the 'holy' in Hinduism. We have noted that Pope John Paul II makes the universal presence and activity of the Spirit and the universal offer of divine salvation through the Spirit important themes in his teaching about other religions. This is always the Spirit of Christ, who offers the salvation found in Christ and who brings about a relation to the Church, as the sacrament of that salvation (*RM* 10). The Pope teaches that:

> The Spirit manifests himself in a special way in the Church and in her members. Nevertheless, his presence and activity are universal, limited neither by space nor time (DEV 53). The Second Vatican Council recalls that the Spirit is at work in the heart of every person, through the 'seeds or the Word,' to be found in human initiatives – including religious ones – and in man's efforts to attain truth, goodness and God himself. (*AG* 3, 11, 15; *GS* 10–11, 22, 26, 38, 92–93) (*RM* 28)
>
> The Spirit's presence and activity affect not only individuals but also society and history, peoples, cultures and religions. Indeed, the Spirit is at the origin of the noble ideals and undertakings which benefit humanity on its journey through history, 'The Spirit of God with marvellous foresight directs the course of the ages and renews the face of the earth.' (*GS* 26) (*RM* 28)

The Church does not teach that other religious traditions are ways of salvation, separate from, or equal and alternative to, the way of salvation found in Christ. Insofar as the Spirit communicates divine grace and makes members of other religious traditions holy and insofar as that holiness is then manifest in other religious traditions, this is always a participation of the holiness of Christ. As the Pope teaches, the Spirit is manifest in 'the "seeds of the Word" to be found in the human initiatives – including religious ones – and in man's efforts to attain truth, goodness and God himself'. In this sense then, Catholics might look to see the holy in the traditions of Hindu theism.

Dhavamony, for his part, offers us a helpful account that affirms the presence of the holy in Hindu *bhakti* religion. His account is important and helpful because it combines both a deep knowledge of Hindu *bhakti* traditions in their historical and theological reality and a sensitivity to the issues facing a Catholic Christian theological account that aims to adhere to normative Christian teaching. Dhavamony relates the central Christian experience of the gift of God's love to the Hindu experience of *bhakti* of divine grace within it. Whereas Christianity and Hinduism clearly differ as objective, or 'thematic', historical religions, they nonetheless meet 'at the horizon of unthematic theological life' where, as Dhavamony puts it, '"theologal" refers to the communion with the living God. This communion surpasses the "natural" capacities of the human being, and is possible only through the gratuitous self-communication of God' (2002, 33). The theologal life experienced by both Christian and Hindu is a common experience of the same God of love and of the gift of God's love. In other words, the *bhakti* experience, which is then expressed in the historical and particular *bhakti* traditions, should be acknowledged to be an encounter with the Spirit, the grace of God, a place where the 'holy' clearly manifests itself in Hinduism. Dhavamony likens the relationship of this common theologal life and the particular experience of the gift of God's love in Christ to the relationship between grace and sacrament. The grace given in the sacrament is more widely experienced than the sacrament, but remains the same grace as given in the sacrament and a participation in the fullness of what is given in the sacrament (2002, 33–41).

This account has the strength that it both recognizes what the evidence of the Hindu *bhakti* religions themselves suggest, while reaffirming the absolute and universal character of Christ as the Way of salvation. At the same time it has to be balanced from a Christian perspective with an affirmation of the qualitative difference that the incarnation and the sacramental economy of the Church make to the communication of divine grace and the realization of salvation for human beings. In other words, the particularity of the saving revelation and action found in Christ and the particular efficacy of the Christian sacraments mean that the relationship between Hinduism and Christianity cannot be reduced adequately to one of a quantitative part-whole relationship or just the difference between implicit and explicit access to the same divine grace, as if it does not really make that much difference at the end of the day whether one is a Hindu or Christian theist.

Indian Christians have themselves felt able to engage with the literary forms, concepts and sentiments found in Hindu devotional theism in order to develop forms of Indian Christian hymns and poets, directed towards the Trinity, Christ and the Blessed Virgin Mary. As we have noted in our discussion of Christian approaches to *dharma*, the egalitarian aspects of the Hindu theism found in the devotional movements have also appealed to Indian Christians concerned with what in Hinduism seems most conducive to social emancipation. This had led to the evolution of an Asian form of liberation theology that finds in the *bhakti* traditions a liberative core within Hinduism. It is in this context that a liberative hermeneutic of religions is favoured by many Indian theologians for determining what kind of inculturation there can be into the traditions of Hinduism. A prominent advocate of this in India, Soosai Arokiasamy ('Theology of Religions from Liberation Perspective' in *Religious Pluralism: An Indian Christian Perspective*, ed. Pathil, Delhi, ISPCK: 1999, 300–323), identifies the *bhakti* movements, themselves usually inspired by members of the lower castes or outcastes, as liberative because God is held to offer salvation equally to all whatever their status, thereby rendering irrelevant the spiritual hierarchy and exclusiveness of the caste system, and because they emphasize the need for social emancipation in this life along with final liberation. Within this perspective *bhakti* has historically often lost its liberative power, when it has been combined with an affirmation of the values of the caste system or a world-transcending spirituality. Nonetheless, this kind of Asian liberation theology in encounter with *bhakti* represents an interesting point of Christian encounter with Hinduism that has the potential to mediate between concerns to engage with Brahmanical Hindu culture and the social concerns of Dalit Christians.

The positive approach to Hindu *bhakti* religion among Indian Christians, such as Dhavamony, contrasts with the condemnation of Hindu theism by earlier generations of European missionaries, for whom Hindu theism represented the epitome of polytheism, idolatry and superstition. Moreover, it stands in contrast with the tendency to favour Advaita Vedānta as *the* Hindu tradition as both the best that Hinduism had to offer and the one with which Christian theologians and contemplatives should engage. This more positive attitude to and engagement with Hindu theism represents a remarkable shift in the Catholic and wider Christian approach to Hinduism and a substantial advance in interreligious understanding of significance both for the Catholic community in India and more widely.

Further Reading

Introductions to Hinduism

Brockington, J. (1996), *The Sacred Thread: Hinduism in Its Context and Diversity*, 2nd ed., Edinburgh: Edinburgh University Press.

Flood, G. (1996), *An Introduction to Hinduism*, Cambridge: Cambridge University Press.

Flood, G. (ed.) (2003), *The Blackwell Companion to Hinduism*, Oxford: Blackwell.

Klostermaier, K. K. (1994), *A Survey of Hinduism*, 2nd ed., Albany, NY: SUNY Press.

Lipner, L. (2010), *Hindus: Their Religious Beliefs and Practices*, 2nd ed., London: Routledge.

Christian approaches to Hinduism and Hindu-Christian dialogue

Brockington, J. (1992), *Hinduism and Christianity*, London: Macmillan.
Coward, H. (1990), *Christian-Hindu Dialogue: Perspectives and Encounters*, New York: Orbis.
Dhavamony, M. (2002), *Hindu-Christian Dialogue: Theological Soundings and Perspectives*, Amsterdam-New York, Rodopi.
Ganeri, M. (2007), 'Catholic Encounter with Hindus in the Twentieth Century: In Search of an Indian Christianity', *New Blackfriars* 88, July.
Robinson, B. (2004), *Christians Meet Hindus*, Delhi: Regnum.

CHAPTER 5

CATHOLICISM AND BUDDHISM[1]

Paul Williams OP

An Overview

Buddhism is the '-ism' that is named after the Buddha. The word *Buddha* is a title. It means an *Awakened One*. It refers to one who has awakened in the deepest, most life-transforming way, to a final understanding of the way things truly are. In coming to this understanding he is held to have brought to an end for himself all the forces that lead to suffering, frustration, disharmony and, in short, all those negative experiences that we would rather do without. These negative experiences that a Buddha has escaped from are and have been ours not just in this life but also in past lives, for Buddhists believe in rebirth, reincarnation. And, Buddhists claim, there is no chronological first beginning to the series of past lives. We have all of us been reborn an infinite number of times. No God is needed, either to start the series off – there was no first beginning – or to explain why there is anything at all rather than nothing. Questioning it is irrelevant to the overriding and severely practical aim of overcoming suffering. We have all experienced infinite suffering, and we shall continue to be reborn and to suffer until we 'see things the way they really are' and bring to a complete and final end the forces within us that have led to so much suffering. These forces are mental acts (*karma*) of greed, hatred and ignorance (or 'delusion'), and they power the physical actions that spring from those 'three root poisons'. Such acts have been ours throughout infinite past time, they lead to our suffering, but they are not essential to us. We can completely eradicate them, and produce instead their opposites – altruism, loving kindness, and wisdom. A Buddha is one who has developed these positive qualities to their highest degree, their perfection.

In achieving this goal the Buddha has not simply abandoned others. Out of his altruism, loving kindness and wisdom the Buddha has also taught the way for others to follow him and achieve for themselves what he has done. His teaching, and also the way things truly are which he discovered and that is expressed in his teaching, is known in Sanskrit as the *Dharma* (Pali: *Dhamma*).[2] This term carries with it the senses of 'Teaching', 'Doctrine', 'The Way It Is', 'Things As They Really Are', and perhaps also a little of the sense of 'Righteousness'. For lay supporters and donors the Buddha taught mainly basic moral teachings, but his particular interest was in establishing an Order of renouncers – monks and nuns – who could devote themselves full time to following the Way he mapped out for them in the Dharma. Inasmuch as this Way sets out to reverse psychological forces that are deeply ingrained habits from infinite lifetimes, the Way requires hard dedicated practice in morality, in meditation and in wisdom. It is not a Way for amateurs. Thus the Buddha also established the *Saṃgha*. The Saṃgha in its fullest sense consists of four parts: the monks, the nuns, and pious and devoted male and female lay supporters, although the term Saṃgha is also commonly used to refer to just the monks and nuns.

These three components, Buddha, Dharma and Saṃgha, are known in Buddhism as the 'Three Jewels'. The minimum requirement for being a Buddhist is truly to 'take refuge' in the Three Jewels. One takes refuge in the Buddha as the one who has come to understand, realize and teach the way things really are, the way that alone leads to final cessation of all suffering. One takes refuge in the Dharma as the correct expression of the way things are, and the way to achieve deep liberative realization of it. One takes refuge in the Saṃgha as the community of exemplars, those who are following this Way and demonstrating in their lives its truth.

The Buddha

I began by talking about *a* Buddha. Anyone who achieves what a Buddha achieves is a Buddha. Since time is infinite, in infinite time there have been many past Buddhas and there will be many (actually, infinite) Buddhas in the future too. Since Buddhism – the Dharma – is considered to be the true way of things, it is not invented by a Buddha but is rather *discovered*. A Buddha discovers this liberating truth, he teaches it, the teaching flourishes but eventually in the course of time it is completely lost. After a long period of time when there is no Buddhism another person becomes a Buddha. He rediscovers and teaches the truth. And so on, throughout all time.

The Life of Śākyamuni Buddha

But I also spoke above about *the* Buddha, the one who actually, in history, established for us the religion we know in English as 'Buddhism'. Scholars are extremely unsure about when exactly the Buddha lived although there is some consensus emerging that he may have died around 400 BC. Tradition names him *Siddhārtha Gautama*, although after he became awakened, or enlightened, Siddhārtha was henceforth known as *Śākyamuni Buddha*. That is, he was the Buddha who was the 'sage' (*muni*) of the Śākya clan. The Śākyas lived in the foothills of what would nowadays be southern Nepal. Tradition also has it that the young Siddhārtha was born a prince. He was certainly born into a prosperous family. The accounts claim that had Siddhārtha not become a Buddha – the supreme achievement of the spiritual world – he would have become a world-conquering monarch, the supreme achievement of the worldly life. We are told he grew up living a luxurious and hedonistic life, and married a beautiful bride who subsequently gave birth to their son. What changed everything was the young man's discovery, in a series of disturbing experiences, that all were bound to suffer in life through such torments as old age, sickness and death. Reincarnation, by this time well established in India, meant such suffering would simply be repeated infinitely unless something was done to bring to an end the whole horrible cycle (a cycle known as *saṃsāra*).

Learning of renunciation of the worldly householder life, of living an ascetic life in the jungle, and through meditation seeking to find the way to eradicate the forces that lead to suffering and rebirth, suggested to Siddhārtha a way out. One night Siddhārtha fled his home, cut off all his hair, donned tan-coloured robes made from discarded rags (both showing the complete renunciation of his previous luxurious life and wealth), and set off into the jungle to find a teacher who could teach him the way to follow. Henceforth, his scant food came from asking for alms. It is said that Siddhārtha studied with many teachers, and indeed surpassed each of his teachers in his mastery of asceticism and deep meditation. From a life of extreme indulgence he now adopted a lifestyle of excessive mortification and acquired several disciples. But still the liberating truth eluded him. Eventually Siddhārtha reflected that extreme mortification was no more effective in attaining the spiritual insight necessary to overcome suffering than was hedonistic indulgence. Overcoming suffering is a matter of the *mind*, not bodily asceticism. He took to eating a moderate diet again, and sat down in meditation under a tree. Thinking that Siddhārtha had given up the struggle, his disciples abandoned him. Siddhārtha was now alone, but it was during this period of deep solitary meditation that Siddhārtha broke through to the deep transformative understanding and insight that enabled him, it is said, to shatter forever the forces of suffering and rebirth. He was now the Buddha, the Awakened One. Emerging from his meditation Śākyamuni Buddha sought out his former disciples, and they were the first to hear what he had discovered. Following his teachings, they too put an end to all suffering and rebirth. They too achieved their final goal.

Śākyamuni Buddha taught all who would hear him, including members of his family. His wife and son both joined the Order he established, and attained enlightenment. He travelled widely in north India and died aged in his early eighties. His body was cremated, and relic shrines set up. Asked to appoint a successor it is said that the Buddha refused. His successor would be the Dharma, the discovery he had made and taught.

The Dharma

What did the Buddha discover? In what follows I shall outline some of the central teachings of Buddhism, teachings that can plausibly be traced back to the Buddha himself. In their broad sense they can be thought common to all Buddhists, the core of what scholars nowadays are inclined to call 'Mainstream Buddhism'.

Many of the basic teachings of Buddhism can be found neatly stated in an early discourse known as the *Discourse Setting in Motion the Wheel of Dhamma*, traditionally held to be the Buddha's first teaching, after his enlightenment. His teachings are organized around what is known as the 'Four Noble Truths'.

(1) *Dukkha* (P): This states the basic starting point, our 'existential malady' which the Buddha, apparently consciously using the image of a 'transcendental doctor', sets out to remedy. *Dukkha* is usually translated as 'suffering'. Absolutely everything, the Buddha wants to say, that pertains to an unenlightened individual is really dukkha. This includes even happy situations such as, for example, laughter and joy if they are the laughter and joy of one who is not enlightened. All unenlightenment is suffering. Buddhists in the modern world are sensitive to the suggestion that this might make them appear rather pessimistic, or perhaps downright miserable. In reality Buddhists, of course, are no more miserable than other religious groups, and one often finds considerable caution about the translation of 'dukkha' as 'suffering'. It is pointed out that Buddhist tradition accepts three sorts of dukkha. First, there is straightforward pain. This is called *dukkhadukkha* – that is, the dukkha which [really] is dukkha, suffering. But there is also the dukkha which is simply that unhappiness which accompanies transience, the mutability of all things, even our happiness. And finally there is the dukkha that is what all unenlightenment is, merely because it is not enlightenment. Hence laughter is dukkha not because it is literally painful, but because all our ordinary unenlightened happiness in the

end ceases. That is why modern translators sometimes prefer English expressions like 'unsatisfactoriness' for 'dukkha'. But it is clear that the word 'dukkha' in its everyday usage does indeed mean 'suffering', pain. That is why the expression 'dukkhadukkha' can be used in this technical context to mean 'the dukkha which *really* [or, we might say, obviously] is dukkha' (as when you step with bare feet on a drawing pin). But clearly as a technical term in Buddhism 'dukkha' has come to have a specialized usage that is wider than simply suffering in the sense of literal raw pain. The term used throughout is the standard one for suffering nevertheless. All unenlightenment is through and through suffering. And Buddhism is first and foremost offered as a solution to this all-pervasive suffering.

(2) *Origin*: If we knew the origin of suffering we should be able to overcome it. The origin of suffering is said to be *craving*.[3] Craving is of course fundamentally something to do with the mind. If Buddhism is all about overcoming suffering, and the cause of suffering is held to be mental, then it follows that Buddhism is all about (working on) the mind. God, or other grand metaphysical 'theories', are irrelevant, but so too is fierce asceticism, torturing the body. Craving is said to include craving for sensual pleasures, but also craving for an eternal life or for its opposite, a sort of suicide, 'a complete end to it all'. Craving, it is said, leads to attachment. And our attachment will inevitably bring about suffering since this attachment is incompatible with a fundamental feature of the world around us – its impermanence. The obvious impermanence of the things that make up our lives and our equally obvious attempts to avoid coming to terms with this, is central to Buddhism. We all crave things that are impermanent, that are certain to perish. When they do perish (including, fundamentally, ourselves and all our loved ones), we suffer. Seeing things the way they really are, in its deepest possible life-transformative manner, leads to letting-go, a cessation of craving and hence of suffering. Thus other early Buddhist sources suggest that what is more fundamental even than craving in bringing about suffering is ignorance, ignorance of the way things really are as represented in the Four Noble Truths – crucially failing to recognize the nature of things as impermanent and suffering. Note, however, that ignorance is not thought to be a first cause in the sense that once there was nothing, and ignorance brought things about. There never was a time in the past when there was nothing. The series of past births is, for each one of us, infinite. But ignorance is the first cause in the sense that once it is overcome by someone there is no more reincarnation, no more rebirth, for that person. Hence suffering for him or her has ended. That is *nirvāṇa*.

(3) *Cessation*: The way to eradicate suffering is through the destruction of its cause, ignorance, and thence the cessation of craving. The result of this is enlightenment (*nirvāṇa*). Fundamentally 'nirvāṇa' simply is the term used for the achievement of a person who has come to see things the way they really are and put a stop once and for all to all the forces of ignorance and craving that lead to continued rebirth and thence continued suffering in life after life. The term refers primarily to the cessation, the 'blowing-out' of those forces of ignorance and craving, in that person's mind. That is all. The person who has attained nirvāṇa, while still alive, is said to have 'nirvāṇa with a remainder', that is, the remainder of his or her psycho-physical constituents (i.e. his body and embodied mind). In other words, he or she has not yet died. After death there is 'nirvāṇa without a remainder'. The psycho-physical constituents have ceased. There is thence no more basis to which words can be attached. After the death of the person who is enlightened there is no more suffering. Nothing more can be said. To attempt to do so is fruitless. Early Buddhist tradition was emphatic that we cannot say enlightened beings continue to exist, but equally we are unable to say they do not exist. Suffering simply does not exist for them anymore. That is all. What more should we (or they) want?

(4) *Way*: The actual way to achieve nirvāṇa is declared by the Buddha in his Four Noble Truths to be the famous 'Eightfold Path of the Noble Ones'. It is said to be the 'middle way' between hedonistic self-indulgence and excessive and fruitless asceticism. The eight dimensions of this path consist of:

(a) Appropriate (or 'right', throughout) view
(b) Appropriate intention
(c) Appropriate speech
(d) Appropriate action
(e) Appropriate livelihood
(f) Appropriate effort
(g) Appropriate mindfulness
(h) Appropriate concentration

The first of these is explained as seeing the truth of the Four Noble Truths, and acting in conformity with it. 'Appropriate intention' is explained as intentions free from attachments to worldly pleasures, selfishness and self-possessiveness, and animated by benevolence and compassion towards all living creatures. 'Appropriate speech' is speech that is not false, divisive, hurtful or merely idle chatter. 'Appropriate action' is refraining from harming living beings, particularly through killing them, refraining from taking what is not given and refraining from sexual misconduct. In the case of monks and nuns this means refraining from all sexual activity. 'Appropriate livelihood' is explained as livelihood not involving the infringement of appropriate speech and appropriate action. Some sources refer to five kinds of trade particularly inappropriate for lay Buddhists (let alone monks and nuns): trade in arms, human beings, flesh, intoxicating drinks (presumably also other 'recreational' drugs) and poison. 'Appropriate effort' consists of effort to prevent the arising of unwholesome mental states (e.g. of greed, hatred and delusion) that have not arisen and effort to abandon unwholesome states that have arisen. It is effort to arouse wholesome states (e.g. of nonattachment and altruism, loving kindness, and wisdom) that have not arisen, and effort to develop and promote wholesome states that have arisen. 'Appropriate mindfulness' is constant mindfulness, awareness, with reference to the body, with reference to feelings, with reference to the mind, and with reference to physical and mental processes. In watching these one is aware of their flowing nature, moments arising and falling, aware of their impermanence and aware of letting them go. In watching in this way one perceives them as they are, and abandons any notion that they might be worth craving, as capable of providing lasting happiness, or as an object of attachment as one's true Self (see below). In knowing, seeing the body, feelings, the mind, and physical and mental processes as they are, one begins to erode any basis for craving, and thus the forces that power suffering and rebirth. 'Appropriate concentration' consists of one-pointedness of mind, the mind focusing unwaveringly on a single object, which can be taken to the point where one can use this ability to attain very advanced stages of meditation.

The Teaching of Not-Self

So far I have spoken about the Four Noble Truths, as elaborated in the *Discourse Setting in Motion the Wheel of Dhamma*. According to tradition the Buddha followed up this initial discourse with another one, known as the *Discourse on the Definition of Not-Self*. In this discourse the Buddha outlined his famous teaching of 'not-Self' (P: *anattā*). This is the central dimension of 'seeing things the way they really are', the discovery that really made the Buddha the Awakened One, and that Buddhists hold distinguishes his teaching from all other non-Buddhist teachings.

The Buddha's teaching of not-Self is sometimes presented in books as a teaching of 'no soul'. The Buddha, it is said, completely denied the existence of a soul. This interpretation should be resisted. The notion of the 'soul' is a complex one theologically and philosophically. It is closely bound up with issues concerning post-mortem survival. The Buddha certainly did not hold that death is the end. He taught rebirth, although he had a very particular explanation of how rebirth occurs. But the Buddha did not know of the (largely 'Western') discussions and concerns relating to the soul, as such. When the Buddha taught *anattā* he was talking about the existence or otherwise of a very particular sort of thing, and that thing is best understood not as the soul, but as the *Self*.

My Self, if there were one, would simply be the real me, unchangingly what I truly am. Now, the Buddha says, take the case of physical things – say, my body and all the physical things around me. Physical things (called in technical Buddhist terminology 'form') cannot be my Self. Rather, form is not-Self. It leads to suffering and moreover the Buddha points out that we have no control over it. It is also impermanent. If physical things were my Self, the real me, they would not lead to suffering, I would have control over them, they would not be impermanent. And the same could be said for four other categories of events that make me up, or that I am involved in: feelings, perceptions, other mental events like intentions, and even consciousness itself. Each of these categories of events consists of events that are not-Self. Since they are not-Self, the Buddha concludes, we should 'become dispassionate' towards them, let them go, cut at the very root any craving for them.

The impermanence of physical events and things, of feelings, perceptions, other mental events like intentions, and consciousness itself – and hence their unsatisfactory nature, and our need to let go of them – is stressed repeatedly in Buddhist thought from the earliest times, with elaborate discussions of just how impermanent they are. Meditating systematically and deeply on it forms the central element of the 'insight' meditation that when developed to its highest and most intense degree cuts once and for all the forces of ignorance and hence craving that power rebirth and suffering. But did the Buddha think there is nevertheless something else in addition to these which does not lead to suffering, which one does have control over, and which is permanent and hence is genuinely worth calling my Self. The overwhelming weight of Mainstream Buddhist tradition is that there is no such thing. The teaching of not-Self is also a teaching of no Self at all. There is no place for a permanent Self in all of this.

Life after Death

What has all this to do with life after death? What happens at death, if there is no Self? Buddhist tradition considers that the issue of life after death, and the issue of the existence or otherwise of a Self, need have nothing directly to do with each other. In my present life, I might think I have a Self, an unchanging thing called the real Me, but actually 'I' am a continuum, an ever-changing and largely uncontrolled stream, of physical events, of feelings, perceptions, other mental events like intentions, and consciousness. Clearly, when death occurs my physical events ('form') cease. But mental events continue, ever-changing and hence not in any sense my *Self*, and they contain within them the 'residual traces' of my previous mental acts (*karma*) of greed, hatred and ignorance (or 'delusion'), or their opposites, that powered my physical actions when I was alive. In accordance with these, as appropriate, a new (obviously changing) body is formed linked to the continuing series of mental events. In other words, we can say for conventional practical purposes that 'I' am reincarnated. And I can be reincarnated not just as a human being, in either pleasant or unpleasant circumstances. Appropriate to the dominant forces of virtuous or vicious former acts I may be reborn in one of many very nasty hells, or as an animal, as a 'hungry ghost', as a human, as a sort of mighty titan or 'anti-god', or as a 'god'. The order here is in general from greater to lesser suffering. A 'god' is not God. It is a form of rebirth, perhaps analogous to the old Graeco-Roman gods and goddesses, in appropriately divine comfort. Since these are all types of rebirth, in accordance with previous acts (karma), when the force of the acts that led to the rebirth runs out death occurs and then rebirth elsewhere. This goes on throughout all eternity unless enlightenment is attained, putting a stop to the whole process.

It follows from all of this that the relationship between the one who dies and the reborn being is one of 'neither the same nor different'. They are clearly not the same person (my rebirth as a cockroach would not be *me*). But they are not completely different, since the rebirth is the result of causal forces (karma) made (in part) by me. If we think of all our births as a river, my rebirth is a later stage of the river or, as Buddhists say, of 'my' continuum. Rebirth is due to a totally impersonal process of *causation*. The causes that bring all this about do not need reference to God. The chain of causes stretches back infinitely into the past and, unless there is enlightenment, the chain will stretch infinitely into the future as well.

The Saṃgha

The Buddha established monks and nuns to create the optimum facilities for practising his path, and to preserve his teachings, as well as to teach the wider community the way of virtue that will lead to welfare in future (through 'good karma') and perhaps even enlightenment. It is *not* considered in Buddhism that only monks and nuns can attain enlightenment, and we have the names of several lay people who eventually became enlightened. Nevertheless, the order of monks and nuns is absolutely central to Buddhism, and historically the principal religious function of the Buddhist laity has always rested in the material support they can give to the monks and nuns who, in theory at least, are required to obtain their food through alms. In return, it is felt that the presence of monks and nuns can give positive benefits to the wider lay community through their teaching, their example of piety and serious Buddhist practice, and crucially through the way they serve as a means of 'making merit' through such acts as donations by others to the monastic order that will lead (through 'good karma' again) to improved welfare in this life and in future lives for the donors. Between the monks and nuns on the one hand, and the wider lay community, there is in Buddhist societies a reciprocal relationship (in their different and appropriate ways) of welfare, care and affection.

To the Buddha himself is attributed the many monastic rules and regulations that are contained within what is now a written Buddhist Canon. The Canon consists of three sections, and hence it is known as the 'Three Baskets' (*Tripiṭaka*). The section concerning matters relating broadly to monastic code is known as the *Vinaya*. The other sections are the *Sūtras*, discourses attributed in the main to the Buddha himself, and the 'Higher Teaching' (*Abhidharma*) relating in particular to issues of philosophical and psychological analysis, composed and assembled probably significantly later than the time of the Buddha himself.

Schisms in Buddhist History Related to Monastic Identity

In the centuries after the death of the Buddha various schisms occurred. In general schisms in Buddhism (literally: 'splitting of the Saṃgha') do not occur over *doctrinal* differences but rather over differences in the *monastic rule*. So, for example, one of the first schisms is said to have been incited in particular by a suggestion that it was legitimate for monks to handle money. If one group insists on allowing this while another does not, and there can be no reconciliation, then the two groups have to separate. They can no longer live together. Eventually their monastic regulations will reflect this difference, and a monk ordained in one or the other will be a monk of *that* tradition, rather than *the other* tradition. Thus we come to speak of a Theravāda monk, or a Mūlasarvāstivāda monk, or a Dharmaguptaka monk, or a monk of one of many other monastic traditions. Each of these refers to a monk ordained according to that particular monastic tradition. Particularly interesting and important are the Theravāda monks. These are, broadly speaking, nowadays the Buddhists of, for example, Sri Lanka, Thailand, Burma and other countries of South East Asia as well as those countries to which Theravāda Buddhism has spread (including now, of course, the West). While it is not a certain way of identification, generally Theravāda monks can be recognized, for example, by their shaven heads and orange, yellow, or brownish robes. One reason for their importance is that the Theravāda is the only Buddhist tradition that preserves its Canon in an ancient Indian language (Pali) akin to that which was spoken by the Buddha himself. Tibetan monks, for example, use Tibetan translations. Chinese monks use Chinese translations. Moreover, while Buddhism was lost in mainland India from about the fourteenth century (to be reintroduced in modern times), Theravāda Buddhism continued within the Indian sphere in, for example, Sri Lanka. Nowadays, Theravāda Buddhism is more often than not closest in day-to-day practice and belief to the Mainstream Buddhism that I have portrayed above.

Becoming a Buddhist Monk

How, for example, does one become a monk in the Theravāda tradition? There are two stages, corresponding to a novice and a fully ordained monk. The postulant first goes through a ceremony called 'going forth'. This is possible at the age of about 7 or 8. After that he is a novice. The ceremony involves reciting the 'Triple Refuge' (in the Buddha, Dharma and Saṃgha) in the presence of a full monk of at least 10-years standing, and taking 10 precepts. These precepts include the 5 basic precepts that (it is piously hoped) all good Buddhists will adhere to: (1) to refrain from harming living creatures; (2) to refrain from taking what is not given; (3) to refrain from all sexual activity (this would obviously be modified for a lay person); (4) to refrain from false speech; and (5) to refrain from intoxicants that cause heedlessness. Additional precepts are specific to the monastic situation. Hair is shaved, and the novice now dresses in orange robes. To become a full monk the novice must be at least 20. The ceremony requires at least 5 full monks of 10-years standing. Possessions are henceforth (traditionally) to be few, in 1 list 8: 3 robes, alms-bowl, razor, needle, belt and water-strainer. One's life is governed by the 227 rules of a monk. The 4 breaches that would involve expulsion are (1) sexual intercourse; (2) taking what is not given; (3) killing another human being; and (4) falsely laying claim to spiritual attainments. Other breaches might involve, depending on seriousness, a period of suspension of full status within the Saṃgha, or some penalty decided by the Saṃgha, or simply confession. Note, incidentally, that in Buddhism monastic vows need not necessarily be taken for life. In some countries a man might even become a monk for a period of just a few months as a summer break. Other monks spend time as 'forest-dwellers', hermits engaged in intensive meditation and living a more austere life than the monastic norm.

Buddhist tradition tends to see the monastic Saṃgha as the prerequisite for the establishment and flourishing of Buddhism in a country or society. The rules force members of the Saṃgha to exist in dependence upon the lay community. Rules also aim to ensure that a monk or nun is approved of by the laity since unless the broader lay community sees the Saṃgha as pure, people will not want to offer alms. Merit gained through almsgiving depends on the worthiness of the recipient. In ancient times when kings became themselves lay supporters of the Saṃgha it sometimes happened that effectively Buddhism was given official state support, although even then royal patronage was not necessarily given exclusively to Buddhism. Equally, the Saṃgha could become involved in supporting the state, and everyday politics, even to the extent of supporting war against enemies of the state who were also (or thus) seen as enemies of Buddhism.

While there are records of enlightened women in ancient times, the order of fully ordained nuns effectively died out in, for example, the Theravāda tradition of South Asia, and also in Tibetan Buddhism. Fully ordained nuns are now generally only found within the monastic traditions of East Asian Buddhism (such as China). In modern times, however, there has been some attempt to reintroduce the order of fully ordained nuns into other parts of the Buddhist world.

Buddhist Meditation

The forces that lead to 'unenlightenment' (*saṃsāra*) are greed, hatred and ignorance or delusion. These are essentially mental, and therefore becoming enlightened involves working on the mind to transform it in a very deep way. This is pre-eminently through meditation. In its broadest sense meditation in Buddhism has two facets (or perhaps 'stages'): (1) calming the mind down, sometimes translated as 'calm abiding'; and (2) using the calm mind to see deeply and in a transformative manner the way things really are. This second facet is known as 'insight' meditation.

Calming Meditation

Calming meditation presupposes such prerequisites as faith in the teaching of the Buddha, and participation in regular Buddhist ethics and religious practice. The first stage is narrowing one's attention through concentrated focusing of the mind, becoming simply – but unwaveringly – aware of the mind's object. Texts list various possible objects of concentration. For example, the important Theravāda manual, the *Path of Purity* (fifth century AD), speaks of forty types of objects for meditative concentration. These can be divided into three groups: (1) those – such as a coloured disc – suitable for people dominated by hatred; (2) those suitable for people dominated by greed, such as a skeleton; or (3) those suitable for people dominated by delusion. Commonly, focused awareness (= 'mindfulness') of the process of breathing is recommended for delusion although particularly in recent centuries mindfulness of breathing has become a general practice recommended for all those beginning meditation as a way to overcome the mind's natural inability to concentrate. Another object for meditation, particularly recommended for those dominated by hatred, is the 'four divine abidings', also known as the 'four immeasurables'. This practice involves developing all-pervading loving kindness, all-pervading compassion, all-pervading sympathetic joy and all-pervading equanimity. The meditator is exhorted to overcome the five hindrances while meditating: sensual desire, ill will, tiredness and sleepiness, excitement and depression, and doubt.

Insight Meditation

Insight meditation involves bringing about a state of meditative absorption where the object of meditation is not one of the, for example, forty or so types of objects mentioned above, but rather the way things really are. This is understood in terms of suffering, impermanence, and not-Self, and their ramifications. Through this one attains 'wisdom' (*prajñā*), the state of mind where one sees things the way they really are. Developed to its deepest degree this will cut the forces that lead to rebirth. Hence there is nirvāṇa.

Mahāyāna

Mahāyāna represents the biggest internal development within Buddhism. We have scriptures dating in origin initially from perhaps the second or first century BC, claiming to be the word of the Buddha and that advocate a vision calling itself *Mahāyāna*. These scriptures are apocryphal – they are not accepted as authentic by all Buddhist traditions. Those who do accept some or all of them as authentic, and hence too the teachings within them, eventually came to see themselves as followers of this *Mahāyāna* (the superior 'Great Vehicle', or perhaps the 'Vehicle leading to the Great'). Nowadays Buddhists who would accept the apocryphal Mahāyāna scriptures, and would advocate that vision as embodying their highest aspirations, are likely to be found among Buddhists in, say, Tibet, China, Japan, Korea and, of course, among Buddhists too in the West.

Followers of Mahāyāna came to portray it as a *vision* of what Buddhism is finally all about, based on one's *motivation* for engaging in the spiritual path. The highest motivation, the Mahāyāna motivation, is *to become not just enlightened but actually a perfect Buddha out of compassion for the benefit of all sentient beings.* Compared with this, any other motivation (such as simply aiming for the ending of one's own suffering, that is, simply aiming for nirvāṇa) is inferior and practised in an Inferior Vehicle, a *Hīnayāna*.[4] Mahāyāna thus consists of a vision of what Buddhism is finally all about expressed in terms of compassion, embarking on the path to become a perfect Buddha in order to help all sentient beings [beings with consciousness] and not just aiming to bring to an end *one's own* suffering. Moreover followers of Mahāyāna eventually concluded that we should all embark on this path. That is, if we can we should all take the vow of a *bodhisattva*. This is the technical term used to refer to one who has vowed, and is actually engaging in the path, to become a Buddha for the simple reason that it is the best way in order to help most perfectly others. Thus we should all follow the same long path that Śākyamuni took benefiting many others on the way, rather than seeking simply to bring to an end our own suffering as quickly as possible. That long path is said to be very difficult, and to take three incalculable aeons of rebirths, gradually developing in wisdom and compassion, from first vowing to become a perfect Buddha to actually achieving the goal. Hence, in the light of this compassion, immediate freedom from rebirth ceases to be the most important aim and concern.

Mahāyāna and the Continued Existence of the Buddha

Possibly one central feature of Mahāyāna is the idea that the Buddha is really still around, and can thus be contacted in meditation (and perhaps, in prayer). He is still around because of his great compassion (which entails he would not abandon us after just 80 years or so), and his superhuman abilities (which entails he could put off death, perhaps forever). He is still around on another plane, known as a 'Pure Land'. Since throughout infinite time there must have been infinite Buddhas, and Buddhas do not abandon their flock, there must be many (indeed infinite) other compassionate

Buddhas still around too, each present in their own individual Pure Lands.

Hence the Buddha is still teaching, and perhaps inspiring new texts and even new practices to suit changed circumstances. With acceptance of the idea that the Buddha is still around, everything changes. It becomes possible not only to receive new teachings, but also (even though he is not seen doctrinally as God, or as a god) to pray to the Buddha and receive help from him out of his great compassion. The Buddha is now defined in terms not only of his wisdom – his insight into the way things really are – but also crucially in terms of his compassion. Hence the Buddha helps beings in all kinds of different ways, ranging from spiritual ways to also granting even ordinary mundane material benefits.

The 'Three Dimensions of a Buddha'

As Mahāyāna thought on the nature of the Buddha evolved, the doctrinal view eventually developed that there are three aspects or dimensions to a Buddha (Williams 2000: 172–176; 2009: ch. 8):

(1) Dharmakāya: The 'dharma-dimension', what we might call a Buddha's real dimension or aspect. This is the Buddha seen in terms of the way things really are. It is what he (like all of us) really is, and what as an enlightened person he really wants us to understand. In other words it is simply the Truth, the final true nature of things itself, spoken of (if you like, 'personified') as a dimension or aspect of the Buddha himself.

(2) The 'Dimension of Communal Enjoyment': Unlike the Dharmakāya, which is in a way abstract, the 'Dimension of Communal Enjoyment' is the actual magnificent visible appearance of a Buddha in his Pure Land. Here a Buddha sits on his lotus throne teaching the Mahāyāna Doctrine to an assembly consisting (perhaps mainly) of advanced bodhisattvas. It is possible for those who are sufficiently advanced in meditation to visit him there, and receive teachings from him. There are many – indeed infinite – such Buddhas.

(3) The 'Dimension of Magical Transformation': A Buddha magically emanates numerous 'dimensions (or 'aspects', or perhaps 'manifestations') of magical transformation', in whatever form is necessary to help beings on any plane. Thus for the Mahāyāna it is commonly said 'our' Śākyamuni Buddha in history was just a magical emanation from a Buddha on a higher plane, from a 'Dimension of Communal Enjoyment' (i.e. the second Dimension, above).

Bodhisattvas, followers of the Mahāyāna path for the benefit of others, are encouraged themselves to gain miraculous abilities (the various magical powers often thought to accompany developed ability in meditation) in order to help others. Eventually very advanced bodhisattvas came to be given names – like Avalokiteśvara, later referred to as '*the* bodhisattva of compassion', or Mañjuśrī, '*the* bodhisattva of wisdom' – and also take on the status of supramundane helpers. Thus in Mahāyāna we find not only many, indeed infinite, kind and compassionate Buddhas still existing and willing to help, but also great advanced bodhisattvas who similarly can help those who have recourse to them. It is explained that this is possible because these Buddhas and bodhisattvas, by virtue of their achievements, have great 'stocks of merit' – resulting from their vast deeds of virtue over so many lifetimes – and they can transfer their merit to other beings like us. Such Buddhas and bodhisattvas form the central themes of Mahāyāna Buddhist art.

How is a Catholic Christian to Approach Buddhism?

Our starting point here has to be the Vatican II document *NA* (Abbott, ed., 1966: 662: sect. 2):

> Buddhism in its multiple forms acknowledges the radical insufficiency of this shifting world. It teaches a path by which men, in a devout and confident spirit, can either reach a state of absolute freedom [enlightenment] or attain supreme enlightenment [perfect Buddhahood] by their own efforts or by higher assistance . . . The Catholic Church rejects nothing which is true and holy in [Buddhism]. She looks with sincere respect upon those ways of conduct and of life, those rules and teachings which, though differing in many particulars from what she holds and sets forth, nevertheless often reflect a ray of that Truth which enlightens all men.

Nevertheless, in order to avoid possible misunderstandings this should be read alongside the statement in the Declaration *Dominus Iesus* (Congregation 2000: 33; italics original):

> With the coming of the Saviour Jesus Christ, God has willed that the Church founded by him be the instrument for the salvation of *all* humanity (cf. *Acts* 17: 30–31). This truth of faith does not lessen the sincere respect which the Church has for all the religions of the world, but at the same time, it rules out, in a radical way, that mentality of indifferentism characterized by a religious relativism which leads to the belief that "one religion is as good as another". If it is true that followers of other religions can receive divine

grace, it is also certain that *objectively speaking* they are in a gravely deficient situation in comparison with those who, in the Church, have the fullness of the means of salvation.

It seems clear that Buddhism, of all the great world religions, at its best and at the most can be understood in the light of the statement of the Vatican II document *LG* (sect. 16; Abbott, ed.: 35):

> Nor does divine Providence deny the help necessary for salvation to those who, without blame on their part, have not yet arrived at an explicit knowledge of God, but who strive to live a good life, thanks to His grace. Whatever goodness or truth is found among them is looked upon by the Church as a preparation for the gospel. She regards such qualities as given by Him who enlightens all men so that they may finally have life.

NA (sect. 2) exhorts Catholics 'prudently and lovingly, through dialogue and collaboration with the followers of other religions, and in witness of Christian faith and life [to] acknowledge, preserve and promote the spiritual and moral goods found among these men, as well as the values in their society and culture'. And as Pope John Paul II has pointed out (1994: 81), it was the intention of the Fathers of Vatican II that the Church should identify the 'seeds of the Word' (*semina Verbi*) in other religions, for 'the Holy Spirit works effectively even outside the visible structure of the Church'.

There are indeed things in Buddhism that can validly be seen as 'seeds of the Word' or as preparations for the Gospel. So dialogue with Buddhists needs to seek for and appreciate the Christ-inspired truth in the precepts and doctrines of Buddhism. The austerity and beauty of Buddhist moral and spiritual cultivation, Buddhist appreciation of the inadequacies of this passing world, even some Buddhist doctrinal positions (such as the compassionate benevolent and salvific role of Buddhas and bodhisattvas in Mahāyāna) can all be understood and welcomed by Catholic Christians.

One Example of a Fruitful Area of Buddhism for Christian Theological Reflection

I want to draw brief attention here, by way of just one example, to an area of Buddhism where Christians have in the past discerned a particularly interesting foundation for exploration and dialogue. This is the Japanese Mahāyāna Buddhism of Shinran (1173–1262). The theologian Karl Barth referred to it as 'the most adequate and comprehensive and illuminating heathen parallel to Christianity' (1956: 340). It is of especial interest to us because while remaining totally Buddhist, Shinran also gives interesting critical comments on some features of Buddhism. His starting point is the sheer difficulty, perhaps impossibility, of practising the austere Buddhist path of virtue and spiritual growth in the world as it is now, particularly as it is bereft of a Buddha in the world who can directly teach us. But of course there are still Buddhas available in their Pure Lands. Thus it makes sense so to practise Buddhism that in one's next life one will actually be reborn in a Pure Land where, able to study with its resident Buddha, enlightenment can be obtained. In particular, Shinran's 'Pure Land Buddhism' aims for rebirth in the Pure Land of a Buddha known as *Amitābha* ('Infinite Light'). This Buddha, and his Pure Land (*Sukhāvatī* – the 'Happy Place'), are thought to provide particularly suitable conditions for attaining enlightenment.

Important to Shinran is a version of a teaching that originated in India but is known in its East Asian form as the 'Buddha Nature' doctrine. This developed in answer to the question 'What is it about sentient beings that enables them to become, and to remain forever, enlightened Buddhas?' The answer is that 'all sentient beings possess the Buddha Nature'. But what is this Buddha Nature? Eventually it was reasoned that the Buddha Nature must itself be the deepest level of our consciousness. One is able to 'become' enlightened, and enlightenment will never cease, because our Buddha Nature is of the very nature of unchanging radiant enlightenment. Like a sky that is never really obscured by clouds, our Buddha Nature never was really obscured by ignorant delusion. It was always radiant, unchangeably liberated. To 'become' enlightened nothing has to be done, nothing has to be changed. One simply has to be what one always really was.

Shinran combined such a Buddha Nature view of enlightenment – our 'Buddha Nature' within us is unconditioned, pure, absolute, eternally enlightened, beyond all conceptuality – with a rigorously determinist view of human nature. Hence he concluded that nothing we ourselves can do will ever actually lead us to enlightenment. It simply cannot be done. Attempts to follow the Buddhist path as a means of bringing about enlightenment only enmesh one more and more deeply in egotism, in selfishness. We are incapable of doing a non-egotistic act, and thus quite incapable of ever acting like (and hence being) a Buddha. Enlightenment is only possible by truly, completely, *letting-go* of any attempt to bring it about, and relying on the infinite merits of Buddha Amitābha. Meditation, monasticism – all are at best irrelevant and quite possibly egotistic blocks to our salvation. We rely not on our 'own-power' but on the 'other-power' of Amitābha. Really letting-go in this way – not as yet another strategy of own-power, but from truly realizing one cannot do it for oneself – Shinran calls *shinjin*. This is commonly translated as 'faith', but it is faith as an act of complete letting-go, complete entrusting, complete 'self-abandonment'. Such a complete letting-go allows the other-power deep within us to do what it has always been doing, to shine-forth but through us free of our own selfish interference. In other words, the 'other-power', Buddha Amitābha, is itself our Buddha Nature, the deepest always-enlightened level of our own consciousness. But here it is realized that this deepest enlightened level of consciousness is not in any sense *me* or *mine*. It cannot be said to be *one's own* at all. It is quite Other.

For Shinran, when *shinjin* truly occurs one is saved. All the selfish forces that might power rebirth are dropped. Thus at death it is not really true that one is reborn into the Pure Land, there to become enlightened in the presence of Amitābha, although it might be expressed that way for the purposes of effective teaching. The Pure Land is itself really the state of Buddhahood. At death there is enlightenment and no more rebirth for me. But the enlightenment is not really *my concern*. There is only Amitābha, as there always was. It is as simple as that.

And while still living we can only hymn forth our gratitude to Amitābha – who has already saved everyone, if only they are willing to let-go and trust in him – in the *nembutsu*. This is to resort to the Name, the utterance *Namu Amida Butsu* ('Reverence to Amitābha [Amida] Buddha'), often repeated incessantly but not, of course, as a *means* of salvation. There are no means to enlightenment. But we are saved nevertheless. For that we can only be grateful to Amitābha.

A deep awareness of one's own failings and incapacity, absolute trusting confidence not in one's own abilities but in the grace of the Perfect Other represented by the figure of Amitābha Buddha who loves everyone no matter how wicked or incapable they may be, reliance on Amitābha expressed through his Name, the Buddha Nature as the salvific Other deep within each of us, an awareness also of the danger of self-inflation or pride, even egotism, in the traditional Buddhist path of strenuous spiritual striving that is so emphatically dependent upon one's own efforts in order make any progress – all these aspects of Shinran's Buddhism and more have suggested fruitful areas for conversation between Christians and Buddhists not only in doctrinal dialogue but also in exploring together ways of being religious in the modern world.[5]

Christian-Buddhist Monastic Interchange

In recent years there has also been close and valuable interchange between some Christian and Buddhist monasteries. Former abbot Christopher Jamison of Worth Abbey observes (2006: 7) that 'the monastic life of celibacy and prayer is strikingly similar in the Catholic and Buddhist traditions', and he speaks of the warm friendship that exists between the Benedictine monks of Worth and the monks at the English Theravāda Buddhist monastery of Chithurst. He adds nevertheless that while '[w]e have good dialogues . . . we recognise that there are differences as well as similarities between us'. In further dialogue and exploration Buddhist and Christian monks have sometimes stayed in each other's monasteries. In reflecting together on their shared experience as monks in the modern world Buddhists and Christians have come to a far greater appreciation than might have been otherwise of what they have in common and what they can together witness and offer to the world notwithstanding some very deep and significant differences. Some, such as Thomas Merton, have found not only in monasticism but also in Christian contemplation and mysticism a welcome point of contact with Buddhists (see, for example, Merton 1974).

Exploring the Differences

Having said all this, I want nevertheless to go on to focus here on some significant differences between Buddhist approaches and those we consider as Catholics to be true. It is common nowadays to want to stress similarities between Buddhism and Christianity, perhaps to the extent of urging similarities and even identity where they are patently lacking. I concentrate here on differences deliberately, for it was an awareness of fundamental differences and hence the need (in grace) to make a choice and to take responsibility for that choice that brought me after over 20 years as a follower of the Dalai Lama's school of Tibetan Mahāyāna Buddhism to convert to Catholicism. We need to be clear that Buddhism and orthodox Catholic Christianity, while they have many features in common – and for all the wonderful virtues of Buddhism – are also fundamentally different in ways that are not incidental but are absolutely central and crucial to the religions concerned. Reflection on these differences might help both Christians and Buddhists, who have in fact made choices, to be clear about what choices they have actually made.

God

Buddhism is all about the mind, not God. As we have seen, in practising Buddhism one never finds talk of God, there is no role in practising

Buddhism for God, and it is not difficult to find in Buddhist texts attacks on the existence of an omniscient, omnipotent, all-good Creator of the universe (see, for example, the discussion of Śāntideva in Williams 2004: 89–100).

As Buddhist doctrine developed specialized technical questions concerning what does and does not really exist *did* lead sometimes to the affirmation of the real, essential and fundamental existence of nirvāṇa. Further, questions about how it is that something that is produced from a cause can be permanent – will never cease – *did* lead in some circles to the affirmation of nirvāṇa as an 'unconditioned phenomenon'. But nirvāṇa as an 'unconditioned phenomenon' in this sense has absolutely nothing to do with some sort of 'negative path' (*via negativa*) leading to an Ultimate Reality that might be thought of as in fact God in a Buddhist guise. And the idea of nirvāṇa creating the world, for example, is in Buddhism a complete absurdity. Hence it makes no sense really to talk of *gratitude* to nirvāṇa, or our existential dependence on nirvāṇa, and certainly not *worshipping* nirvāṇa, or a *personal loving relationship* with nirvāṇa, or nirvāṇa as our Father. Nirvāṇa is to be realized by each person individually, not worshipped. One speaks of attaining nirvāṇa, not loving nirvāṇa.

The Buddhist Rejection of God, as Our Loving Creator

I want therefore to focus here on God as a *loving* Creator (for more details see Williams 2004). Given that there are things, God is the answer to the question 'Why is there something rather than nothing?' If there are things, then we as Christians argue that there is this fundamental *causal* question to which 'God' is the answer. Buddhism is very interested in causality, and yet this causal question 'Why is there something *at all* (i.e. anything at all, including even the mind itself with all its layers), at *any* time, rather than nothing?' is as far as I can see never really asked, and hence never answered, within Buddhism. Everything is simply the result of its own natural causes – the tree from the seed, the baby from its parents, the mind at this moment from the mind at a previous moment, and so on to infinity. The fact that natural causal processes in Buddhism include moral causation – virtuous causes bring about good (pleasant) results, vicious causes bad (unpleasant) results, in accordance with karma – just is the way it always is and must be. There is no additional reason for it being that way rather than not.

Indeed from the beginning Buddhists have attacked the very notion of a Creator – loving or otherwise – as unnecessary, contradictory and absurd.

In teachings attributed to the Buddha himself, in some of the very earliest of Buddhist texts, there is a mocking attempt to explain the origins of the notion of a creator God. The idea of a Creator springs from an elementary and foolish confusion on the part not only of his worshippers, but also on the part of 'God' himself. Buddhism accepts no first beginning to the process of unenlightened rebirth. But it does accept the Indian notion of 'cosmic cycles', an endless series of cosmic evolution, collapse and devolution. All this occurs due to impersonal causal processes. At the beginning of the current cosmic cycle a being, due entirely to karmic causes relating to previous deluded deeds, was reborn in a sort of heaven. This was Brahmā. He was there all by himself. So he thought to himself that it would be lovely if there were some company. At that very moment other beings, also due to karmic causes, were born around him. He thus inferred that he must have created them solely by wishing that they should be there. They, for their part, assumed that since he was there already, by himself, he must have created them. Thus Brahmā came to be worshipped as God. But actually, of course, there is no creator God. All happened due to impersonal causes, based on previous karma. In another of these early attempts to mock the creator God, a monk travels to visit Brahmā's heaven to ask him a question. Brahmā simply keeps repeating 'I, brother, am Brahmā, Great Brahmā, the Supreme Being, the Unsurpassed, the Chief, the Victor, the Ruler, the Father of all beings who have been or are to be'. The monk, receiving no answer to his specific question, eventually gets quite fed up. Whereupon Brahmā takes him on one side and explains that actually he, Great Brahmā, has not the faintest idea what the answer to the monk's question is. But Brahmā does not want to be seen by his worshippers to be ignorant, since they think he knows everything. Truly, if the monk really wants to know the answer to his question he should return and ask the Buddha. There is certainly no one else who knows it.[6]

But for a Christian who is remotely traditional, who believes in the God of, for example, the Bible and of the Catholic Catechism, God as our loving Creator is essential to our understanding of who God is and what is owed to Him. It is not an incidental extra to Christianity, which we can take or leave depending on our metaphysical tastes. It is what Christianity is all about. Hence Buddhism is radically different from Christianity in ways that really count. A more important difference it would be hard to imagine.

That said, notwithstanding the doctrinal position, if we look at real, lived Buddhism we shall often find Buddhists acting *as if* Buddhas or bodhisattvas are in fact (from a Christian perspective) God. Buddhas are often approached as absolutely supreme loving saviours and protectors on whose benevolence we depend and rely. In Chinese Buddhism confession to the Buddhas for misdeeds committed is traditional and commonplace. As the Jesuit theologian Henri de Lubac puts it '[f]inally, one senses in Buddhism that quivering of the spiritual being in contact with the mysterious and the sacred' (quoted in Grumett 2007: 143). And of course, God – the actual living God of Abraham, Isaac and Jacob, not vague abstract principles, or a deification of the mind itself – God unknown, unrecognized, really *is* present in Buddhism. Admittedly, Buddhists would disagree with this, but that is not the point here. Buddhists are reaching out for God, just as God is reaching out for them. Of course they are, and in Buddhism – even in Buddhist doctrine sometimes – as everywhere else we see His traces and in deeply spiritual Buddhist lives their response. For as Augustine said (*Confessions* 1.1), 'you [God] made us for yourself and our hearts [will] find no peace until they rest in you'.

Rebirth Offers No Hope for the Individual Person

It was while working on a paper called 'Altruism and rebirth' (in Williams 1998) that, for the first time, I think I truly appreciated the significance of the Buddhist claim that the rebirth cannot be said to be the same person as the one who died (see Williams 2002). Indeed I cited influential Buddhist scholars who have argued explicitly that the rebirth is a *different* person to the one that died. And that must be correct, whatever the point about a rebirth being in the same *continuum* as the one who has died. None of this in itself means the Buddhist position is wrong. But what it does mean is that, if the Buddhist position is right, unless we attain a state (such as nirvāṇa) where in some way or another our rebirth will not matter, our death in this life is actually, really, the death of *us*. Death will be the end for us. Traditionally, at least on the day-to-day level, Buddhists tend to miss appreciating this fact through using language such as '*my* rebirth', and 'concern for *one's* future lives'. But actually any rebirth (say, as a cockroach in South America) would simply not be *oneself*, that is, this person, the person one currently is, at all. The person I am, me, will have quite simply ceased to exist.

I began to see that if Buddhism were correct then unless I attained enlightenment or something like it is this life *I – this* person, the person *I* am – would have no hope. Clearly I was not going to attain enlightenment in this life, and most Buddhists would say exactly the same thing about themselves too. It takes a very, very long time to achieve enlightenment and across the Buddhist world the real concern is with attaining a favourable rebirth after death. So I (and all my friends and family) have in themselves no hope. Not only that. Actually from a Buddhist perspective in the scale of infinite time the significance of each of us as such, as the actual person we are, converges on nothing. Even if a Buddhist might think I was unduly preoccupied with myself and my own survival in all of this, nevertheless for me Buddhism was literally *hope-less*.

Rebirth is Incompatible with Catholic Orthodoxy

Reincarnation (rebirth) was well known in ancient Greece and Rome, and has never been part of Christian orthodoxy. Indeed it is at variance with some traditionally important themes of Christian life and practice. It could not be compatible, for example, with the resurrection of the body. For clearly with rebirth being the case, which of our many bodies would be resurrected at the future time when Christ appears again and there is a 'new heaven and a new earth' (Rev. 21.3)? The Buddhist notion of rebirth not only is incompatible with personal identity across lifetimes, it is incompatible with the infinite preciousness we hold as Christians for *each* and *every* individual person, created by God with an individual purpose. Rebirth is incompatible with the loving creator God revealed to us as our Father by Our Lord Himself. Rebirth is also incompatible with the significance of our actual human bodies in making us the persons we are. These are all variations on a theme, and that theme springs also from the Buddhist rejection of an all-good and loving creator God. If there is no Creator then we cannot affirm that the world, as His creation, is fundamentally *good*. If the world is not as such good, then we as the individual persons we are cannot be fundamentally good, and all the aspects that go to make us up as the individual persons we are – including, of course, our bodies and our relationships – are not fundamentally good either. Effectively, no matter how much someone may love us, or we may love them, in the balance of infinite time as the individual unenlightened and hence suffering persons that we are, we are insignificant and disposable things. Thinking otherwise is simply not 'seeing things the way they really are'.

Suffering

Buddhism, of course, starts from suffering and the need to overcome it. Christians traditionally have not thought that suffering is completely incompatible with creation by an all-good and all-powerful God. Christianity is not about the mind. It is *all* about God and His dealings in history with His creation. As it relates to each one of us, Christianity is all about our relationships with God and hence His creation, and it is all about bringing our lives into harmony with God's intentions and wishes for us. In the light of this, the issue of suffering is not *as such* the problem. It is perfectly possible that in the fallen world in which we now live individual cases of suffering may be God's intention, and thus *in those contexts and under those circumstances* suffering may be something if not to be welcomed nevertheless that should be accepted – even affirmed as the right thing – rather than axiomatically wrong, to be avoided or overcome.

Suffering in Buddhism (as in Gnosticism) is a sign of imperfection

For the Buddhist a person suffers precisely because he or she is not enlightened. It makes no sense to talk about fully enlightened people, those who have attained the ultimate final goal, really actually suffering. Suffering is to that extent a sign of imperfection. More than that, suffering is (very often, perhaps always) a direct result through karma of vicious deeds in the past. The further one advances on the Buddhist path the less one does vicious deeds, and correspondingly eventually the less one suffers.[7] There is a direct similarity here not with orthodox Christianity but rather with some of the early Christian heresies such as those classed under Gnosticism. As Basilides, a second-century Gnostic, put it the man who is absolutely sinless, without even the desire to sin, could never suffer. Thus for Gnostics Jesus Christ as such simply could not have suffered, and various strategies were adopted to explain what happened at the crucifixion such that either it was not the sinless Jesus who was crucified but rather someone else, or that the crucifixion did not really involve Jesus suffering but merely appearing to do so. For Buddhists too, in the modern world, wishing to respond to the figure of Jesus, there is a major problem of how to explain the orthodox Christian view that He *actually suffered*. Christian interest in that suffering – shown in the use of the crucifix – is to Buddhists a source of fascinated incomprehension.

A Buddhist approach to suffering is incompatible with the orthodox Christian view of the sufferings of Jesus, and their redemptive role

Jesus for a Buddhist was not, of course, God Incarnate. He must have been simply a good man at the most. But however one looks at it, if He really suffered He must also have been far from enlightened. For a Mainstream Buddhist position all the sufferings of Christ at the crucifixion would have resulted naturally and quasi-automatically from vicious former acts ('due to karma'). There is a Mahāyāna approach that could see Him either as a bodhisattva working His way towards Buddhahood, or an emanation from either a 'celestial bodhisattva' (like Avalokiteśvara, the bodhisattva of compassion), or from a Buddha, on the model of the 'Dimension of Magical Transformation'. The problem with these strategies, from a Christian point of view, is that quite apart from the denial of Christ's divinity each would be radically unsatisfactory to Christian orthodoxy. If Jesus Christ was a bodhisattva working towards Buddhahood, His suffering, due to karma, entails that He must have been very much a beginner. He was far indeed from the exalted state of a Buddha. But if He really was an emanation, from either a bodhisattva or a Buddha, He was simply a magical creation, a beneficial 'conjuring trick'. He did not suffer, of course, but simply because He was presumably incapable of any real feelings or genuine emotions at all. Jesus did not suffer simply because He was not a fully embodied human being. This position is indeed identical to one well-known Gnostic strategy, the early Church heresy known as *docetism* ('appearance-ism').

The inability of Buddhism to cope with the suffering of Jesus, together with its similarity in this respect to certain well-known Gnostic approaches deemed quite clearly heretical by the early Church, suggest that Buddhism and orthodox Christianity as it was from the very beginning are really radically at variance in their understanding and treatment of suffering. For orthodox Christianity Christ suffered. A Buddha, finally and *qua* Buddha, does not.[8] Jesus Christ's suffering is central to His salvific activity. We might say that it so turned out Christ was effective as a saviour *inasmuch* as He suffered. A bodhisattva can experience suffering, for even bodhisattvas have to begin somewhere and someone might have fairly recently started out on their bodhisattva path to Buddhahood. But a bodhisattva who truly suffers is still a beginner without the great abilities to benefit others of advanced bodhisattvas. Therefore the bodhisattva suffers inasmuch as he or she is as such *ineffective* as a bodhisattva.

Is suffering always bad? A Christian response

The wider issue of the theology of suffering in Christianity is far too big a topic for the present context. I refer those who are interested to Pope John Paul II's 1984 apostolic letter *Salvifici Doloris*. Particularly important, though, is the way in which *Salvifici Doloris* (drawing on the Suffering

Servant passages in *Isaiah*) brings out the many central positive features of suffering in Christianity. Pope John Paul is even prepared to refer to it as 'good': '[S]uffering . . . has a special value in the eyes of the Church. It is something good, before which the Church bows down in reverence with all the depth of her faith in the Redemption' (sect. 24). In fact, 'each man, in his suffering, can also become a sharer in the redemptive suffering of Christ' (sect. 19). And drawing on the theology of St Paul (e.g. Col. 1: 24) Pope John Paul speaks of suffering as 'a vocation':

> Christ *did not conceal* from his listeners *the need for suffering* . . . These persecutions and tribulations will also be, as it were, a *particular proof* of likeness to Christ and union with him . . . Christ has overcome the world definitively by his Resurrection. Yet, because of the relationship between the Resurrection and his Passion and death, he has at the same time overcome the world by his suffering . . . Down through the centuries and generations it has been seen that *in suffering there is concealed* a particular *power that draws a person interiorly close to Christ*, a special grace . . . A result of such a conversion is not only that the individual discovers the salvific meaning of suffering but above all that he becomes a completely new person. He discovers a new dimension, as it were, of *his entire life and vocation*. (sect. 26; italics original)

Is the goal of Christianity absence of suffering?

In suffering, anyone (and not just a Christian) can associate themselves with Christ's act of redemption. It is by no means the case that suffering is axiomatically always to be to be turned away from. But, it may be objected, surely the *goals* of Buddhism and Christianity are the same inasmuch as they are themselves associated with the final overthrow of all suffering?

I am not sure that is obviously the case. From a Christian point of view there is a need to distinguish between the state of the Saints – including their post-mortem state – in the current situation of the Church still embattled, and the 'final scene of heavenly glory'. Thomas G. Weinandy argues persuasively that under the current state of the Church Christ, as its Head, must continue in a way to suffer, as do all the Saints: 'While Jesus is gloriously risen, and thus beyond sin and death and so evil, yet as head of his body, which is still suffering under the constraints of sin, evil, and death, he too, as the head, is still, in some real sense, suffering' (2000: 252). Moreover, Weinandy points out, through the Communion of Saints, the Saints too 'in solidarity with the 'earthly' body . . . indeed continue to suffer in union with Christ their head' (2000: 256, n. 26). Thus we might say that in 'attaining Heaven' after death, Catholic Christians do not consider that they absolutely go beyond all suffering. Christianity is not about happiness. It is about holiness.

The vulnerability of love and the possibility of suffering

But what of the 'final scene of heavenly glory' mentioned, for example, in Revelation 21.3–5? That certainly looks like a state beyond all suffering. Isn't it then finally the same as the goal of Buddhism? I think not. I want to draw here on something that was said by Pope Benedict XVI, when still Joseph Cardinal Ratzinger, in the final pages of his book *Salt of the Earth*:

> Indeed, love means being dependent on something that perhaps can be taken away from me, and it therefore introduces a huge risk of suffering into my life. Hence the express or tacit refusal: Before having constantly to bear this risk, before seeing my self-determination limited, before coming to depend on something I can't control so that I can suddenly plunge into nothingness, I would rather not have love. Whereas the decision that comes from Christ is another: Yes to love, for it alone, precisely with the risk of suffering and the risk of losing oneself, brings man to himself and makes him what he should be. I think that is really the true drama of history. In the many opposing fronts it can ultimately be reduced to this formula: Yes or no to love. (Ratzinger 1997: 282–283)

What Ratzinger is saying here is that love necessarily entails risks, and hence love *necessarily* entails the chance of suffering. When God, who is Love, created mankind He took risks. God Himself did not sidestep risks. And God Himself suffered, as Second Person of the Trinity, not of course *qua* impassible God as such, in His divine nature, but inasmuch as the human and divine natures were united in the person Jesus Christ who was God Incarnate and who certainly underwent suffering. But if love necessarily entails taking risks, and risks necessarily entail the complete and open possibility of suffering then a perfect community of love would be a community where each is utterly open to each other and hence utterly exposed to risk, utterly vulnerable, utterly in the hands of everyone else, and hence supremely capable of suffering. That, perhaps – I am only speculating here – may be the final scene of heavenly glory, where 'God . . . will wipe away all tears from their eyes'. This is not a world with no possibility of suffering. It is a world with (in a way) *every possibility* of suffering, since it is a world of complete trust and love, a world of complete vulnerability to each other. But it will through the grace of God be a world with no *actuality* of suffering. For in that world of perfect love vulnerable trust, with those who inhabit that world, will never be betrayed.

But the enlightened person in Buddhism, finally – in their final state, their very final achievement as enlightened persons – *by definition* simply cannot suffer. If Pope Benedict is right, it follows that the enlightened person in Buddhism by definition, necessarily, finally simply cannot really love. Love is always open to the possibility of suffering. Where suffering is actually impossible there can be no love. Finally, an enlightened person like a Buddha risks nothing in helping others. Inasmuch as he has achieved the goal of Buddhism he simply cannot, by definition, suffer. But if a Buddha cannot suffer then he is simply incapable of making himself vulnerable and hence taking risks in the way that necessarily must accompany true love.

Is the final goal of Christianity the same as that of Buddhism?

I am suggesting that in making his or her goal the final cessation of all suffering, a Buddhist (whether he or she realizes it or not) also has to aim for the final cessation of love. This is because the vulnerability of love is too open to suffering for compatibility with Buddhist enlightenment, whether it be simple nirvāṇa or the state of a Buddha. I want to argue that the final goals of Buddhism and Christianity here are therefore utterly different. Even where the final goals involve no suffering – as in the final Buddhist enlightenment and the final state of heavenly glory in the 'new heaven and new earth' – the differences could not be more marked. On the one hand no suffering necessarily entails no love. The enlightened person is, in terms of taking risks *for himself*, invulnerable, and hence *in that respect* wrapped up in himself. But total vulnerability, absolute openness to others, makes suffering completely possible for the Christian in a way in which for the enlightened Buddhist it is a logical impossibility. In the final heavenly state, suffering is a contingent – not a logical – impossibility. With genuine lovers, in the presence of holiness tested in the crucible of Sainthood, abusing the vulnerability of others does not happen.

The communal nature of the Christian goal

And note that the final scene of glory in God's restored Kingdom on earth is just that – a *community* of lovers. It is not a state of mind, defined in terms of freedom from greed, hatred and delusion. It is not simply some sort of eternal mystical experience either. An eternal mystical experience, which could easily be a state of our own disembodied minds, would not require the 'new heavens and a new earth' that we are promised God will bring for those that love Him. Here we meet another absolutely central difference of Buddhism from Christianity. Christianity is not about the mind, but is about God. Consider the following 'thought experiment': Imagine that it turned out to be true that there existed only one thing – one's own mind (in philosophy this view is called *solipsism*). It is not important whether any Buddhist tradition actually holds this perspective, although there are some that do come quite close to it. Either way, if solipsism were true then in that world, a world of just one's own mind, one could still obtain the goal of Buddhism. This is because Buddhism is all about the mind and its transformation, so providing one's own mind exists it could in principle be transformed in the appropriate way. But if solipsism turned out to be true, the goal of Christianity would be quite impossible and Christianity would be completely false. With solipsism there could not be a loving relationship with God and His creation in a community of love, a community precisely of the new Israel in a newly recreated world, with a new heaven and a new earth, in which we will all be present to each other in the vulnerability of love.

And this newly recreated, redeemed, world is one that Our Lord instituted in His resurrection. It is already in formation. As Christians we are called to take part now in the work for justice and righteousness that will bring about the full presence, the full and final incarnation, of God's eternal Kingdom on earth. Just as our goal is not simply to do with the mind, so our actions here and now are not simply to do with the mind either. It should be clear now why this is the case. Christian involvement with the world in the cause of righteousness stems from a Christian belief in God and the embodied goodness of His Creation, together with a belief that the final goal will involve this very embodied Creation. It is a final goal already inaugurated by God Himself in the resurrection of His Son, a goal that we Christians are required to cooperate with to its conclusion. And that cooperation with God – who has no need of our help but who welcomes it for our own sakes – may well entail our suffering too just as God in Jesus Christ suffered and triumphed over suffering (see Col. 1.24). In a way, if Buddhism is all to do with the mind then Christianity is all about the body. Christian involvement with the world in the cause of righteousness springs naturally from the very essence of Christianity, from all those ways in which we have seen Christianity is radically at variance with Buddhism.[9]

On Meditation

Christians sometimes think of taking up Buddhist meditation. By this they usually mean calming meditation. Calming meditation leads relatively quickly to calm, relaxation, and much improved concentration. It is reasonable to suggest that these are qualities we could all benefit from. They would be of obvious value, therefore, to Christians too.

Calming meditation, and Christian religious concerns

This seems to me to be indisputable. Therein, in a way, lies the problem. Yes, being calm, relaxed and having improved concentration are valuable. What they are not in themselves is *religiously* valuable. So the first problem with Christians taking up Buddhist meditation practices is that inasmuch as the practices teach useful techniques applicable to just about everyone they may come to substitute for what religiously a Christian should be doing which is nurturing a deep and rich prayer life – prayer directed to the living God, a God who meets us not when we are cross-legged but rather when we are one way or another on our knees or flat on our faces in fear, trembling and adoration – and engaging in God's work of ushering in the Kingdom of justice and righteousness. There is nothing wrong with learning to relax. But learning to relax bears as much relationship to prayer as having a glass of wine after a hard day's work bears to taking communion in the Holy Mass.

There is of course a wonderful *Christian* tradition of advice for prayerful enrichment of the spiritual life, from the early Church onwards. It seems to me no Catholic should be contemplating taking up Buddhist meditation if they have not lived and prayed their way through, for example, Thomas à Kempis's *Imitation of Christ* and St Francis de Sales' *Introduction to a Devout Life*, to mention just a couple of my own favourites. Which Catholic has perfected the practice of *Lectio Divina*, the Rosary, Stations of the Cross, saying the Divine Office, daily Mass attendance, or even praying using the Jesus Prayer that derives from Eastern Orthodoxy and the Church Fathers? Of course, there is also a Christian tradition of deep, silent, wordless, meditation. But it is an *advanced* stage, infused with grace, and is precisely a Christian meditation tradition that can only be developed within a rich and specifically Christian liturgical, doctrinal and pedagogical context (see the Catechism on contemplative prayer, CCC paras 2709–2719). Why should a Christian *need* to think of practising Buddhist meditation?

Some possible dangers in Christians adopting Buddhist meditation practices

And there is a second problem that may occur with Christians taking up Buddhist meditation. This is not inevitable, but in my experience it is a real danger and to avoid it requires some care. As a person begins to appreciate 'Buddhist' calming meditation they may perhaps start to adopt other presuppositions or tenets of so-called eastern religions found expressed or assumed in 'meditation circles', alongside and eventually in substitution for Christian truth. We sometimes find, for example, the suggestion that meditators discover that all religions lead to the same ineffable goal. Dogmatic differences are simply words, and there is an Absolute accessible in mystical meditative experience that is radically beyond all words and at variance with them. Really, religion, *all* religions, are just so many means for accessing a particular nonconceptual *experience* although it is suggested that Buddhism (or perhaps some forms of Buddhism, such as Zen) offers particularly pure and potent ways of bringing that experience about. Hence, of course, all expressed truth – and thus the teachings of the Church – are finally false. The meditator knows in his or her own personal experience the truth, effectively a private truth that stands over and against the teachings of the Church. Further, this can lead to the claim that since the Absolute is beyond all words, Jesus Christ cannot have been God (except in the sense that we are all 'God', since 'God' is just another name for the truth discovered in our own inner experience). Jesus does not reveal God to us in any definitive and unique way. He was just a good man, one of many such good men. There will be many more, and indeed we can all realize the 'Christ Nature' – modelled, perhaps, on the Buddha Nature spoken of in Buddhism – within us. The founder of my meditation school, or my guru, or maybe I myself – we are all finally, really, equal to Jesus Himself.[10]

But in reality God is not *my experience*. God is not our own enlightened minds, or our own subjective depths. That is idolatry, replacing God with a creature. God is absolutely objective, and *qua* God Wholly Other than us, as 'the reason why there is something rather than nothing'. And of course if someone were really to meet God, the *Living God*, in meditation such a person would not remain seated on a meditation cushion. While 'sitting quietly in the presence of the Lord' clearly is an appropriate form of Christian prayer (contemplative prayer), the meditator needs careful attention in fact not to substitute what is actually a passive awareness of him- or herself for a real meeting with God. Benedictine Fr Gabriel Bunge, himself a hermit since 1980, suggests here a stern note of warning (2002: 194):

> Anyone who devotes himself to 'practices' and 'methods' that are not home-grown in the soil of his own faith will imperceptibly be led toward that 'faith' which developed these practices as a genuine expression of itself. Today plenty of people are going through this painful experience, even though many do not dare admit even to themselves that they have strayed from the path.

Someone can come to *prefer* Buddhist meditation to prayer. Hence instead of nurturing one's relationship with God and His creation a person simply nurtures their relationship with themselves. As the Congregation for the Doctrine of the Faith, under Joseph Cardinal Ratzinger, put it (1990: 4–5):

> Christian prayer is always determined by the structure of the Christian faith, in which the very truth of God and creatures shines forth. For this reason it is defined, properly speaking, as a personal, intimate and profound dialogue between man and God. It expresses therefore the communion of redeemed creatures with the intimate life of the Persons of the Trinity. This communion, based on Baptism and the Eucharist, source and summit of the life of the Church, implies an attitude of conversion, a flight from 'self' to the 'You' of God. Thus Christian prayer is at the same time always authentically personal and communitarian. It flees from impersonal techniques or from concentrating on oneself, which can create a kind of rut, imprisoning the person praying in spiritual privatism which is incapable of a free openness to the transcendental God.

The Congregation (1990: 23) also notes that 'genuine prayer as the great spiritual masters teach, stirs up in the person who prays an ardent charity which moves him to collaborate in the mission of the Church and to serve his brothers for the greater glory of God.' None of this needs Buddhist meditation, and Buddhist meditation might detract from it. Actually '[t]he prayer of Jesus has been entrusted to the Church . . . This is why when a Christian prays, even if he is alone, his prayer is in fact always within the framework of the 'Communion of Saints' in which and with which he prays, whether in a public and liturgical way or in a private manner' (Congregation 1990: 8).

St Francis de Sales shows just how very different Christianity is from Buddhism in all of this when he urges that finally private practices like meditation are relatively unimportant compared with the public, communal, *actual* meeting with God in, for example, the Mass (1956: 86):

> Indeed, to speak once for all, there is always more benefit and comfort to be derived from the public offices of the Church than from private devotions. God has ordained that communion of prayers should always have preference to every kind of private prayer.

We cannot storm heaven with our meditations. God comes to us freely, in grace. And if we want really to see God we see Him in or through the publicly and sacramentally available figure of Jesus Christ. As de Sales puts it (1956: 54–55):

> By making [our Lord] often the subject of your meditation, your whole soul will be filled with Him. You will learn His ways and frame your actions according to His model. He is 'the light of the world'. It is therefore, in Him and by Him and for Him that we must be instructed and enlightened . . . [B]y keeping close to our Saviour, by meditation and observing His words, actions, and affections, by the help of His grace, we shall learn to speak, to act, and to will like Him.

Christian meditation is for coming closer to Christ, not in strange 'enlightenment' states, or 'mystical' experiences but in our acts, in increasingly Christlike behaviour, so that we may eventually be fitting inhabitants of His Kingdom.

Christian Buddhists?

There are those who think it is possible to be both a Christian and a Buddhist at the same time. I have even met some Christian-Buddhists (or Buddhist-Christians). This short introduction to some of the themes should indicate a number of areas where Christianity would need considerable reinterpretation if it were ever to be truly compatible with Buddhism as Buddhism has existed in doctrine, practice and history. For those who hold in an orthodox way to the faith of the Catholic Church such a reinterpretation of Christianity is, it seems to me, impossible. Hence choices are necessary.

I have described elsewhere in detail the reasons why I converted to Roman Catholicism (Williams 2002). That book has a threefold structure: (1) I came to believe in God; (2) I came to believe in the unique actual historical event of the resurrection, which led me to Jesus Christ; and (3) I came to the Catholic Church as the Church led by the Holy Spirit and intended by Our Lord. In coming to believe in God, the real living personal God of Christian orthodoxy, He gave me hope. This is hope not for an endless abstract series of reincarnations, a series that would make *me* simply nothing. This is hope for me and in God's grace hope for all those I know and love. God exists, and we shall never be thrown away. And all the little things of day-to-day life are significant in a way that they never were in the infinite time and space of Buddhism. As the Jesuit poet Gerard Manley Hopkins put it, 'The world is charged with the grandeur of God'. It is a grandeur that brings forth deep gratitude. The world is now important, and the world as God's world is fundamentally good and will not ever be abandoned by Him. It has been rescued and redeemed, and it will be renewed. Indeed this is already happening. In the incarnation He came to rescue me from my own inability to make any spiritual progress by myself. He made promises to *me*, promises that I trust, and in the resurrection showed that He is Lord even over the impermanence, death and suffering that obsesses Buddhists so much. And in coming into the Catholic Church I really came Home and found all and more that I had been looking for so far from home in Buddhism. That was over ten years ago now, and I have never ever regretted the choice I then made.

Notes

1 This chapter is a shortened and considerably revised version of my booklet *Buddhism from a Catholic Perspective*, published in 2006 by The Catholic Truth Society, London. I am grateful to Fergal Martin and the CTS for permission to reuse this material.
2 Where a source used is in the Pali language, I shall *normally* use the Pali (P) term, where it is in Sanskrit, the Sanskrit (S). The 'default' position is Sanskrit.
3 Some books give this as 'desire'. That is a mistranslation. Even the Buddhas have *desire*. What they lack is *craving* (Williams 2000: 44).
4 *Hīna* really does mean 'inferior', and Mahāyāna use of it is derogatory.
5 See not only the Protestant Barth but notably the Catholic Henri de Lubac, who devoted a whole book (de Lubac 1955; cf. Grumett 2007: ch. 7) to the subject of Pure Land Buddhism.
6 See the *Brahmajāla* and the *Kevaddha Suttas* of the Pali Canon, both cited and discussed in Williams 2004: 99–100.
7 Hence even though in Mahāyāna those who have taken the bodhisattva vow to become perfect Buddhas might be thought positively to opt for future rebirths in order to attain their distant goal, still in aiming for the higher achievement as they advance along it their ability to suffer *decreases* progressively.
8 There is evidence from very early Buddhist sources that Śākyamuni Buddha *did* feel pain, although even there he was not held to *suffer* at all.
9 Note, however, that in the modern world some Buddhists, at least partially in competition with Christianity and influenced by it, have developed their own forms of Buddhist social, economic and political engagement often referred to as 'engaged Buddhism'.
10 For further examples, and discussion, see Congregation 1990: 10ff.

References

Abbott, Walter M., SJ (ed.) (1966), *The Documents of Vatican II*, London and Dublin: Geoffrey Chapman.
Barth, K. (1956), *Church Dogmatics*, 1, 2, trans. G. T. Thomson and Harold Knight, Edinburgh: T&T Clark.

Bunge, Gabriel, O. S. B. (2002), *Earthen Vessels: The Practice of Personal Prayer According to the Patristic Tradition*, trans. Michael J. Miller, San Francisco: Ignatius Press.

Congregation for the Doctrine of the Faith (1990), *Christian Meditation: Letter to the Bishops of the Catholic Church on Some Aspects of Christian Meditation*, London: Catholic Truth Society.

Congregation for the Doctrine of the Faith (2000), *Declaration 'Dominus Iesus': On the Unicity and Salvific Universality of Jesus Christ and the Church*, Vatican City: Libreria Editrice Vaticana.

De Lubac, H. (1955), *Aspects du bouddhisme 2: Amida*, Paris: Seuil.

Grumett, D. (2007), *De Lubac: A Guide for the Perplexed*, London: T&T Clark.

Holy See (1994), *Catechism of the Catholic Church*, London: Geoffrey Chapman.

Jamison, Abbot Christopher (2006), *Finding Sanctuary: Monastic Steps for Everyday Life*, London: Weidenfeld & Nicholson.

John Paul II, Pope (1984), *Apostolic Letter 'Salvifici Doloris' of the Supreme Pontiff John Paul II to the Bishops, to the Priests, to the Religious Families and to the Faithful of the Catholic Church on the Christian Meaning of Human Suffering*, available online at http://www.vatican.va/holy_father/john_paul_ii/apost_letters/documents/hf_jp-ii_apl_11021984_salvifici-doloris_en.html (6 July 2010).

John Paul II, Pope (1994), *Crossing the Threshold of Hope*, trans. J. and M. McPhee, London: Jonathan Cape.

Merton, T. (1974), *The Asian Journal of Thomas Merton*, London: Sheldon Press.

Ratzinger, Joseph Cardinal (1997), *Salt of the Earth: Christianity and the Catholic Church at the End of the Millennium*. An interview with Peter Seewald, trans. Adrian Walker, San Francisco: Ignatius Press.

Sales, St Francis de (1956), *Introduction to the Devout Life*, trans. and ed. John K. Ryan, London, New York and Toronto: Longmans, Green and Co.

Weinandy, Thomas G., OFM, Cap. (2000), *Does God Suffer?*, Edinburgh: T&T Clark.

Williams, Paul (1998), *Altruism and Reality: Studies in the Philosophy of the Bodhicaryāvatāra*, Richmond: Curzon.

Williams, Paul (2002), *The Unexpected Way*, Edinburgh and New York: T&T Clark/Continuum.

Williams, Paul (2004), 'Aquinas meets the Buddhists: Prolegomenon to an authentically Thomas-ist basis for dialogue', in Jim Fodor and Frederick Christian Bauerschmidt (eds), *Aquinas in Dialogue: Thomas for the Twenty-First Century*, Oxford, Malden, MA, and Carlton, Victoria: Blackwell Publishing, 87–117.

Williams, Paul (2009), *Mahāyāna Buddhism: The Doctrinal Foundations*, 2nd ed., London and New York: Routledge.

Williams, Paul, with Tribe, A. (2000), *Buddhist Thought: A Complete Introduction to the Indian Tradition*, London and New York: Routledge.

Further Reading on Buddhism

Bechert, H., and R. F. Gombich (ed.) (1984), *The World of Buddhism: Buddhist Monks and Nuns in Society and Culture*, London: Thames and Hudson.

Carrithers, Michael (1983), *The Buddha*, Oxford: Oxford University Press.
Gethin, R. (1998), *The Foundations of Buddhism*, Oxford and New York: Oxford University Press.
Gethin, R. (2008), *Sayings of the Buddha*, Oxford and New York: Oxford University Press.
Keown, Damien (1997), *Buddhism: A Very Short Introduction*, Oxford: Oxford University Press.
Rahula, Walpola (1967), *What the Buddha Taught*, London: Gordon Fraser. Recently reprinted by Oneworld Publishing.

CHAPTER 6

CATHOLICISM AND THE NEW AGE MOVEMENT

Stratford Caldecott

Introduction

The New Age movement is spoken of less today than, say, 20 years ago, but that is only because the ideas and practices of the movement have seeped into the mainstream and have become commonplace. Surveys of the population in 1990 showed that around one in three people in Britain believed in reincarnation (up from 18 per cent in 1968). The proportion was even higher among Catholics![1] The European Values Survey results for 2010 will show whether that proportion has risen or fallen in the subsequent decade. But the enormous success of Dan Brown's *The Da Vinci Code* and *The Lost Symbol*, which are based partly on New Age ideas, the recent popularity of books predicting the end of the world in 2012 based on New Age interpretations of the Mayan calendar, not to mention increasing numbers of television dramas and films about the occult, show that the movement is far from over, and that its influence on popular culture continues to grow.[2]

In fact the flirtation of Catholics with the New Age is one aspect of a wider cultural phenomenon. The Church is still trying to understand and respond to the cultural crisis that engulfed her after the 1960s. One important element in that crisis was the widespread rejection of the Church's authority in matters of sexual morality after the publication of *Humanae Vitae* by Pope Paul VI in 1968. Another aspect concerned the liturgy. An attempt to simplify and make more accessible the formal liturgy of the Church and an increased emphasis on community-building led to the virtual elimination in many parishes of a sense of mystery and wonder from the Mass. Though the intentions of the reformers were good, decreased attention to the mystical or transcendent dimension of the liturgy seems to have rendered Catholicism less attractive not only to the old, who were often deeply attached to the former style of liturgy, but also to many of the young for whom the revisions had been designed. This contributed to an exodus from the churches, in the direction either of secular hedonism or a vaguely defined 'spirituality'.

An important document titled *Jesus Christ the Bearer of the Water of Life: A Christian Reflection on the 'New Age'*, published by the Pontifical Councils for Culture and for Inter-Religious Dialogue at the Vatican in

2003, points out that the New Age movement is far from 'new'. Nor is it a 'religious movement' in any very coherent sense. It is, rather, an eclectic mix of influences and ideas from Asia, from pagan religions and ancient Gnosticism (see below). The only new elements come from a particular modern spin that is placed on these ideas. The New Age draws on Darwinian evolution, depth psychology, quantum mechanics, feminism and ecology to construct a spirituality that suits our own historical period. Disillusionment with political institutions and even with conventional allopathic medicine contributes to its appeal. And, as the document admits, Christian communities themselves are largely to blame, for paying inadequate attention to the 'spiritual dimension and its integration with the whole of life . . . the link between human beings and the rest of creation, the desire for personal and social transformation' and so forth (Foreword to the document). 'People feel the Christian religion no longer offers them – or perhaps never gave them – something they really need' (sect. 1.5).

The document therefore tries to be fair. 'The existence and fervour of *New Age* thinking and practice', it writes, 'bear witness to the unquenchable longing of the human spirit for transcendence and religious meaning, which is not only a contemporary cultural phenomenon, but was evident in the ancient world, both Christian and pagan' (1.3). Yet immediately it goes on to add that the results of this fervour are almost always at loggerheads with orthodox Christianity ('a new way of practising Gnosticism'), and have seriously undermined authentic Christian spirituality by their influence within retreat houses and religious communities – the Enneagram (a system of analysis based on nine personality types, formulated most recently by Oscar Ichazo in the 1960s) is singled out for mention in this connection (1.4).

While the New Age seeks the transformation of the self, it often denies the transcendence of God, which alone could make a real transformation possible for human beings. Along with the transcendence of God goes the 'otherness' of religion, the fact that it addresses us from beyond ourselves and can tell us things we do not know, and may not want to know. The Vatican document contrasts the appeal of Aquarius the Water Carrier with the appeal of the One who offers us the 'water of life'. 'If the Church is not to be accused of being deaf to people's longings, her members need to do two things: to root themselves ever more firmly in the fundamentals of their faith, and to understand the often-silent cry in people's hearts, which leads them elsewhere if they are not satisfied by the Church. There is also a call in all of this to come closer to Jesus Christ and to be ready to follow Him, since He is the real way to happiness, the truth about God and the fullness of life for every man and woman who is prepared to respond to his love' (1.5).

The term 'New Age' is more frequently used by those outside the movement – sociologists or church-going Christians – than those within it, for reasons that will be apparent as we go along. Nevertheless, the term is a convenient one if used with caution. As a blanket description of the search for alternatives to orthodox Christianity, it expresses the legitimate frustration many feel in the face of materialism, individualism and reductionism in our post-Christian society, but also with the distortions of Christianity itself – including fideism, moralism and fundamentalism.[3] While relativism (the idea that no truth is absolute) might seem to be a typical New Age assumption, many New Agers nevertheless cling to the idea of 'secret teachings' that offer certainties beyond the reach of ordinary religion and science. The challenge for Catholics is to rediscover and represent the authentic theological and moral vision of Christianity in a way that addresses, as far as may be possible, these legitimate concerns.

The present chapter attempts to study and understand the appeal of the New Age, and then to discern the elements of truth that may attract Catholics to it, comparing these where possible with the mystical and spiritual teachings of the Catholic tradition itself.

What is the New Age?

In order to understand the modern New Age movement in relation to Christianity, we have to start at the beginning. Christianity is a religion founded by a man who was born without a human father, who was crucified by the Romans and came back to life. He came back not just to life of the old sort, but a radically *new kind of existence* that is no longer subject to illness or death, and in which the body is so completely spiritualized that it can appear and disappear where it chooses. Furthermore this new state of existence is offered to all who place their love and trust in the same man, submitting themselves as he did to the will of his heavenly Father.

Now that is quite a lot to believe. Add to it the claim that Jesus sent his Holy Spirit to protect the Church of his followers from ever falling into serious doctrinal error (no matter how sinful its leaders happened to be at any given time), and the claim that in order to seal his new covenant, Jesus gave his members his own resurrected body and blood to eat and drink in the Eucharist, and you can see why Christianity seemed 'to the Jews an obstacle they cannot get over, to the pagans madness' (1 Cor. 1.23).

The Gnostic Legacy

By contrast with this, the various movements grouped together under the heading of 'Gnosticism' taught something that appealed more readily both to reason and to imagination: that is, salvation through knowledge (*gnosis* in Greek). The Gnostic movements arose in the Middle East in the few centuries before Christ and flourished around the whole Eastern Mediterranean region during the few centuries after. They were condemned both by early Christian theologians of the second century such as St Justin Martyr and Irenaeus, and by neo-Platonists such as Plotinus.

As in the case of today's 'New Age', the label 'Gnostic' was more useful to the critics than the proponents of the movement. (Something similar could be said of the label 'Modernist' at the end of the nineteenth century.) The term *gnosis* was used by Clement of Alexandria and other early Church Fathers to refer to the direct or spiritual knowledge of God that comes through faith – Jesus Christ being the 'knowledge', the 'Logos' or Word, of the Father – but the Gnostics emphasized knowledge as *opposed* to faith, and rejected the authority of the Church. The Gnostics regarded the material world as the product of a fall or emanation from the deity (in some versions this was the fault of a female spiritual entity known as Sophia or Wisdom). They taught a process of spiritual ascent (at least for the elite) through the different levels of the cosmos by the invocation of helpful spirits, until matter itself could be transcended. Some versions of Gnosticism, such as that of Marcion, who separated the God of the Old Testament from that of the New, tended towards a kind of dualism rather than emanationism or pantheism. More explicitly dualistic still, however, were ancient Zoroastrianism and the eclectic religion founded by the Persian Mani in the third century (Manichaeanism), in which dark and light principles were presented as equal and opposed, until a final separation of the two took place at the end of time.[4]

Gnosticism was judged heretical by Christians for several reasons. Its fanciful mythology (undoubtedly a stimulus for the imagination) was deemed absurd, and its identification of matter and the body with evil simplistic and misguided. The Christian Gospel taught that matter was created by a good and supreme Creator, but that the harmony of creation had been disrupted by a purely spiritual evil – the sin of pride. Evil, however, was not a rival principle but merely the absence of good (so that the Devil is good insofar as he exists, but evil insofar as he lacks those goods which he should have possessed, such as humility and love). It taught that the Son of God had assumed a fleshly body among men in order to redeem the world of matter. The whole world is destined to follow the Son through bodily death to a resurrection of the flesh. All of these teachings – including that of the actual incarnation of the divine Son – were denied by the Gnostics. In fact it was partly by responding to the intellectual and pastoral challenge of Gnosticism that the early Christian apologists laid the foundations for the definitions of orthodoxy promulgated by the early Ecumenical Councils.

Gnosticism was never definitively defeated. Instead it continued to flourish at the margins of Christian society, to influence other religious movements, and to throw up new heresies from time to time through the centuries. The medieval heresy of the Cathars or Albigensians based in southern France is a case in point. The Cathars (who were probably influenced by the Manichaeans just mentioned)[5] were violently suppressed in the first 'internal crusade' of Christendom at the end of the eleventh century, but they also provided the stimulus for the foundation both of the Dominican Order, dedicated to the intellectual exposition and defence of the true faith (Thomas Aquinas was a model Dominican in this sense), and of the Franciscans, with their extreme emphasis on poverty and the humanity of Christ.

Meanwhile, another series of controversies in the early centuries had forced the Church to define with increasing precision exactly what Christians believed about the nature of Christ. Was he a man inhabited by a divine Spirit, or a God who adopted the illusion of a human body? Was he divine or human? By the time of the Council of Chalcedon in 451 the Church had found a way of saying that he was both of these at one and the same time: fully divine and fully human. The two were not incompatible. In order for that to be possible without self-contradiction, they had to make a crucial distinction between *person* and *nature*. Jesus was a divine person (in Thomistic terms a 'substantial relation') who had assumed a human nature (including therefore both body and soul).[6] Those who rejected this solution were labelled heretics, to distinguish them from those who held the ancient and orthodox faith of the Church, now definitively clarified.

Medieval and Renaissance Influences

But the heretics did not go away, and heretical ideas continued to ferment underground even as the Church became the established religion of the Empire (or what was left of it after the collapse of Roman power). These influences were to resurface in the Renaissance, with the rediscovery of pagan civilization, later in the period of Romanticism, and again in the time of Post-modernism. By the beginning of the thirteenth century, other influences had also come to bear, including the revolutionary ideas of the Cistercian Abbot, Joachim of Fiore (or Flora), who died in 1202. Clearly a holy man, Joachim nevertheless with the encouragement of several popes developed an interpretation of history based on scripture and numerology that probably qualify him as the first real New Ager. In the words of the online *Catholic Encyclopedia*, he taught that:

> There are three states of the world, corresponding to the three Persons of the Blessed Trinity. In the first age the Father ruled, representing power and inspiring fear, to which the Old Testament dispensation corresponds; then the wisdom hidden through the ages was revealed in the Son, and we have the Catholic Church of the New Testament; a third period will come, the Kingdom of the Holy Spirit, a new dispensation of universal love, which will proceed from the Gospel of Christ, but transcend the letter of the Gospel, and in which there will be no need for disciplinary institutions.[7]

This 'new dispensation' or 'new age' was supposed to be already at hand. Joachim's detailed prophecies failed to materialize, his simplistic interpretation of world history was refuted within 50 years or so by St Thomas Aquinas, and the 'spiritual Franciscans' he influenced were suppressed by St Bonaventure, but the potent idea of an Age of the Spirit in which the rule of law would be abolished and universal love would reign remained extremely attractive. Freemasons, many Protestant sects, anarchists and New Agers can all trace their ancestry back to Joachim.

The flowering of the Jewish mystical teachings known as Kabbalah in twelfth-century Spain and southern France introduced another potent idea: that of a cosmic diagram of the forces and numbers underlying the cosmos. Thought to be of immense antiquity, going back by oral tradition to Moses himself, this was the first of many revivals of 'ancient' or 'lost' knowledge – a constant theme in esoteric writing ever since.[8] The masons and architects responsible for the Gothic cathedrals themselves looked back to the musical and mathematical knowledge of Plato and Pythagoras. Contact between Jewish, Christian and Islamic scholars in Moorish Spain and contact with the East brought about by the Crusades enriched Christendom with lost texts of Aristotle in Arabic translation, and with improved forms of mathematical notation (including Arabic numerals and zero, which had been developed in India and adopted by the Arabs).

The medieval period gave way to the Renaissance, which brought this process of 'retrieval' to fever-pitch, as its name suggests. The rediscovery of Classical wisdom combined with an extraordinary creative confidence led to a flourishing of the arts and sciences, but also of occult and magical speculation, driven by the desire to understand or even control the forces of nature. It was the age not just of artistic geniuses like Leonardo and Michelangelo, Raphael and Botticelli (all of them profoundly influenced by Classical learning and mystical ideas) but of sages and mages, magicians and astrologers, Christian Kabbalists and alchemists who looked back to the supposed Hermetic wisdom of ancient Egypt – men like Paracelsus, John Dee (the magus in the court of Elizabeth I) and Nostradamus.[9] In 1439, having met the leading neo-Platonist Gemistus Plethon when the latter was attempting to overcome the East-West schism at the Council of Florence, Cosimo de Medici tried to re-establish the Platonic Academy in Florence with the energetic young Marcilio Ficino at its head. Ficino's writings and translations (he made the works of Plotinus, for example, available for the first time in Latin to Christian readers)[10] had an enormous influence in Renaissance Italy and throughout Europe, especially as he always managed to keep just on the right side of Catholic orthodoxy (unlike his pupil, Pico della Mirandola, most famous for his oration *On the Dignity of Man* and for developing a Christian version of the Kabbalah).

Dawn of the Age of Science

Renaissance alchemy and astrology proved to be the seed-bed for the modern sciences of chemistry and astronomy, but as science became more rationalistic and empirical, the more intuitive, spiritual and magical approach became the province of secret societies such as the Freemasons and occult brotherhoods like the Rosicrucians, which flourished during the Enlightenment period. The two streams of speculation were never entirely disentangled, however, and Isaac Newton, for example, was involved in both. Sometimes termed 'the last magician', his extensive work on alchemy, the Philosopher's Stone, the cosmic properties of Solomon's Temple and the interpretation of the Apocalypse seems to have been of greater importance to him than his scientific research. Newton's approximate contemporary, the Swedish visionary Emanuel Swedenborg, also had a distinguished career as a scientist. Johannes Kepler, the founder of modern astronomy, was not entirely 'modern' in this respect either, his work largely being inspired by a faith in Pythagorean numerology and a search for the music of the spheres.[11]

The seventeenth and eighteenth centuries nevertheless saw the emergence of a more purely quantitative and empirical approach to scientific research, one oriented increasingly towards technological innovation and power over nature, rather than contemplation and intuition. Whatever else he may have believed, Newton's work in optics and his theory of gravity were landmarks in the development of the modern scientific method. After Descartes, anything less than mathematical certainty and clarity began to seem unacceptable in science. On a human level, this understandably left many people feeling dissatisfied and alienated. The poet William Blake spoke of England's 'dark Satanic mills' and 'Newton's sleep'.[12] In fact Blake may have been the first in the modern period explicitly to herald the 'New Age', thus:

> Rouze up, O Young Men of the New Age! set your foreheads against the ignorant Hirelings . . . We do not want either Greek or Roman models if we are but just & true to our own Imaginations, those Worlds of Eternity in which we shall live for ever in Jesus our Lord . . . 'Would to God that all the Lord's people were Prophets.'[13]

The Romantic movement with which we associate Blake and poets such as Coleridge and Wordsworth (and in Germany, of course, Goethe, many of whose ideas were later developed by Steiner) gathered to itself many of the influences already discussed – Platonism, Hermetic wisdom claiming to come from ancient Egypt, the Kabbalah – feeding the development of numerous secret and not-so-secret societies and brotherhoods during the Victorian era. Hungry for some kind of wisdom or spiritual fulfilment which neither science nor Christianity seemed able to offer, many respectable people were also attracted to spiritualism, frequenting mediumistic séances where they tried to communicate with the dead using ouija boards, and some believed in fairies. Arthur Conan Doyle, the inventor of *Sherlock Holmes*, was an avid proponent of such things, and G. K. Chesterton as a young man was also drawn to the occult in the last decade of the nineteenth century, though he soon rejected it in horror.

The most influential societies of this type were the Hermetic Order of the Golden Dawn, which included the poet W. B. Yeats, and the Theosophical Society. The Society was founded in New York in 1875 by the Ukrainian-born occultist Madame H. P. Blavatsky (1831–1891), drawing on wide experience among Freemasonic and other secret societies and occult fraternities, and the knowledge acquired during her travels in India and Egypt. The movement, led in the early twentieth century by Annie Besant (converted from Marxism by meeting Blavatsky) and C. W. Leadbeater, divided and subdivided. A boy called Jiddu Krishnamurti (d. 1986) was groomed by the Society to be the next great teacher of mankind, but renounced the title in 1929 and went on to teach that *gurus* are unnecessary. The French metaphysician René Guénon, influenced by Theosophy and Freemasonry, joined a Sufi Order and in 1930 moved to Cairo, where he continued to be a leading figure in the movement sometimes called Perennialism or Traditionalism.[14]

In another very important schism, the German clairvoyant Rudolf Steiner left the Theosophists to found the more Christian-oriented Anthroposophical Society in 1923. Anthroposophy has become one of the most interesting movements with the New Age, and in many ways the closest to orthodox Christianity, despite Steiner's insistence on the doctrine of reincarnation, for which anthroposophists claim to find some evidence in the Bible. Steiner regarded Christ as the central figure in world history and St Thomas Aquinas as the greatest philosopher. His writings and lectures have borne fruit in the Waldorf schools, in biodynamic agriculture, in associative economics and in the arts. Through Owen Barfield, a member of the Oxford Inklings, he can be said to have influenced C. S. Lewis slightly. Many of his followers have been Christian or have converted to Catholicism, including the Russian anthroposophist Valentin Tomberg, whose *Meditations on the Tarot* will be mentioned later.[15]

The Age of Aquarius

The term 'New Age' in its modern sense was popularized by Alice Bailey in the 1930s, founder of another offshoot of the Theosophical Society. It was picked up by Baba Ram Dass (alias Richard Alpert) and others in the 1960s, when it was popularly identified with the coming astrological 'Age of Aquarius'. In that Age, it was prophesied, mankind would finally become mature enough to renounce the use of force and establish a new world order of peace and harmony, an era of higher or cosmic consciousness and universal love. Eventually mankind would evolve to leave matter behind, and all would be light.

Again, other influences came to bear during the twentieth century: the depth psychology of Carl Jung, the evolutionary cosmological speculations of scientist-theologian Teilhard de Chardin, yoga, ecology and feminism. The scriptures of other religions, alongside the writings of Kabbalists and mystics, became widely available in translation. In the wake of Swami Vivekananda and the Vedanta Society, which propagated a version of Hindu wisdom to a growing intellectual audience in the West at the end of the nineteenth century, new gurus appeared from the East (G. I. Gurdjieff,[16] the Maharishi Mahesh Yogi, Bhagwan Sri Rajneesh). In some cases, these teachers were helped to prominence by celebrity 'converts', most famously, in the case of the Maharishi, the Beatles. A wave of interest in Zen Buddhism (fostered in California by the writings of Alan Watts and D. T. Suzuki) and Sufism (associated with Pir Vilayat Khan, Idries Shah and Frithjof Schuon), prepared the ground for exiled Tibetan *rinpoches* and the Dalai Lama himself to create centres of Buddhist meditation and ritual in the

West – even entire monasteries complete with golden dragons, like Samyé Ling in Scotland.

Meanwhile, the erosion of Christian faith and practice continued apace, while, beginning in California, the practice of humanistic psychology flowered in the 'human potential movement' (associated with Abraham Maslow, Fritz Perls, Robert Assagioli, Viktor Frankl and R. D. Laing). The therapeutic systems founded by Freud, Jung and Adler were by now well established. Jung in particular may be viewed as one of the major influences on the New Age, having broken with Freud after beginning to see the Unconscious less as a repository of repressed sexual energy than as a bridge to the mystical, patterned by universal archetypes or primordial images.[17] This led him into the study of Chinese philosophy (the divination system known as the *I Ching* was translated by his friend Richard Wilhelm), ancient Gnosticism, medieval alchemy and astrology, and even UFOs, all of which he treated as expressions of symbolic thinking indicative of human wholeness. To some extent, the exploration and release of human potential in these therapeutic movements from Freud onwards took on many of the traditional functions of religious faith and practice, including meditation, confession and catharsis, offering the hope of some kind of secular redemption or personal transformation (Jung called it 'individuation').[18]

The fascination with mediumistic phenomena and spiritualism so prominent at the end of the nineteenth century re-emerged under the cloak of parapsychology, the academic discipline founded by J. B. Rhine in the 1930s, and then rather less respectably in the 1980s fashion for 'channelling' disembodied entities calling themselves Ramtha, Lazaris, Seth, and so on (following the popularity of the American psychic Edgar Cayce with his 'channelled' teachings in the early twentieth century). Books such as the hugely popular *A Course in Miracles* recording the revelations of these entities (in the case of the *Course* claiming to be 'Jesus') became bestsellers.

An interest in native American traditions involving he use of hallucinogenic drugs led (through the writings of self-styled anthropologist Carlos Castaneda beginning with his book *The Teachings of Don Juan*, which purported to be a doctoral thesis though it was later assumed to be a work of fiction) to a growing interest on shamanism, with its attempt to mediate between this world and the world of spirits and natural forces. Ancient shamanistic and animistic beliefs and practices in Europe were also rediscovered (and to some extent, given the paucity of documentary evidence, reinvented), and these were successfully promoted as offering a viable spiritual option for modern men and women disenchanted with 'patriarchal' and 'institutional' Christianity. Known as neo-Paganism and Wicca (witchcraft), these supposedly native European pre-Christian religions are now regarded by many academics as forming a significant religious minority, with as many as 20,000 exponents in the United Kingdom alone.

In Eastern Europe, partly because the prevailing ideology in the Soviet Union was a strongly materialist one, parapsychology flourished, since it seemed to offer a respectably empirical and scientific route to the whole world of extraordinary phenomena. Thus, with the suppression of Christianity in Soviet Russia, the ground was prepared for the explosion of religious sects and occultism that took place after the fall of Communism in 1989.[19] An additional factor here was the influx of Western New Age ideas, sometimes presented in the form of management training and business seminars for aspiring Russian entrepreneurs. And while Catholics and Orthodox argued about the return of Church property, wealthy sects including the long-established Mormons and Jehovah's Witnesses did their best to fill the religious vacuum among the young.

In parallel with all this, the development of sciences such as physics and biology during the twentieth century has itself fed the New Age movement. Many of the leading physicists responsible for quantum mechanics were profoundly interested in mysticism and especially Asian and Chinese philosophy (e.g. Erwin Shroedinger, James Jeans, Niels Bohr, Max Planck and Wolfgang Pauli), a story that was later told by physicist Fritjof Capra in his 1970s bestseller *The Tao of Physics*. Einstein himself, who had overturned the Newtonian view of the universe in 1905 with relativity theory, was a theist of a more Western cast of mind, though not a believer in what he called a 'personal God'. (He allegedly objected to the use of probability theory in quantum mechanics saying, 'I don't believe God plays dice with the universe.')[20]

The 'new physics' inspired similar developments in chemistry (Nobel prizewinner Illya Prigogine) and later in biology (Rupert Sheldrake, with his suggestion of 'morphogenetic fields' responsible for the growth and transmission of form).[21] These perfectly legitimate developments and hypotheses were sometimes picked up by non-scientists looking to give extra credibility to New Age ideas (see next section), and provided a host of new metaphors and analogies for the New Age to elaborate upon – as in the case of relativity theory, which was wrongly taken to imply that 'all is relative', and James Lovelock's Gaia Hypothesis, which became confused with the assertion that the Earth itself – or rather the ecosystem – was consciously alive and possibly divine.

Some New Age Ideas

Partly in its reaction to the mind-body dualism and the problematic materialism that the Enlightenment left in its wake, the New Age leans towards idealism and monism, referring frequently to the identity of *Atman* and *Brahman* (Self and God) in Vedanta, and seeking the 'God within' through various forms of meditation. In 1908, G. K. Chesterton satirized the Theosophical obsession with the God within in the following terms:

> Of all conceivable forms of enlightenment the worst is what these people call the Inner Light. Of all horrible religions the most horrible is the worship of the god within. Anyone who knows anybody knows how it would work; anyone who knows anyone from the Higher Thought Centre knows how it does work. That Jones shall worship the god within him turns out ultimately to mean that Jones shall worship Jones. Let Jones worship the sun or moon – anything rather than the Inner Light; let Jones worship cats or crocodiles, if he can find any in his street, but not the god within. Christianity came into the world, firstly, in order to assert with violence that a man had not only to look inward, but to look outwards, to behold with astonishment and enthusiasm a divine company and a divine captain. The only fun of being a Christian was that a man was not left alone with the Inner Light, but definitely recognized an *outer* light, fair as the sun, clear as the moon, terrible as an army with banners.[22]

Of course, the impulse for self-realization is also present in Christianity, culminating in the 'deification' of the person by grace, but as Chesterton indicates this is achieved by looking and turning outwards, in self-giving love, rather than trying to lose oneself in the Inner Light as many Theosophists seemed to do. Mrs Besant, says Chesterton, referring to the leading Theosophist of his day, 'does not tell us to love our neighbours; she tells us to be our neighbours'.[23] Though an amusing caricature, and something of an oversimplification, like many that appear in Chesterton's writing, there is a serious point here that applies to many less sophisticated New Agers, who do regard universal brotherhood as the fruit of a realization that there is but one true life – the 'Christ life' as some put it, or 'cosmic consciousness' – in all alike, and that selfishness is based merely on the illusory perception that we are each distinct.

We may get a clearer fix on New Age ideas by looking in more detail at one of its exponents. In England, a leader and inspirer of the New Age movement for much of his long life was Sir George Trevelyan (nephew of his namesake, the well-known historian). Trevelyan (d. 1996) was the founder of the Wrekin Trust, one of a number of important New Age centres that include Findhorn in Scotland and Dartington Hall in England (an intellectual hub of the new Age). Trevelyan sums up the New Age world-view thus:

> Behind all outwardly manifested form is a timeless realm of absolute consciousness. It is the great Oneness underlying all the diversity, all the myriad forms of nature. It may be called God, or may be deemed beyond all naming ... The world of nature, in short, is but a reflection of the eternal world of

> Creative imagining. The inner core of man, that which in each of us might be called spirit, is a droplet of the divine source. As such, it is imperishable and eternal, for life cannot be extinguished. The outer sheath in which it manifests can, of course, wear out and be discarded; but to speak of 'death' in relation to the true being and spirit of man is irrelevant.[24]

Implied here is one of the most popular beliefs associated with the New Age movement, namely, reincarnation. As Sir George expresses it: 'The soul belongs properly to higher and purer spheres. It incarnates for the purpose of acquiring experience in the density of earth matter – a necessary educational phase in its development. Such incarnation, of course, entails drastic limitation of a free spiritual being. Birth into a body is, in fact, more like entry into a species of tomb' (6). He explains the anthropology that lies behind this belief as follows: 'More precisely, we must recognise man as a threefold being of body, soul and spirit . . . The immortal "I" is neither the soul nor the transient personality. In order to descend into the density of the phenomenal world, it must clothe itself, so to speak, in a protective sheath' (ibid.). The 'soul' is therefore the sheath or 'astral body' which the eternal 'I' draws about it in order to experience the psychological level of reality. It also draws around itself an 'etheric' body of vital forces to hold together the physical body.

In Christianity, the unique personality constituted by the unity of a human spirit or soul with the body it animates is not transient, as in the theories of reincarnation, but is promised an eternal resurrection. But Sir George writes: 'If the earth plane is indeed the great training ground of the soul, it is unlikely that we should come here only once. One lifetime is hardly sufficient to reap all the harvest of experience that earth can offer' (36). He traces the idea that the earth is a school for reincarnating spirits back to the German theologian G. E. Lessing in 'The Education of the Human Race', published in 1780. At the end of chapter 4 he writes:

> To summarise what we have said, the eternal essence of the human being makes a descent into a series of earthbound lives, thus building up a personality with which to confront the pressures of the world. The whole 'object of the exercise' is, through long experience and suffering, to master and dissolve this lower self and transmute the soul into an organ in which the Higher Self, the true spiritual being of man, can operate. The ordinary personality is obviously too ephemeral to reincarnate. But at death we carry forward a seed of real individuality which, developing in the life between death and rebirth, can, when time is ripe, make the descent again.

It may descend to improve itself or to serve others, or to do both.

The idea of reincarnation has always been popular in parts of Asia, but there it has traditionally been regarded in a negative rather than a positive light, as a sign of spiritual failure. For most Buddhists, for example, the goal of a human being should be to escape reincarnation by achieving enlightenment. In any case, since reincarnation as a human being, rather than as a lower animal, is regarded as extremely unlikely, another earthly life is not necessarily something to be anticipated with pleasure. What transformed the popular understanding of reincarnation in the West was the theory of evolution, with which it became entangled. Sir George comments that 'it is fitting for our western minds that evolutionary thinking should colour our understanding of reincarnation. Consciousness evolves from age to age, and this consciousness is carried in individual souls. Each, therefore, can enter the stream of earth life as a creative deed to lift the race as a whole one step further' (38). Thus the doctrine of reincarnation in the form now held by a quarter of the European population is not simply an idea taken over from the Oriental religions, but an application of the idea of progressive evolution to the human soul.

Sir George believes we will eventually leave all our need for a gross material body, but he quotes St Paul (1 Cor. 15.52) to the effect that we shall be one day clothed in an incorruptible spiritual body, and looks forward to the new heavens and the new earth of the book of Revelation. One with the Oneness through spiritual communion, we will also retain our individuality as creatures of the One. In this way he tries to integrate Christian and Asian teachings with the discoveries of modern science.

Whether it is true of not, the idea that the 'I' (even if this does not refer to the self of everyday consciousness) has many lifetimes in which to learn from its mistakes and discover its communion or even identity with the 'God within' can seem immensely attractive – especially if the apparent alternative is either to vanish after a brief span on earth, or to be judged for ever on the basis of decisions taken in ignorance. (The latter is a popular misinterpretation of the Christian doctrine of the afterlife, missing the point of the Church's teaching that no one will be condemned for doing something they could not help or avoid.)[25]

There is also in the New Age a perfectly legitimate desire for spiritual healing. This lies behind much alternative or complementary medicine, as well as the therapies devised by the successors of the founders of modern psychology. In line with the 'holistic' perspectives of the New Age, similar principles must apply to the healing of the whole earth. The science of ecology, and the realization that irresponsible industrialization may have irreparably damaged the earth's ecosystem (a major concern of the hippies in the 1960s but now, through John Paul II and Benedict XVI, fully incorporated in Catholic social teaching), have taken the place of the Cold War and the arms race as a topic of near universal concern. Within the New Age movement, the transformation of the individual through therapy or changes in diet and lifestyle is linked to transformation of the planet, through the restoration of balance in the 'earth-energies' and the creation of a new, sustainable and environmentally friendly civilization. Generally, the aim is to achieve this not by a top-down restructuring of the global economy, but through the spiritual influence of personal example, invocation or prayer.

The confluence of environmentalism with the feminist idea that the ecological crisis is due to the historical predominance of 'patriarchical' structures responsible for the 'rape of the earth' (a confluence branded 'eco-feminism') leads many in the New Age to promote matriarchal forms of religion and society. A Mother-Goddess – sometimes known as Gaia, the personification of Nature and of the living planet – takes the place of the Father-God and his Son, and a female priesthood develops to represent her (the role of the priestess in any of the ancient traditions usually being one of invocation and healing rather than sacrifice). All of this in turn leads to a corresponding movement among *men*, also linked to the revival of shamanistic traditions and the appropriation and reinterpretation of ancient myths and folktales (Joseph Campbell's *The Masks of God* and Robert Bly's *Iron John* are classics of this genre). Catholics, too, have bemoaned the loss in modern society of the strong male role-model that might once have been provided by the father of a large family. Though the New Age 'men's movement' sometimes takes the form of an initiation into feminism for men,[26] the use of traditional tales and myths about male heroes reminds us that there are characteristic virtues in masculinity that have been suppressed in a society where everyone is supposed to behave in the same way and feel the same things.

Throughout the New Age movement a similar dynamic is apparent. Modernity or the rationalistic civilization of the Enlightenment is perceived as, in one way or another, diseased – the cause being identified variously as industrialization or materialism or patriarchy, or all three together. The world is regarded as an organic whole in need of healing, and 'therapy' must start at the level of the individual. While the therapies and solutions on offer may at times be rather wild, the assumptions of the diagnosis are quite compatible with Christianity. Even feminism, which in its extreme form rejects all patriarchal authority and certainly that of the Church, is rooted in a discontent which many Catholics share. Pope John Paul II's 1995 encyclical *Evangelium Vitae* called for a 'new feminism' which 'rejects the temptation of imitating models of "male domination"'. This was no mere attempt to steal feminism's thunder, but based on the recognition that feminism was an understandable reaction to the brutalization of men and their abuse of authority.[27]

The Da Vinci Code *Phenomenon*

The runaway success of Dan Brown's thriller, *The Da Vinci Code*, highlights the perennial challenge that some aspects of New Age thinking pose to Christians. The *Code* is fiction, but bases itself on speculations that have been put forward in other books (notably *Holy Blood, Holy Grail*) and are taken seriously by millions. The 'secret' that the Church has supposedly been hiding all these centuries – in order to protect its own power – concerns the true nature of the Holy Grail. Far from being the miraculous chalice in which is preserved drops of blood from the side of the dying Christ (the object of the legendary Quest of the knights of King Arthur, and a mystical symbol of the Eucharist), the Grail turns out to be the *sang real*, the royal bloodline of Jesus Christ passed down through marriage with Mary Magdalen, through the Merovingian dynasty of French monarchs, down to the cryptographer Sophie Neveu (the main love-interest in the book). Or rather the Grail is the Magdalen herself, the receptacle of the bloodline, giving Brown a chance to tap into the New Age interest in the 'sacred feminine' and the Gnostic Gospels.

Jesus, in this version of events, was not divine and not celibate. His divinity was falsely proclaimed by the Emperor Constantine several centuries after his death. The true importance of Mary Magdalen was suppressed, and along with her a doctrine of sacred sexuality, the balancing of yin and yang through sexual intercourse, and the equality of the sexes, which led to the massacring by patriarchal authorities of 5 million women as witches. The alleged secret was known to the Templars and by their offshoot, the ancient Priory of Sion, of which Leonardo Da Vinci was a member (actually the real Priory was only founded in the twentieth century), and Catholics are ready to commit murder to prevent it being revealed even today.

A whole raft of New Age ideas are combined in this page-turning potboiler, including the love of secret societies, coded messages and conspiracies involving well-known historical figures, the hatred of patriarchal authority and the interest in sex-magic that has always been a part of occult lore. A more subtle agenda is the feminist resentment against the figure of the Virgin Mother, here dethroned in favour of the Magdalen. The allegations have been refuted many times.[28] For example, the cult of the Virgin Mother and Child did not result in a devaluation of sexuality: it was the medieval Church that defended sacred sexuality against the Gnostics and Cathars who denied it. Opus Dei is also misrepresented: there are no 'monks' in the community, let alone any 'advance absolution' for murder (which is impossible in the Catholic understanding of absolution anyway). The distortions of Church history (and even art history) are so egregious that it would take pages to enumerate them. But the popularity of the book exposes the desire of many to believe that the truth must be the opposite of what the Church teaches. That is one of the traits commonly found in the New Age movement, as it is among many others who resent the Church's moral authority for whatever reason, and needs to be taken into account by Christians seeking to enter into dialogue with it.

Escaping the Cage of Modernity

What I have been attempting to describe as if it were a unified movement is not, of course, anything of the sort. It is certainly highly unstable, and my own impression, based on a large amount of anecdotal evidence, is that it has a tendency to break up in at least three main directions. Some members tend to lapse back (or move on) into more traditional religious allegiances, becoming Buddhists, or Christians, or Muslims. A second group consists of those who are 'captured' by one of the extreme religious sects or new apocalyptic cults (ranging from Scientology and the People's Temple to the Unification Church). A third group simply merge back into (and subsequently influence) the mainstream culture.

The New Age has an innate tendency to become big business. Pop stars (e.g. the Beatles, Madonna) and film stars (e.g. Shirley MacLaine, Tom Cruise) have helped to promote it. Chains of shops have appeared, selling books, crystals and records of New Age music. Publishers have responded to a growing market by investing heavily in the production of new titles, employing the 'New Age' as a marketing device. In fact, this was a major factor in the rapid growth of the movement during the 1980s. However, the very success of New Age products – many of them collected in the *Whole Earth Catalog* founded in 1968 by Steward Brand (and now available online) – was taken by many in the movement itself as evidence for the growth of the new global awareness.

The New Age 'festivals' or 'fairs' that first took place during the 1980s expressed very clearly the coming of age, not of mankind, but of the New Age itself as a self-conscious movement. This was the spiritual quest married to consumerism: a marriage arranged and consummated in America but soon on honeymoon in the rest of the world. The compatibility of the two partners, after all, runs very deep. Life in a market economy (mirrored in the thinking of post-modernist intellectuals) dissolves the sense of personal identity by increasing mobility, instability and consumer choice. For the armchair tourist, culture itself becomes a commodity.

Existentialist philosophers had claimed that 'existence precedes essence', that we are what we choose: the modern consumer lives out that understanding in everyday life. When the consumer embarks on a spiritual quest (the search for a deeper reality or transcendent unity), this naturally tends to take the form of a review of different religious options and belief systems, with a view to choosing an alternative lifestyle that will suit his individual tastes. The deeper level where '*all is one*' corresponds to the all-embracing unity of the market economy, and the radical plurality of the available spiritualities matches the goods on display in any shopping mall or supermarket.

A Brief History of Individualism

The New Age movement, despite the fact that is woven of influences from the far past and the Far East, can therefore be called a phenomenon of the modern West: in its essence it is a revolt by some aspects of modernity against others. Its origins lie in the Reformation and the Enlightenment, even if it draws on deeper and more ancient traditions. The Protestant Reformation favoured subjective judgement (the private interpretation of scripture) over the external judgement of Church authority, while the succeeding Age of Reason broke with the authority of scripture too. Thenceforth, the hero of the story modernity told about itself was always a man of genius, an individual, someone who thinks and imagines freely – an artist in his garret, a scientist in his laboratory, a Leonardo, a Galileo, an Einstein.

Christianity had introduced into history the idea of the infinite worth and immortal destiny of each human person. A growing concern with human subjectivity – the consciousness and inviolable conscience of the individual – was therefore both inevitable and desirable. Unfortunately, as Louis Dupré shows in his book *Passage to Modernity*, from the fourteenth century onwards this concern was diverted into an increasingly narrow bed by the Nominalist philosophers and those influenced by them.[29] Galileo's separation of primary from secondary qualities and Descartes' mathematicization of nature contributed to the progressive lack of concern with the interiority of things – whether this was the metaphysical interiority of nature, opening on to the horizons of divine purpose and the beauty of cosmic Wisdom, or the psychological interiority of human persons, opening on to spiritual kingdoms above and below the conscious mind. The acting person was imagined to be a mere 'individual', a social atom, determined solely by external relations, even as the world of matter was being similarly reduced to a series of indivisible particles impacting upon each other like billiard balls.[30]

By the beginning of the twentieth century, with the 'discovery' of the unconscious mind by Freud and Jung and the splitting (at first conceptually, and later physically) of the atom, this mechanical model of the universe had begun to break down. But the natural sciences had long since emancipated themselves from theology and philosophy, and so the new scientific approach did not immediately result in a recovery of either Christian cosmology or Christian psychology.

The philosopher Charles Taylor has charted these developments in *The Sources of the Self* and *A Secular Age*.[31] As he makes clear, individualism and the modern 'turn to the subject' were by no means completely negative developments. A new sense of freedom and of personal dignity expressed as inalienable rights were among the positive gains. However, the cult of the individual also led to extremes such as the fetishism of 'art for art's sake', free love and revolutionary violence. In the end, no self-respecting individualist would accept the authority of objective truth. 'True' must only mean true 'for me', or true 'because it works'. The same applied to all other values; to beauty and goodness as well as to truth: it was all a matter of subjective taste. Thus what was really enthroned in the Age of Reason was not in fact Reason at all: it was the Self, and the Age of Self is an Age of Unreason. The New Age movement is both a product of this situation and a reaction against it.

Escape to Nowhere

The New Age – understandably and probably rightly – attempts to overcome the split between mind and matter, and in this way to overcome the isolation of the spiritual self in a world of material forces. But often it remains trapped in the modernity shaped by Galileo and Descartes: trapped, that is, between the two poles of the opposition between matter and spirit. Either it remains dualistic, and – like the Gnostics criticized in the second century by St Irenaeus – seeks to escape from the oppression of matter through some kind of spiritual liberation (e.g. reincarnation culminating in reunion with the divine consciousness), or it tries to turn materialism on its head by absorbing matter into mind, declaring the very distinction to be unreal (a form of idealism or spiritual monism). These two paths can also be combined by making dualism merely a preliminary, a 'lesser truth' destined to be left behind in the higher stages of spiritual enlightenment.

The New Age can therefore partly be understood as a reaction to the atomic individualism of post-Enlightenment modernity, and to the social fragmentation and alienation associated with this. In its negative aspect, it presents a picture of the self desperately battering against the bars of its own cage, trying to find a way out, but too often constrained by one or other still-unexamined assumption of modernity. It seeks to submit to an authority (a guru, for example), in order to overcome the isolation of the self, but will no longer look in the one place where genuine authority may still be found – the Roman Catholic Church. It seeks love, but it cannot bring itself to make a lifelong commitment. It seeks to respect and venerate nature, but at the same time it wants to escape the constraints that nature imposes. It wants to become immortal, but at the same time it wants to evolve into something different from (and better than) itself.

All of this can be recognized in the attitudes of the '60s generation', for the 1960s were the time that New Age went mainstream. Wealthy teenagers growing up in a world that technology had brought easily within reach, emancipated from their own cultural traditions and conventions, felt (in the words of Tom Wolfe's famous words from *The Electric Kool-Aid Acid Test* in 1968) that they were 'the first wave of the most extraordinary kids in the history of the world', and set off in search of new lifestyles, new values, new knowledge. The Hippy Trail stretched from California through Afghanistan to India and beyond. These were 'angelheaded hipsters burning for the ancient heavenly connection',[32] a connection that they could no longer find in Christianity.

The Search for Authority

Much New Age literature is accordingly concerned with the search for a spiritual teacher, to whom submission must be made for the sake of reaching the ultimate state of knowledge. Tales of an encounter with true authority form, of course, a venerable tradition in every religion. One classic example would be in the Tibetan biography, *The Life of Milarepa*,[33] whose teacher Marpa puts him through a series of demanding and dispiriting ordeals before giving him the initiation he craves. Similar examples abound in the legends of the Desert Fathers and the Christian saints, as they do among New Age teachers such as Gurdjieff. But although the New Age can accept the idea of individuals possessed of spiritual authority (either self-authenticating or proved by supernatural powers), it tends not to accept the notion that an institution, such as a Church, may be similarly endowed, or may by the same right of genuine authority require sufficient humility from the seeker of ultimate truth.

The picture of Jesus and his band of 12 intimate disciples, who are taught by him the secret meaning of the parables that make up the bulk of his public or exoteric teaching, is very appealing to New Agers, and much has been made of it in those circles. The fact that one of the disciples, Peter, was invested by Jesus with the authority of the Holy Spirit and made the foundation-stone of a Church that was explicitly intended by him to endure infallibly through time is easily and conveniently dismissed as a later interpolation.

Not that the New Age guru needs to appear in the flesh. One of the most commercially successful channelled teachings allegedly from an invisible entity is to be found in the *Course in Miracles*, a series of books which have sold in many hundreds of thousands since their publication by the Foundation for Inner Peace in 1975, and have generated an extensive secondary literature. The author identifies himself with Christ. 'I am the only one who can perform miracles indiscriminately, because I am the Atonement', he says, continuing: 'You have a role in the Atonement which I will dictate to you. Ask me which miracles you should perform. This spares you needless effort, because you will be acting under direct communication . . . *Lead us not into temptation* means "Recognize your errors and choose to abandon them by following my guidance."'[34]

According to some New Age authors, then, 'the Christ' who spoke through Jesus of Nazareth was the highest of true teachers, and still works invisibly on earth, though of course not through the Church. In *Esoteric Christianity*, Annie Besant writes:

> The historical Christ, then, is a glorious Being belonging to the great spiritual hierarchy that guides the spiritual evolution of humanity, who used for some three years the human body of the disciple Jesus . . . who drew men to Him by the singular love and tenderness and the rich wisdom that breathed from His Person; and who was finally put to death for blasphemy, for teaching the inherent Divinity of Himself and of all men.[35]

More recently, and from a very different point of view (deeply influenced by Gurdjieff), Professor Jacob Needleman writes of an 'intermediate level of Christianity' that can produce 'real change in human nature, real transformation'.[36] The official guardians of Christianity, he explains, have continued to teach us what Christ wanted us to *do* (to love each other, and so on), but they omitted to transmit the intermediate teachings that would have given us the *power* to do those things. As a result, the religion of Christ has been reduced to the promulgation of empty moral rules no one can obey, softened by an equally vacant sentimentality. What we need is to discover those who have the authority to teach the methods of putting Christianity into practice. Perhaps they may be found in a remote and secret monastery, but in any case we need to search high and low if we wish to find them.

Such views are representative of a large body of opinion to the effect that Christianity must have lost something vital in the early centuries – and it is with the claim to have rediscovered or reconstructed this 'lost Christianity', to have discarded the dry husk but found the living kernel of truth, that many New Age groups begin. Against this must be set the view of many converts from the New Age – I am referring to myself and my friends here, and therefore relying once again on anecdote – that it is precisely in Christianity that the practical spiritual help may be found that is so lacking elsewhere. We have found it not only in the ancient monastic tradition of practical spiritual guidance, but in the practice of a regular life of prayer anchored in the sacraments and the continuing *real presence* of Jesus Christ, who feeds us with his body and blood under the forms of bread and wine. This is the same Lord who promised his disciples that he would send them the Spirit to guide them into all truth (Jn 16.13), and we have found that the guidance of the Holy Spirit more than compensates for a dearth of human gurus.

Catholicism and the New Age

The Roman Catholic Church became more open to some of the influences I have been describing in the period after the Second Vatican Council (1962–1965). Pope John XXIII no doubt hoped the Council would prove a preliminary to the reintegration of divided Christianity – the overcoming at source of the historical divisions of Christendom, in order to open the way for a new global evangelization in the twenty-first century. The idea was that the Church would open herself to the modern world in order to absorb, understand and ultimately transform the cultural ferment around her.

The more immediate result of the Council was perhaps inevitable: previously sheltered Catholic universities, schools and seminaries were exposed to the forces of secularization and the lure of alternative spiritualities for the first time. The spirit of the age, which had been held at bay or driven underground during the first half of the century, seems to have taken advantage of the Church's openness. In the period after the Council, then, Catholics hungry for spiritual experience began to turn to Yoga, Zen, Tibetan Buddhism, and neo-Pagan rituals that promised a greater measure of self-transcendence. Some tried, with greater or lesser success, to adapt for Christian use insights and techniques of the Eastern religions (among the most respected would be Thomas Merton, Bede Griffiths and John Main). Others eventually left the Church altogether – as was the case, for example, with Matthew Fox. This renegade American Dominican argued for a reinterpretation of the Christian tradition that would place emphasis on God's 'Original Blessing' of the creation in the first chapter of Genesis, rather than on the doctrine of Original Sin which he attributed exclusively to St Augustine. Influenced by feminism as well as 'deep ecology' he was equally open to various forms of Western paganism and nature-religion, including Wicca (through the witch Starhawk).[37]

The influence of the Eastern religions and New Age movement on Christian spirituality naturally became a focus of controversy within the Church. In an address to the Bishops of the United States on 28 May 1993 (reported in *L'Osservatore Romano*, English edition, 2 June 1993), Pope John Paul II spoke of it in balanced and measured tones:

> It is not an exaggeration to say that man's relationship to God and the demand for a religious 'experience' are the crux of a profound crisis affecting the human spirit. While the secularization of many aspects of life continues, there is a new quest for 'spirituality' as evidenced in the appearance of many religious and healing movements which look to respond to the crisis of values in Western society. This stirring of the *homo religiosus* produces some positive and constructive results, such as the search for new meaning in life, a new ecological sensitivity, and a desire to go beyond a cold, rationalistic religiosity. On the other hand, this religious re-awakening includes some very ambiguous elements which are incompatible with the Christian faith.
>
> Many of you have written Pastoral Letters on the problems presented by pseudo-religious movements and sects, including the so-called 'New Age Movement'. New Age ideas sometimes find their way into preaching, catechesis, workshops and retreats, and thus influence even practising Catholics, who perhaps are unaware of the incompatibility of those ideas with the Church's faith. In their syncretistic and immanent outlook, these parareligious movements pay little heed to Revelation, and instead try to come to God through knowledge and experience borrowed from Eastern spirituality or from psychological techniques. They tend to relativize religious doctrine, in favour of a vague world-view expressed as a system of myths and symbols dressed in religious language. Moreover, they often propose a pantheistic concept of God which is incompatible with Sacred Scripture and Christian Tradition. They replace personal responsibility to God for our actions with a sense of duty to the cosmos, thus overturning the true concept of sin and the need for redemption through Christ.
>
> Yet, in the midst of this spiritual confusion, the Church's Pastors should be able to detect an authentic thirst for God and for an intimate, personal relationship with him. In essence, the search for meaning is the stupendous quest for the Truth and Goodness which have their foundation in God himself, the author of all that exists. Indeed, it is God himself who awakens this longing in people's hearts. The often silent pilgrimage to the living Truth, whose Spirit 'directs the course of the ages and renews the face of the earth' (*Gaudium et spes*, n. 26), is a 'sign of the times' which invites the Church's members to examine the credibility of their Christian witness. Pastors must

honestly ask whether they have paid sufficient attention to the thirst of the human heart for the true 'living water' which only Christ our Redeemer can give (John 4:7–13). They should insist on the spiritual dimension of the faith, on the perennial freshness of the Gospel message and its capacity to transform and renew those who accept it.

Saint Paul tells us that we must 'seek the things that are above, where Christ is seated at the right hand of God' (Col. 3:1). To neglect the supernatural dimension of the Christian life is to empty of meaning the mystery of Christ and of the Church: 'If for this life only we have hoped in Christ, we are of all people most to be pitied' (1 Cor. 15:19). Nevertheless, it is a sad fact that some Christians today are succumbing to the temptation 'to reduce Christianity to merely human wisdom, a pseudo-science of well-being' (*Redemptoris Missio*, n. 11). To preach a version of Christianity which benignly ignores, when it does not explicitly deny, that our ultimate hope is the 'resurrection of the body and life everlasting' (Apostles' Creed) runs counter to Revelation and the whole of Catholic tradition.

Indeed, if we follow the Pope's instructions and example, and look more closely at the original message of the Gospel as it was understood by Church Fathers and mystics well before the modern period, we find something that does not quite fit the consensus of New Age thinking. I want to try to state this as clearly as possible, before going on to the next section to talk about the ways in which we might try to retrieve some of the insights and intuitions of the New Age for the sake of a new apologetics.

The incarnation has always been something of a scandal. The Christian emphasis on a particular man of flesh and blood, his gruesome death and empty tomb – unless interpreted as a purely symbolic narrative – strikes many people as absurd or even unwholesome. Yet it is in this emphasis on the physical incarnation that the foundation of Christian mysticism can be discovered. And here, I think, we can rediscover the most authentic Christian way out of the modern dilemma. Certainly, if we do not take this as our starting point, any use made of the elements of other traditions is likely to result in a dilution or distortion of the distinctive message of Christianity.

Right from the start, of course, the Jewish religion attributed great importance to history. It was after all founded on history: the Covenant and its periodic renewal; the liberation from slavery in Egypt; the giving of the Law through Moses. The Jews also believed that history would come to a *conclusion*: the restoration of David's kingdom by the Messiah. For Christians, the life of Jesus of Nazareth was the continuation, and the beginning of the fulfilment, of Israel's long history.[38] The precise Christian claim is easy to state, but difficult to grasp: that Jesus, the long-awaited Messiah, was a human being, a man, but also God: a divine Person, the Second Person of the Trinity. In him, the Creator of the cosmos became (and will eternally remain) a man of flesh and blood like us. 'The Christian is immersed in wonder at this paradox, the latest of an infinite series, all magnified with gratitude in the language of the liturgy: the immense accepts limitation; a Virgin gives birth; through death, he who is life conquers death forever; in the heights of heaven, a human body is seated at the right hand of the Father.'[39]

For dualists and monists alike, this claim is scandalous. If true, it means that Jesus is more than any Jewish prophet; more than an 'Avatar' (to use the Indian term that has recently acquired a new meaning in popular culture thanks to the most popular movie of recent times, James Cameron's *Avatar* in which the consciousness of a human soldier is projected into an alien body grown for this purpose in a chemical vat). The Supreme Reality has not merely revealed itself on earth as though in a mirror, but has stepped, like Alice through the Looking Glass, into the very realm of shadows. It has done more: it has brought (or promised to bring) the realm of shadows back with it to the real world, the 'truly real' world of the Absolute, or of God's Eternity. The implication of the Resurrection and Ascension, linked to the incarnation, is that no event in the earthly, historical life of Jesus can ever be 'over and done with'. The elements of his life no longer lie in the past, in historical time alone, for they have been raised up *with his human flesh* to God's right hand.

These facts change the way we think of our destiny. Our highest aspiration is no longer to be liberated from the body in order to merge our particular spirit with the universal Spirit. There is a higher destiny than *nirvana*. The latter is not equivalent to the Christian concept of 'salvation'. If *nirvana* corresponds with anything in Christian theology, it is to the controversial doctrine of 'limbo', the doctrine that there exists a perfect state of purely natural happiness reserved for unbaptized children. This idea was introduced as a way of coping with the difficulty of imagining how God could admit such children, who had never made an act of faith or had one made on their behalf, into the highest state of beatitude.[40] For what baptism makes possible is a *supernatural* fulfilment: the Beatific Vision of God.

Thus if my reading is correct, Christianity does not offer the same as the other religions, but more. When the Church Fathers wrote that 'God became man so that man might become God', they did not mean that we will one day awaken to the fact that we were God all along. They meant that we were *not* God, but may become so by the most intimate kind of participation: God by grace not by nature. This is the implication of St Paul's teaching that we shall see God 'face to face': 'I shall understand fully, even as I have been fully understood' (1 Cor. 13.12). As St Thomas explains this and similar New Testament texts, we shall know God with God's own knowledge of himself (i.e. his essence takes the place of the intelligible form by which we know him).[41] Once divinized through the indwelling of the Holy Spirit, the divine nature in which we share is undivided, and yet we remain eternally distinct from every other person, human or divine. Through losing ourselves in the contemplation of the Beloved, we receive an eternal identity (a 'new name') in the Communion of Saints.

Notice in particular how, if the cosmic relationship of Self and Other, of Subject and Object, is to be transcended, as oriental religions and many in the New Age believe, 'eternal life' must consist of extinction – sometimes described as the extinction of a raindrop in the ocean. This is a unity of absorption: the Lover is absorbed into the Beloved. But at that point love itself comes to an end: loves turns out to have been merely a longing for unity with God, which is now satisfied. There is no Lover any more: only the Beloved. But while a Christian may agree that duality – the separation of Self and Other – is not the end of the story, only a Christian knows the 'happy ending'. The incarnation has revealed a distinction in God between Father, Son and Spirit. The message is that Lover and Beloved *can* live happily ever after. Love does not merge with the Self into the Other, but preserves them in relationship.

In place of the unity of absorption, Christianity places a mystery of unity without confusion, and proclaims that love need never come to an end (cf. 1 Cor. 13.8). Our relationships are the most important things about us; love is the way, the only way, to enter into eternal life.

Evangelizing the New Age

It is easy to see why numbers attending Mass and studying for the priesthood are at an all-time low in Western Europe. What we seem to be seeing is a collapse of cultural Catholicism under the onslaught of consumerism. By *cultural Catholicism* I mean the passing on of the faith peacefully from one generation to the next within countries or social enclaves that have defined themselves as Catholic for many generations. Culturally, Catholicism always appears fairly strong right up until the moment it collapses. Its weakness lies in the fact that it is based on an unexamined and almost habitual faith, one not able easily to defend itself against the culture that supplants it from within the TV set, the iPod and the shopping mall.

When that happens, some priests are tempted to compete with the new culture in its own terms – to make Christianity more outwardly engaging, exciting not boring. That is usually a mistake. Christianity is never going to be able to compete for long in the entertainment stakes. The interior or mystical dimension is the most vital part of religious experience, and there is a risk of losing that dimension if all the emphasis is placed on outward manifestation. Too often it has been lost already, since habitual faith that is easy to supplant is a faith in which outward observance has become disconnected from the inner life.

What happens after the collapse of cultural Catholicism and the alienation of a whole generation from the faith of their fathers? The religious search and yearning that is natural to humanity cannot be suppressed for long. Secularism is shot through with religiosity, now detached from tradition. Or rather, there is no longer a single overarching tradition to give shape and coherence to the whole society, against which another religious tradition would define itself as a subculture or minority. *Every* religion finds itself in the position of a subculture.

When the Pontifical Councils for Culture and for Inter-Religious Dialogue addressed the challenge of evangelizing the New Age in 1993, they chose as their fundamental reference in scripture the following passage from the Gospel of John (Jn 4.13–15), where Jesus is talking with a Samaritan women – an outsider, not one of God's People, and someone who was very definitely not living the traditional teaching on marriage. Referring to the well next to which they are standing, Jesus says to her: 'Everyone who drinks of this water will thirst again, but whoever drinks of the water that I shall give him will never thirst; the water that I shall give him will become in him a spring of water welling up to eternal life.' The woman replies simply, 'Sir, give me this water, that I may not thirst, nor come here to draw.'

In order to offer the men and women of our day the 'living water' that is faith in Jesus Christ, those of us who have been blessed with that faith need to appreciate the situation of the ones we are addressing – as Jesus did, seeing into the very soul of the Woman at the Well and understanding her attitude to him. The New Age is growing for a combination of negative and positive reasons. The negative reasons: many people are understandably repelled by the face of Christianity they see around them and in the history books. They consider that Christians throughout the ages have been responsible for religious wars and persecutions, and that even among today's believers a majority seem to be only nominally or culturally Christian, lacking any visible spirituality or moral integrity beyond the average. In recent years we have been made particularly aware of the scandalous behaviour of some priests who betrayed the trust that was placed in them. To set against this, there is also much evidence within the Church of genuine sanctity, often heroic, and frequently attested by miracles. However, sanctity (in the Catholic tradition particularly) is associated in the minds of many with an extreme asceticism and a cult of sentimentality that they also find repulsive.

There are, however, also positive reasons that might attract someone to search out alternatives to Christianity. A need for healing, or just a desire for freedom and adventure; a need for community and greater participation (do-it-yourself rituals are a common feature of New Age spirituality). A sense, too, that the Truth must be greater than any human words can express, which goes with a preference for mythology, storytelling and poetry over seemingly prosaic dogma. Above all, perhaps, a hunger for a higher level of consciousness than that of the everyday mind, so preoccupied with trivial affairs, and for first-hand religious experience, for access to invisible worlds and beings, rather than second- or third-hand accounts of this experience.

The Holy Spirit may have already responded to this hunger in his own way, or so it seems to many Christians in the Charismatic Movement – a worldwide phenomenon beginning in 1960 that spread to the Catholic Church by 1967, marked by spontaneous prayer, speaking in mysterious tongues, miraculous healings and enormous outpourings of devotion. Critics question the degree to which such phenomena can be induced by emotional manipulation or group hysteria, but the Church has been careful to regulate the life of the charismatic communities that have sprung up, and they seem to bear much good fruit. Many who have been touched by the Spirit in this way find themselves in a much deeper and more personal relationship with Jesus, and their lives are marked by a lasting charity.

The Charismatic Movement is not the only movement raised up by the Holy Spirit in the Catholic Church during the past half century. Communion and Liberation, Focolare, Sant Egidio, L'Arche, the Neocatechumenal Way, The Legionaries of Christ, Youth 2000, the Faith Movement and a dozen others, not to mention the prelature Opus Dei and numerous secular institutes, each with members worldwide sometimes numbered in many hundreds of thousands, form what Pope John Paul II called a 'new Pentecost' of ecclesial movements of the faithful – each with a particular charism or spiritual gift. Some have experienced tensions with local bishops, some (notably the Legionaries after revelations in 2010 concerning the private life of their founder) have been through a crisis that almost destroyed them.

There are always dangers involved with becoming part of a group that views itself as special on the grounds that it possesses some important gift from God. The attraction of becoming part of an elite group, of sharing a secret knowledge, of acquiring special powers or influence – these are temptations familiar the world over and in the New Age movement especially. Yet the Church needs such movements. She cannot depend on authority and tradition alone. A living Church, animated by the Holy Spirit, will always throw up new expressions of faith that need to be discerned, respected and incorporated (and where necessary purified and reformed).

It is in movements of this sort – rather than simply in the parishes – that New Agers may find the kind of community and transformative activity within the Catholic Church that they have been looking for. They will recognize other phenomena too. The Catholic Church does not permit channelling and mediumistic phenomena, yet she admits miracles and apparitions of the saints, especially the Blessed Virgin Mary, and allows the faithful to believe a number of private revelations that have been granted to individuals, including Bernadette Soubirous (Lourdes), Margaret Mary Alocoque (the Sacred Heart devotion) and the children of Fatima. Apparitions and locutions happening since 1981 in Medjugorge have yet to be formally assessed. In all such cases – and there are many – the Church has the authority to judge the authenticity of a phenomenon, or at least to decide when it is dangerous to the faithful. Converts like myself who once moved in New Age circles are grateful for the presence of an authority capable of exercising careful and measured discernment.[42]

The attempt of Pope Benedict XVI to 'reform the reform' of the Catholic liturgy, by paying attention once again to its mysterious, sacred and sacrificial elements and to the aesthetic dimension may also be appealing to New Agers at the present time. My impression is that some of the growth of the New Age movement in recent times was partly caused by misguided attempts to demythologize and 'de-mystify' Christianity. The New Age seeks a transforming contact with mystery (that which transcends us) and with the supernatural – a hunger for true love, for beauty, for healing, for saints and miracles . . . for poetry not prose. It therefore appeals to the imagination in a way that Christianity in a period of cultural decline and commercial secularism finds it increasingly hard to do. There is a tendency among some Christians to react against the modern world and its temptations by emphasizing reason and the will, naked truth and virtue, at the expense of feeling and the imagination, which come to be regarded as an irrelevance or a distraction, if not actually demonic. A new apologetics or evangelization directed at the New Age would offer for consideration instead a sacral liturgy, together with the example of modern *mythopoeic* writers such as George MacDonald, Coventry Patmore, G. K. Chesterton, C. S. Lewis, J. R. R. Tolkien and Charles Williams, and the more ancient tradition of the great poet-theologians from St Ephrem and

Romanos to St Thomas Aquinas, Dante, St John of the Cross and Gerard Manley Hopkins, whose work expresses the mystery without reducing it to lifeless abstractions.

No matter how devoutly we celebrate the rituals of the Church, how carefully we observe her teaching and abide by her moral rules, our spiritual life will constantly tend to freeze over if it is not warmed from within. In order to penetrate to the source of that inner warmth we must continue to grow in the faith, cultivating a deeper prayer life and a more personal relationship with Christ, never resting content with what we have known and understood already. Ultimate truth is not a thing that can be possessed on a piece of paper. Truth is transcendent, always exceeding what we can grasp by our own power. There are indeed hidden mysteries that await our discovery. As Henri de Lubac writes of Holy scripture, 'it will always have new mysteries to teach us, and the grandeur of these mysteries will always exceed us. This is the way with anything that is divine. This is the way with the secrets of God's Wisdom.'[43]

Those concerned with the passing on of the faith should take all of this into account, and consider what it implies for their own preaching and teaching ministry. For Catholics it implies the need for a more conscious emphasis on the beauty and solemnity of the Mass, which helps to communicate the presence of an interior meaning. It calls us to renewed clarity in apologetics (the intellectual defence of the faith) and catechesis (religious instruction). But it also challenges us to develop a 'new' apologetics; a way of presenting the faith less as an intellectually satisfying set of ideas than as a way of life, personal healing and self-transformation. (And we must be aware that the greatest obstacle to faith is often Catholics themselves, when they fail to exemplify the transformative power of grace or the joy that flows from a deep intimacy with Christ. For that reason we should try to focus on the lives and example of the saints rather than ourselves.)

The New Age also challenges us to develop again the ancient practice of 'mystagogy' – the careful unfolding of the mysteries of the liturgy and the sacraments. In this work the *Catechism* is a good foundation, because it shows us the boundaries and lineaments of faith, but we need to go further, using mystical theology and metaphysics. This kind of work will not appeal to everyone, but for many who come from outside the tradition, from a radically post-modern, New Age and neo-Pagan milieu, it will be important to see Catholics engaged in it. The popes have set an example to us, for example, when John Paul II unfolded the 'theology of the body' implied in the creation account of Genesis, and Benedict XVI connected the liturgy with the cosmos and turned once again to the Patristic method of biblical exegesis.[44]

Three Examples

There are three specific examples I would give where elements of New Age interest are in the process of being made available for the articulation of Catholic truth – though with the proviso that great care and discernment are needed in this task.

My first example is the exegesis of religious symbolism that we owe to writers influenced by René Guénon, Frithjof Schuon and their 'Perennialist' school. This would include the art historian A. K. Coomaraswamy (who in turn influenced Catholics such as Eric Gill and Thomas Merton), Huston Smith (whose writings on comparative religion are widely used and respected) and S. H. Nasr (a leading figure in the dialogue between Muslims and Christians). Perennialism, following Guénon, has been particularly significant in France, and I want to draw attention to two French writers in particular from among the many who come from this background. Jean Hani, a critic of the modern Catholic liturgy, has done a great deal to explain the detailed symbolic and cosmological language of traditional church architecture and liturgical form.[45] Jean Borella is a Catholic philosopher, formerly under the influence of Schuon and Guénon but now somewhat critical of them, who has successfully distinguished the valuable from the less valuable elements in the Perennialist writings about Christianity, producing an orthodox yet esoteric systematic theology of great beauty and power.[46]

A second example is the work being done by several writers on symbolic properties of numbers and shapes, on arithmetic and geometry and their relation to arts such as music and architecture. Sacred Geometry has long been a subject of fascination in the New Age, coming into the category of 'the lost knowledge of the ancients' that has more often than not been assumed to have been suppressed by the Catholic Church. Fascination can easily lead to obsession, and there are plenty of websites devoted to fanciful attempts to decode the prophecies of the Bible or the geometry of the Great Pyramid. However, the basic principles of Sacred Geometry are fairly clear and seem to have been widely used in the construction of ancient buildings, images and texts.[47]

The third example is the Russian Valentin Tomberg, who died in 1973 after converting to Catholicism from anthroposophy and writing (anonymously) a massive work titled *Meditations on the Tarot*.[48] This was intended to reintegrate the lost wisdom of the Hermetic tradition with the orthodox Christianity of St Teresa, St Francis and St Bonaventure. It can stand as a harbinger, perhaps, of other attempts to retrieve and purify the legacy of the esoteric movements. In a foreword to the German edition of the book, Hans Urs von Balthasar praised it as the insightful work of a 'thinking, praying Christian of unmistakable purity'. Hermeticism had led Tomberg to realize that the free investigation of spiritual truth eventually leads to an agreement with the teachings of Catholicism: that there are guardian angels; that there are saints who participate actively in our lives; that the sacraments are effective; that prayer is a powerful means of charity; that the ecclesiastical hierarchy reflects the celestial order; and that Christ abides with the Church and instructs his disciples there.[49] By means of 22 meditations, in the form of 'letters to an unknown friend', he integrates his vast store of esoteric knowledge, gleaned from years of spiritual training in New Age groups, within the orthodox Catholic vision of faith. The Tarot cards are used, not for divination, but as symbolic encapsulations of the wisdom he has learned. Thus the High Priestess warns us of the danger of Gnosticism in teaching the discipline of true *gnosis*. The Empress evokes the dangers of mediumship and magic. The Emperor warns us of the will-to-power and teaches us the power of the Cross.

Tomberg draws an important distinction between three forms of mystical experience: union with Nature, with the transcendental human Self and with God. The first is pantheism; the second lies at the heart of the Eastern religions, and leads to metaphysical distortions when Westerners take the Self to be identical with God. The third is the goal of Christianity, and is inevitably dualistic because it involves the union in love between two distinct beings. Characteristic of this third kind of mystical experience, he thinks, is the 'gift of tears', whereas the 'advanced pupil of yoga or Vedanta will forever have dry eyes'.

* * *

The readers of Dan Brown, the millions who follow the 'channelled' teachings of the spirit world, the dabblers in new cults and therapies, the believers in conspiracy theories, reincarnation and the occult – broadly speaking, the members of the New Age movement I have been describing – bear witness to the continuing search for meaning and healing in the modern world. Through this search many will rediscover the nature of contemplation and the interior life. Mystagogy and living the Christian life is a process of learning more deeply, loving more truly. It is this alone that will bring New Agers into the Church and keep them there. And it is this desire to go deeper that many of us Christians need to learn from the New Age.

Notes

1 Based on a summary of the European Values Study at www.spiritual-wholeness.org/faqs/reinceur/reineuro.htm

2 I am thinking of movies such as *Ghost, Constantine, 2012, Hellboy, Harry Potter* and *Twilight, New Moon*, and so on, and TV shows such as *The X-Files, Buffy the Vampire Slayer, Angel, Fringe* and *the Sixth Sense*. The genre increasingly merges with SF in popular shows like *Lost* and *Heroes* – but then, as Arthur C. Clark famously said, science whenever sufficiently advanced is indistinguishable from magic. Many aspects of the New Age movement were brilliantly satirized by Umberto Eco in his 1998 novel *Foucault's Pendulum*.

3 These are three of the main ways of detaching faith from reason. The *fideist*, who can give no 'reason for the hope that is in him' (1 Pet. 3.15) but adheres to faith by sheer force of will or habit, can persuade no one to take it seriously. The *moralist*, who reduces faith to a set of moral rules, can appeal to no one who wants to behave differently. The *fundamentalist*, who insists on such a simplistic literal interpretation of scripture that he is forced to gloss over evident contradictions in the text, makes faith repulsive for the intelligent person.

4 See Kurt Rudolph, *Gnosis: The Nature and History of Gnosticism* (New York: HarperSanFrancisco, 1987).

5 See Friedrich Heer, *The Medieval World: Europe for 1100 to 1350* (London: Weidenfeld & Nicolson, 1962), 161–164.

6 See, for example, St Thomas Aquinas, *Summa Contra Gentiles* (South Bend: University of Notre Dame Press, 1975), Book 4, ch. 41, 'How One Should Understand the Incarnation of the Son of God'.

7 Article: Joachim of Flora, accessed February 2010 – www.newadvent.org/cathen/08406c.htm. On Joachim see Marjorie Reeves, *Joachim of Fiore and the Prophetic Future* (San Francisco: Harper, 1976).

8 In order to establish authority for a spiritual teaching, one has to claim either that it has been newly revealed by some higher being, or that it possesses a significant pedigree in tradition. Broadly speaking most New Age teachings fall into one of these two groups.

9 The term 'Hermetic', associated with this tradition, is derived from the figure of Hermes, the Greek god identified with the Egyptian Thoth and often taken to have been a pagan prophet from the time of Moses who revealed the mysteries of the universe. Paracelsus (d. 1541), an itinerant Swiss physician, botanist and astrologer, is regarded as one of the founders of modern medicine thanks to his experiments with the use of minerals and chemicals for the treatment of disease, though his medical theories were based on the ancient Greek doctrine of cosmic correspondences and the four humours. John Dee's life and influence in Elizabethan circles has been chronicled by Frances A. Yates in her books *The Rosicrucian Enlightenment* (London: Routledge & Kegan Paul, 1972) and *The Occult Philosophy in the Elizabethan Age* (London: Routledge & Kegan Paul, 1979). Nostradamus (d. 1566) was a seer and healer best known for his prophecies of the future. Other figures might be mentioned, including Cornelius Agrippa (d. 1535), an influential successor of Ficino and Pico. Interestingly, the researches of these men into magic and Hermeticism

were in general not condemned by the Church. Far from being seen as 'black magicians', these were scholars on the cutting edge of contemporary thought.

10 These works, along with many others including the Platonic dialogues themselves, were translated into English by Thomas Taylor in the early nineteenth century, influencing in turn William Blake and the English Romantics, the American Transcendentalists and early Theosophists.

11 See Arthur Koestler, *The Sleepwalkers: A History of Man's Changing Vision of the Universe* (Harmondsworth: Penguin, 1989), 227–411; also Fernand Hallyn, *The Poetic Structure of the World: Copernicus and Kepler* (New York: Zone, 1990).

12 'May God us keep From Single vision & Newtons sleep', he wrote to Thomas Butt in 1802, contrasting the reductionism of science with the 'fourfold vision' of ancient times. The 'dark Satanic Mills' of the Industrial Revolution are mentioned in his 1808 poem *Jerusalem* (originally part of the preface to *Milton*).

13 From the Preface to 'Milton', in *Blake: Poems and Letters*, ed. Jacob Bronowski (Harmondsworth: Penguin, 1958), 161–162.

14 The literature and influence of this group is extensive, and I will mention them again later. An attempt was made to explore its history by Mark Sedgwick in *Against the Modern World: Traditionalism and the Secret Intellectual History of the Twentieth Century* (Oxford: Oxford University Press, 2004), but this was flawed by an obsession with the political dimensions of the movement and a lack of appreciation of its more central metaphysical concerns.

15 The history of the Theosophical Society, the Golden Dawn and related organizations has been well and sympathetically told in Joscelyn Godwin, *The Theosophical Enlightenment* (Albany, NY: State University of New York Press, 1994). Two other books from SUNY Press are particularly worth mentioning here, both by Antoine Faivre: *Access to Western Esotericism* (1994) and *Theosophy, Imagination, Tradition: Studies in Western Esotericism* (2000). (Both books formed part of a single study in the original French.)

16 To understand the impact of Gurdjieff, which continues to this day, see P. D. Ouspensky, *In Search of the Miraculous: Fragments of an Unknown Teaching* (London: Routledge & Kegan Paul, 1950).

17 There is a line that leads from Jung to the 'archetypal psychology' of James Hillman and Henri Corbin, with other influences coming in from Martin Heidegger and Persian theosophy. See Andrew Samuels, *Jung and the Post-Jungians* (London: Routledge & Kegan Paul, 1985); Robert Avens, *The New Gnosis: Heidegger, Hillman, and Angels* (Dallas: Spring Publications, 1984). Corbin was a major influence on Kathleen Raine and the Temenos Academy in London – and through her also on the Prince of Wales and his circle up to the present.

18 While Jung went beyond Freudian reductionism in his notion of the Unconscious, Traditionalists and others accuse him of failing to distinguish within the unconscious realm between the infraconscious and supraconscious, and thus between the Psyche and God, though with his concept of 'synchronicity' he seems to have been reaching for a synthesis in which the archetypes order the physical universe as well as the psychical realm.

19 I am basing this assertion on information I was given during several trips to Eastern Europe in the 1990s.
20 See Ken Wilber, ed., *Quantum Questions: Mystical Writings of the World's Great Physicists* (Boston and London: Shambhala, 1984) for a collection of relevant texts. Arthur I. Miller's *Deciphering the Cosmic Number: The Strange Friendship of Wolfgang Pauli and Carl Jung* (New York: W. W. Norton, 2009) describes the explorations of one leading physicist into numerology and Kabbalah to discover the secrets of the collective unconscious. One of the most interesting of modern physicists from a Catholic point of view was David Bohm (d. 1992), who like Einstein rejected the anti-realist Copenhagen interpretation of quantum reality, and sought an alternative account in hidden variables implying an 'implicate order' uniting all diverse phenomena. His book *Wholeness and the Implicate Order* (London: Routledge & Kegan Paul, 1980) was extremely popular despite its some times technical nature. Bohm engaged in dialogue with New Age figures such as Jiddu Krishnamurti, but also with Catholic thinkers (see David L. Schindler, ed., *Beyond Mechanism: The Universe in Recent Physics and Catholic Thought*, Lanham, MD: University Press of America, 1986), developing with Karl Pribram a theory of the 'holographic' nature of the brain, while never losing his credibility as a scientist. More recently Catholic mathematical physicist Wolfgang Smith has sought to reconcile modern cosmology with perennial metaphysics in books such as *The Quantum Enigma: Finding the Hidden Key* (Hillsdale, NY: Sophia Perennis, 2005).
21 Fritjof Capra provides an overview of organismic, holistic thinking about biological systems in *The Web of Life: A New Synthesis of Mind and Matter* (London: HarperCollins, 1996).
22 G. K. Chesterton, *Orthodoxy* (New York: Garden City, 1908), 138.
23 Ibid., 244.
24 Sir George Trevelyan, *A Vision of the Aquarian Age* (London: Coventure, 1977), 5–6. The book is online at www.sirgeorgetrevelyan.org.uk/books/thtbk-VAA00.html
25 'To die in mortal sin without repenting and accepting God's merciful love means remaining separated from him for ever by our own free choice' (CCC, n. 1033). Hell is *self-exclusion* from God's presence, and 'God predestines no one to go to hell' (n. 1037). Responsibility for a mortal sin is mitigated by ignorance (n. 1735). Even the most hardened sinner may experience a death-bed conversion or change of heart. Theologians dispute whether we may in fact hope that in the end hell will prove to be empty, since so many appear to be dead set on going there, but they agree that God does all that he can to save everyone, and not just those who are visibly baptized.
26 I remember attending a men's workshop during the 1970s in which we were required to hug each other in order to discover our 'feminine side' (an idea that perhaps goes back to Jung with his doctrine of the *anima/animus*).
27 See Léonie Caldecott, 'Sincere Gift: The Pope's "New Feminism"', *Communio* 23 (Spring 1996) and online at www.secondspring.co.uk. The author cites Catholic poet Gertrude von le Fort: 'The feminist movement had its spiritual roots in the dullness and narrowness of the middle-class family. Its economic backgrounds do not concern us here. From the stress of their starving souls, the women of that period cried out for a spiritual purpose in life and for an

activation of their capacity for love. It was a tragic motivation, for these women sought out a share of responsibility in the man's world, and sought it outside the family which could no longer shelter and satisfy them.'

28 See, for example, Carl Olson and Sandra Miesel, *The Da Vinci Hoax: Exposing the Errors in The Da Vinci Code* (**San Francisco: Ignatius Press, 2006**).

29 Louis Dupré, *Passage to Modernity: An Essay in the Hermeneutics of Nature and Culture* (New Haven: Yale University Press, 1993). See also Kenneth L. Schmitz, *The Recovery of Wonder: The New Freedom and the Asceticism of Power* (Montreal: McGill-Queen's University Press, 2005).

30 Hans Urs von Balthasar sums it up thus: 'During the Nominalist period the universe lost its theophanic radiance – the devout no longer encounter God outside but only within themselves. At the same time, the universe loses its hierarchic gradation and collapses into "matter" which, itself without essence, becomes that which is merely mathematically calculable and which is present to be exploited by man' (*The Glory of the Lord*, Vol. 5, San Francisco: Ignatius Press, 1991), 452.

31 Charles Taylor, *Sources of the Self: The Making of the Modern Identity* (Cambridge University Press, 1989); *A Secular Age* (Cambridge, MA: Harvard University Press, 2007).

32 Allen Ginsberg, 'Howl', in *Collected Poems 1947–1980* (San Francisco: Harper & Row, 1984).

33 Labsang P. Lhalungpa, trans., *The Life of Milarepa: A New Translation from the Tibetan* (New York: Dutton, 1977).

34 Anon., *A Course in Miracles: The Text, Workbook for Students and Manual for Teachers* (London and New York: Routledge & Kegan Paul, 1985), 7.

35 Annie Besant, *Esoteric Christianity* (London and Benares: Theosophical Publishing Society, 1905), 140–141.

36 Jacob Needleman, *Lost Christianity: A Journey of Rediscovery to the Center of Christian Experience* (New York: Doubleday, 1980), 4. The Christian teacher encountered by Needleman in his book is a fictional device, but similar claims are made by Robin Amis in *A Different Christianity: Early Christian Esotericism and Modern Thought* (Albany, NY: SUNY Press, 1995): 'a study of certain ideas and methods known in the early Church but lost, in one way or another, to modern Christianity' (4). Amis draws on the Philokalia and other authentic Eastern Christian spiritual writings, but is strongly influenced in his interpretations by Boris Mouravieff, a student of P. D. Ouspensky.

37 See, for example, Ted Peters, *The Cosmic Self: A Penetrating Look at Today's New Age Movements* (San Francisco: HarperSanFrancisco, 1991), 120–131.

38 See CCC, nn. 436–440.

39 John Paul II, *Orientale Lumen*, 1995, n. 10.

40 Limbo is not a dogma of the Church but a *theologoumenon*, a theological opinion, and one which many today find unappealing. The *Catechism* skims over this point in section 1261, encouraging us to hope for the full salvation of children who die unbaptized.

41 Thomas Aquinas, *Summa Contra Gentiles* (Notre Dame: University of Notre Dame Press, 1975), Book 3, Part 1, ch. 51.

42 The investigation of miracles and the phenomena associated with holiness can lead some people to faith. See Patricia Treece, *The Sanctified Body* (New York: Doubleday, 1989).

43 Henri de Lubac, *Medieval Exegesis*, Vol. 1 (Grand Rapids: Eerdmans, 1998), 76.
44 See John Paul II, *Man and Woman He Created Them: A Theology of the Body* (Boston: Pauline, 2006); Joseph Cardinal Ratzinger, *The Spirit of the Liturgy* (San Francisco: Ignatius Press, 2000); Joseph Ratzinger/Pope Benedict XVI, *Jesus of Nazareth* (London: Bloomsbury, 2007).
45 Jean Hani, *The Divine Liturgy: Insights into Its Mystery* (San Rafael, CA: Sophia Perennis, 2008); *The Symbolism of the Christian Temple* (San Rafael, CA: Sophia Perennis, 2007). I should refer also in this connection to the work of another leading member of the school, Titus Burkhardt, author of *Sacred Art in East and West* (London: Perennial Books, 1967), and *Chartres and the Birth of the Cathedral* (Ipswich: Golgonooza Press, 1995). Earlier, Coomaraswamy had written numerous works on symbolism, art and architecture, both Christian and Hindu, and Guénon had explored the nature of religious symbolism in *Symbols of Sacred Science* (San Rafael, CA: Sophia Perennis, 2004). These writers tried to show that the symbolic properties of traditional art and design contained a universal metaphysical meaning. Their works are mostly now available from Sophia Perennis in California or World Wisdom Books in Indiana.
46 See Jean Borella, *The Sense of the Supernatural* (Edinburgh: T&T Clark, 1998); *The Secret of the Christian Way: A Contemplative Ascent through the Writings of Jean Borella*, ed. G. John Champoux (Albany, NY: SUNY Press, 2001); *Guénonian Esotericism and Christian Mystery* (Hillsdale, NY: Sophia Perennis, 2004).
47 See Michael S. Schneider, *A Beginner's Guide to Constructing the Universe: The Mathematical Archetypes of Nature, Art and Science* (San Francisco: HarperPerennial, 1994); John Michell with Allan Brown, *How the World is Made: The Story of Creation According to Sacred Geometry* (London: Thames & Hudson, 2009); Robert Lawlor, *Sacred Geometry: Philosophy and Practice* (London: Thames & Hudson, 1982). I have argued in my own book, *Beauty for Truth's Sake: On the Re-enchantment of Education* (Grand Rapids: Brazos, 2009), that a better appreciation of symbolic mathematics would be desirable.
48 Anon., *Meditations on the Tarot: A Journey into Christian Hermeticism* (New York: Amity House, 1985). See also a lesser work by the same author, Valentin Tomberg, *Covenant of the Heart: Meditations of a Christian Hermeticist on the Mysteries of Tradition* (Shaftesbury: Element, 1002). Tomberg died in 1973 in Reading.
49 Cf. *Meditations on the Tarot*, 281.

Further Reading

Books not already included in the footnotes.

Balthasar, Hans Urs von (ed.) (1990), *The Scandal of the Incarnation: Irenaeus Against the Heresies*, San Francisco: Ignatius Press. Selections from St Irenaeus with commentary by Balthasar bring out the contemporary relevance of the Patristic polemic against Gnosticism.

Bouyer, Louis (1990), *The Christian Mystery: From Pagan Myth to Christian Mysticism*, Edinburgh: T&T Clark. A profound historical and theological survey by an expert on Christian spirituality.

Caldecott, Stratford (2006), *The Seven Sacraments: Entering the Mysteries of God*, New York: Crossroad. An attempt to reveal the inner coherence of scripture and tradition in a way designed to appeal to seekers of lost wisdom.

Clément, Olivier (1993), *The Roots of Christian Mysticism*, London: New City Press. A brilliant compendium of Patristic spiritual teaching by a leading lay orthodox theologian.

Congregation for the Doctrine of the Faith (1990), *Letter to the Bishops of the Catholic Church on Some Aspects of Christian Meditation*, London: Catholic Truth Society. Criticizing the reliance on 'techniques' of prayer.

Davie, Grace, Paul Heelas and Linda Woodhead (eds) (2003), *Predicting Religion: Christianity and Alternatives in the West*, Aldershot: Ashgate.

Ferguson, Marilyn (1981), *The Aquarian Conspiracy: Personal and Social Transformation in the 1980s*, London: Routledge & Kegan Paul. One of the classic texts of the nascent New Age movement.

Hauke, Manfred (1988), *Women in the Priesthood? A Systematic Analysis in the Light of the Order of Creation and Redemption*, San Francisco: Ignatius Press. Includes much relevant material on the feminist strands of New Age thought.

Heelas, Paul, and Linda Woodhead, with Benjamin Seel, Bronislaw Szerszynski, Karin Tusting (2005), *The Spiritual Revolution: Why Religion is Giving Way to Spirituality*, Oxford: Blackwell.

Kemp, Daren (2004), *New Age: A Guide*, Edinburgh University Press. A useful sociological study and guide to the extensive literature.

Lewis, James R., and J. Gordon Melton (eds) (1992), *Perspectives on the New Age*, Albany, NY: SUNY Press. A collection of papers surveying the movement in different countries at the beginning of the 1990s.

Martin, Francis (1995), *The Feminist Question: Feminist Theology in the Light of Christian Tradition*, Edinburgh and Grand Rapids: T&T Clark and Wm Eerdmans. Important for insights into aspects of the Enlightenment, against which much of feminist (and New Age) theory is a semi-conscious reaction.

Saliba, John A. (1999), *Christian Responses to the New Age: A Critical Assessment*, London: Geoffrey Chapman. An ecumenical survey.

Schönborn, Christoph, OP (1995), *From Death to Life: The Christian Journey*, San Francisco: Ignatius Press. Includes a helpful Catholic perspective on reincarnation.

Thomas, Keith (1971), *Religion and the Decline of Magic: Studies in Popular Beliefs in Sixteenth- and Seventeenth-Century England*, Harmondsworth: Penguin. A landmark study that showed how much of what we think of as 'New Age' was around in our culture centuries ago.

See also the 'Deeper Christianity' series published by the Catholic Truth Society in London, and a special issue of *The Chesterton Review* (XXVI, 1 and 2), February/May 200, 'The Light Within: The New Age and Christian Spirituality'.

Index

'Abduh, Muhammad 79
Abraham 17, 18, 37, 55, 78
Abrahamic Covenant 36, 62
Abrahamic theism 18
Abû Hâmid Muhammad ibn Muhammad al-Ghazâlî 79
Advaita Vedānta 130
Ahmad, Mirza Ghulam 87
al-Adawiyya, Rabi'a 87
al-Hallaj, Hussain Mansur 88
'Ali Talib, 'Ali ibn 86
al-Sirhindi, Ahmad 88
Āḷvārs 120
Antiochus, Emperor 46
anti-Semitism 6, 16, 60–1
Aristotle 23, 183
Arokiasamy, Soosai 139
Assagioli, Robert 187
Assisi, prayer meeting 25, 26
Avalokiteśvara 156, 166

Baba Ram Dass 186
Bailey, Alice 186
Bar Kochba revolt 57
bar Yochai, Rabbi Shimon 49
Barfield, Owen 186
Barth, Karl 11, 157
Basilides, the Gnostic 165
ben Eliezer, Rabbi Israel 48
Benedict XVI (Pope) 6, 12, 18, 25, 57, 61, 125, 168, 169, 191, 206, 207
Benedictine monks 160
Benjamin, Tribe of 34
Bernard of Clairvaux 136
Besant, Annie 185, 198
Bhagavad Gītā 111
Bhagwan Sri Rajneesh 186
Blake, William 185

Blavatsky, Madame H. P. 185
Bohr, Niels 188
Borella, Jean 208
Botticelli, Sandro 184
Brahmanical Hinduism 108–9, 111, 114, 129, 139
Brand, Steward 194
Brown, Dan 178, 193
Buddhism 15, 18, 141–76, 169
Buonarroti, Michelangelo 184

Callistus III (Pope) 60
Calvin, John 11
Campbell, Joseph 192
Capra, Fritjof 188
Carmelite tradition 18
Castaneda, Carlos 187
Cayce, Edgar 187
Chardin, Teilhard de 186
Chari, S. M. Srinivasa 122
Charismatic Movement 205
Chesterton, G. K. 185, 189, 206
Cistercian monastic order 25
Clement of Alexandria 3, 181
Coleridge, S. T. 185
Confucianism 19
Conservative Judaism 48–9
Constantine, Emperor 99, 193
Coomaraswamy, A. K. 208
Council of Chalcedon 182
Council of Elvira 59
Council of Florence 2, 184
Council of Jerusalem 64
Council of Nicaea 59
Coventry Patmore 206

Dalit Christians 128–9
Dante Alighieri 107
Daoism 19

De Leon, Moses 49
de Nobili, Roberto 128
de Smet, Richard 129
de Soto, Domingo 4, 5
de Vitoria, Francisco 4, 10
Descartes, René 185, 195, 196
Dharmaguptaka Buddhism 150
Dhavamony, M. 136, 137–8, 139
Dominicans 4, 23
Doyle, Arthur Conan 185
Druzes, Lebanese 87
Dupré, Louis 195
Dupuis, Jacues 30n22

East Asian Buddhism 152
Ecumenical Councils 182
Einstein, Albert 188
Eusebius of Caesarea 19

Feeney, Leonard 8
Ficino, Marcilio 184
Flood, Gavin 108
Four Noble Truths 145
Fourth Lateran Council 59
Fox, Matthew 199
Frankl, Viktor 187
Freud, Sigmund 187

Galileo Galilei 195, 196
Gandhi, M. K. (Mahatma) 107
Gill, Eric 208
Gnosticism 49, 165, 181–2
Goethe, Johann Wolfgang von 185
Grant, Sara 129, 131
Greco-Latin heritage 24
Greek philosophy 3
Greek tradition 22
Griffiths, Bede 199
Guénon, René 185, 208
Gurdjieff, G. I. 186, 198

Hadith 71
Hanbalites 73
Hani, Jean 208
Hasidim 48
Hasan al-Basri 87
Hermetic Order 185
Hermeticism 49, 209

Hindu Nationalism 107
Hinduism 15, 17, 106–39
Holy Office (Congregation for the Doctrine of the Faith) 8
Hopkins, Gerard Manley 207

Ibadites 87
Ibn 'Arabi, Andalusian Muhy al-Din 88
Ibn Hanbal 103n4
Ichazo, Oscar 179
Islam 14, 15, 16–17, 71–104

Jainism 21
Jamison, Christopher 159
Japanese Buddhism 23, 157
Jeans, James 188
Jesuits 23
Joachim of Fiore (or Flora) 183
Johanns, Pierre 129
John XXIII (Pope) 60, 199
John Paul II (Pope) 6, 13, 16, 17, 18, 61, 124, 125, 129, 137, 157, 166, 191, 192, 200, 205, 207
Judah, Tribe of 34
Judaism 15, 16, 34–70
Julian of Norwich 136
Jung, Carl 186, 187

Kabbalah 49–50
Kantian Enlightenment 6
Kepler, Johannes 184
Khan, Pir Vilayat 186
Krishnamurti, Jiddu 185
Kṣatriyas 109

Laing, R. D. 187
Lama, Dalai 160, 186
Las Casas, Bartolomé de 4
Le Saux, Henri (Swami Abhishiktananda) 23, 130, 132
Leadbeater, C. W. 185
Leo XII (Pope) 60
Leonardo da Vinci 184
Lessing, G. E. 190
Lewis, C. S. 186, 206
Lovelock, James 188
Lubac, Henri de 163, 175n. 5, 207

MacDonald, George 206
Maharishi Mahesh Yogi 186
Mahāyāna Buddhism 153–4
Maimonides, Moses 39, 40
Main, John 199
Martyr, Justin 20
Marx, Karl 24
Maslow, Abraham 187
Medici, Cosimo de 184
Merton, Thomas 23, 160, 199, 208
Messalianism 24
Messianic Judaism 50
Mirandola, Pico della 184
Monastic Interreligious Dialogue 25
Mosaic Covenant 37, 62
Muhammad, The Prophet 71–9, 82, 84, 86, 87, 91, 96–7
Mūlasarvāstivāda Buddhism 150

Nasr, S. H. 208
Nāyaṇmārs 120
Needleman, Jacob 198
New Religious Movements 19
Newton, Isaac 184
Nostradamus, Michel de 184

Pāñcarātra system 122
Paracelsus, John Dee 184
Patañjali 118
Pattinattar 128
Paul VI (Pope) 124, 178
Pauli, Wolfgang 188
Perennialism 208
Perls, Fritz 187
Pius IV (Pope) 60
Pius XI (Pope) 60
Pius XII (Pope) 10, 23
Planck, Max 188
Platonism 185
Political Hinduism 107
Pontifical Council for Culture 178, 204
Pontifical Council for Social Justice 126
Prigogine, Illya 188
Protestant 22, 38, 183
pseudo-Gnosticism 24
Purāṇic Hinduism 120

Qur'an 71
Qutb, Sayyid 85

Rabbinic Judaism 43
Rahner, Karl 10
Ramana Mahārshi 130
Rāmānuja 23, 118
Raphael, Raffaello Sanzio da Urbino 184
Ratzinger, Joseph Cardinal 125, 168, 173 *see also* Benedict XVI
Reform Judaism 48
Rhine, J. B. 187
Roman tradition 22
Romanos 207

Śaivism 119
Śākta 122
Śākyamuni Buddha 142–3, 154
Sankara 23, 24
Schuon, Frithjof 186, 208
Second Vatican Council 6–13, 60, 90–1, 122
Semitic theism 17
Shah, Idries 186
Shari'a 80
Sheldrake, Rupert 188
Shia Muslims 72
Shroedinger, Erwin 188
Sikhism 19, 25
Smet, Richard de 131
Smith, Huston 208
Śrī Vaiṣṇavism 119, 120, 133
St Ambrose of Milan 58
St Augustine 2, 3, 11, 12, 55
St Bernadette 52
St Bonaventure 208
St Cyprian 58
St Cyril 54
St Ephrem 206
St Francis de Sales 171, 173, 208
St Irenaeus 181, 196
St John Chrysostom 58
St John of the Cross 207
St Justin Martyr 181
St Margaret Mary Alacoque 52
St Paul 63
St Peter 63

St Teresa 208
St Thomas Aquinas 4, 9–10, 15, 17, 20, 23, 125, 182, 186, 207
Steiner, Rudolf 185, 186
Śūdras 110
Sufism 26
Suhrawardi, Shihab al-Din 88
Sunni Muslims 72
Suzuki, D. T. 186
Swami Vivekananda 107, 186
Swedenborg, Emanuel 184
Synod of Breslau 59
Synod of Narbonne 59
Synod of Ofen 59

Talmud 41
Tanakh 38
Tantric Hinduism 112, 113, 120
Taylor, Charles 196
Temple Judaism 43
Theistic Vedānta 133
Theodosius I, Emperor 99
Theosophical Society 185
Theravāda Buddhism 150, 160
Thomism 129
Tibetan Buddhism 151, 160
Tolkien, J. R. R. 206

Tomberg, Valentin 186, 208
Torah 38
Trappist tradition 23
Trevelyan, Sir George 189, 190–1
Trinitarian foundation 7, 9, 25, 93, 96, 130, 131, 132, 133, 134
Turkish Alevites 87

Vaiśyas 110
Vatican II 1, 11, 13, 19
Vedic Hinduism 108, 109, 110
von Balthasar, Hans Urs 209
von Stietenchron, Heinrich 106

Watts, Alan 186
Weinandy, Thomas G. 167
Western Latin tradition 22
Williams, Charles 206
Wolfe, Tom 197
Wordsworth, William 185

Yeats, W. B. 185

Zaidiyya 87
Zen 23, 172, 186, 199
Zoroastrianism 181

Made in the USA
Las Vegas, NV
01 August 2021